inside moves

Microsoft®

AGE of EMPIRES™

Revised and Expanded Edition

Steven Kent

Microsoft Press

PUBLISHED BY
Microsoft Press
A Division of Microsoft Corporation
One Microsoft Way
Redmond, Washington 98052-6399

Library of Congress Cataloging-in-Publication Data
Kent, Steven
    Microsoft Age of Empires: Inside Moves / Steven Kent. -- Rev. and
Expanded Ed.
       p. cm.
    Includes bibliographical references (p.) and index.
    ISBN 0-7356-0569-6
    1. Microsoft Age of Empires.   2. Title.
GV1469.25M54K46   1998
793.93'25369--dc21   98-38728
                                                                                      CIP

Printed and bound in the United States of America.

1 2 3 4 5 6 7 8 9   MLML   3 2 1 0 9 8

Distributed in Canada by ITP Nelson, a division of Thomson Canada Limited.

A CIP catalogue record for this book is available from the British Library.

Microsoft Press books are available through booksellers and distributors worldwide. For further information about international editions, contact your local Microsoft Corporation office or contact Microsoft Press International directly at fax (425) 936-7329. Visit our Web site at mspress.microsoft.com.

Acquisitions Editor: Kim Fryer
Project Editor: Saul Candib

Dedication

In loving memory of my father in-law Mark Barberich,
Moe meka hoku lani.

Steven Kent

Acknowledgments

I would like to thank Steven Kent for another incredible effort in such a short time-frame. I also wish to thank the many others who contributed, behind the scenes, to the creation of *Age Of Empires: Rise of Rome Inside Moves*.

At The PC Press, Inc.: Lance Elko, Project Editor; Kathleen Ingram, Managing Book Coordinator; Kim Davis, Art Director.

At Microsoft Press: Kim Fryer, Acquisitions Editor and Saul Candib, Microsoft Press Project Editor.

And lastly, Steven and I would like to thank the entire Microsoft Games group, especially: Tim Znamenacek, Program Manager; Robert Howg; Bryan Trussel and Mark Thomas. Thanks also to the people at Ensemble, including: Tony Goodman, Founder, CEO, President, Lead Art Director, and Generally Good Father at Ensemble; Chris Rippy, the guy at Ensembe who does the sounds and thinks up the levels; Duncan McKissick, Dave Pottinger, and Chea O'Neill of the Ensemble hit squad; and thanks to John Romero, the Tony Goodman of ION Storm.

Robert C. Lock
President and Editor-in-Chief
The PC Press, Inc.

Contents

Introduction

ROAD TO GLORY

This image's head was of fine gold, his breast and arms of silver, his belly and thighs of brass, His legs of iron, his feet part of iron and part of clay.
—Daniel 2:32-33

Sometime between B.C. 604 and 561, King Nebuchadnezzar of Babylon had a remarkable dream in which he saw a great statue with a head of gold, a chest of silver, a belly of brass, legs of iron, and feet of iron and clay. Theologians have long interpreted his dream to refer to the great empires of the world.

The golden head has long been thought to represent Babylon—a splendid but short-lived empire that lasted less than 100 years. The silver breast is believed to represent the Medes and Persians. The brass stomach, torso, and thighs are thought to represent Greece—the noble empire of Alexander the Great. And the iron legs are said to represent Rome—the last great empire.

Whether you believe that Nebuchadnezzar's dream was the result of prophecy or a disagreeable late-night snack, one thing is certain: the empire business went down the tubes after the fall of Rome. No other empire has managed to conquer the world so completely, rule the world so methodically, and last as enduringly as Rome. As my high-school European Studies teacher used to say, "Do you know why Italy is shaped like a boot? Because Rome kicked everybody's butt."

Academic wisdom aside, it is with a certain reverence that I approach this book. The original Microsoft's Age of Empires was not merely a great game, it was a landmark merging of entertainment and education. It had great play mechanics, but it also offered information about Xenophon's March and Hammurabi's Code. You could not play the campaigns without learning a little something about history.

AGE of EMPIRES

There is no way of knowing how many people knew the difference between a phalanx and a cataphract before playing Age of Empires, but it's certain that more than a half million people know now.

Microsoft's Rise of Rome builds on that original Age of Empires formula by adding the great empire that brought peace to the world—Roman peace (pax Romana). To belong to the Roman Empire meant paying taxes and accepting the Roman definition of order—but it also placed you in the often respectful care of one of the greatest civilizing forces in history. Rome was a terrible enemy, but also a far more merciful conqueror than the nations that ruled before her.

It's certain that you will enjoy the Age of Empires Expansion Pack: Rise of Rome. It is the perfect conclusion to the first chapter of the Age of Empires saga—the finale of the ancient world and the beginning of modern society.

Chapter One

TIME, INDUSTRY, AND RELIGION

You may want to skip this chapter of the book if you read the strategy guide for the original Microsoft's Age of Empires. This section consists solely of nuts-and-bolts historical background covering the time periods depicted in the game.

If you are new to Age of Empires, you will likely find this information interesting and helpful—although it is unlikely to improve your playing, it will help you understand the game and provide context.

The Ages

In Denmark, in 1836, the curator of Copenhagen's National Museum, Christian Jurgensen Thomson, devised a method for classifying historical objects by ages. He classified crude tools as being from the "Stone Age," early metal items as being from the "Bronze Age," and more advanced metal work as being from the "Iron Age." Even though Thomson did not have grandiose ambitions of changing the way mankind views history, his system was adopted by historians and archeologists, and it did change the way people view pre-history.

Archeologists embraced Thomson's system and expanded it. Today, terms like Stone Age and Iron Age are commonly used descriptions. Fred Flintstone would not have been a member of an "average Stone Age family" if it weren't for Thomson. Instead, the Flintstones would simply have been classified as cavemen.

Random Map games, multiplayer death matches, and many of the scenarios in the campaigns require players to guide their civilizations through multiple ages. The game presents rough approximations of the technologies of the Stone, Tool, Bronze, and Iron Ages, and then uses those approximations to depict the combat of that day.

One of the keys to winning in multiplayer and single-player games is learning how to progress through the early stages of society more quickly than your opponents—be they real or virtual.

If natural selection has an ally in Age of Empires, it's technology. You can cut through a swarm of Stone Age clubmen with a few Tool Age axemen—but let your axemen run into the Bronze Age cavalry, and they're dead. Those cavalrymen, on the other hand, would not stand a chance against a phalanx.

This portion of the book will discuss ways to maximize your power through each stage of the game—but before we can talk about holding off the entire Roman Army with a clubman and a prayer, let's look briefly at some of the important facets of each time period.

The Stone Age

The Stone Age, which began approximately two million years ago, did not vanish all at once. The Middle East and parts of Asia emerged from the Stone Age in B.C. 6000, while the isolated civilizations of the Americas did not emerge from Stone Age culture for another three to four thousand years.

The Stone Age in Age of Empires is more precisely known as the Mesolithic or Middle Stone Age. Humanity still gathered food by hunting and gathering during the Mesolithic Era, but their hunting activities broadened to include fish and shellfish as well as the animals and berries that had sustained men for the last two million years.

Men already had clubs and sharp stones used as knives during the Paleolithic (or first) Stone Age. Mesolithic man improved these instruments by imbedding rows of sharp stones into them. When you see clubmen attacking each other in Age of Empires, they're not just generally smashing away, they're hacking their enemies to bits.

The Tool Age

The period that Age of Empires refers to as the Tool Age is more correctly stated as the Neolithic or New Stone Age period. This was the final era of the Stone Age, a time characterized by the beginnings of agriculture and specialized tools. By the Neolithic Period, ancient man abandoned the sharp rocks and began making hammers, axes, spears, and other tools with polished stone blades.

Improvement in tool-making was not the only change occurring during this period—this was the era in which certain societies began making pottery, farming, and domesticating animals. It is widely held that Egypt and Sumer led the way in this evolution, closely followed by Greece.

The Bronze Age

The civilizations in Age of Empires sort of skip a grade. In real history, most civilizations had a Copper Age before they started working with bronze. Soft and malleable, copper does not require melting—you can simply pound it into shape.

There is no record to explain exactly how bronze was discovered. It may have been a serendipitous accident.

As an alloy (a mixture of tin and copper), bronze is more rigid than copper. Bronze changed the way wars were fought. Soldiers' helmets became lighter and more protective, and weapons once used for clubbing enemies suddenly became rigid enough to hack and slice. Soldiers wielding bronze swords would have been able to smash through their enemies' primitive armor.

Bronze was not the only innovation that occurred during its namesake age. Trade routes grew during this period, and great nations such as Babylon and Greece rose to power.

The Iron Age

The Iron Age would have preceded the Bronze Age if iron had been easier to make. Iron is actually more common than copper or tin, the minerals that form bronze—but working with iron requires melting raw ore, a process that requires a strong source of heat.

The first people to perfect the use of iron were the Hittites, who developed this talent shortly before they were wiped out of existence by invaders known as the Sea People.

Learning about working iron offered societies several advantages. Iron was more rigid than bronze. Iron helmets could deflect blows that would cause a bronze helmet to cave in. Iron was also more plentiful, meaning that it could be used for building purposes and not just for weapons and ornamentation.

The Need for Food: Foraging to Farming

Early man was known as a hunter/gatherer, meaning he looked for fruits, nuts, berries, roots, and vegetables as well as hunted small animals. Tribes could find enough food to feed themselves during good years, but hunting and gathering could not produce sufficient food during droughts. As mankind searched for

more efficient means of providing for itself, both changed—hunting evolved into animal husbandry and gathering evolved into farming.

Of course, this did not happen overnight. During the Neolithic Period, hunters slowly switched from chasing animals that traveled in herds to hunting forest animals.

Agriculture, practiced successfully, was one of the foundations of a thriving society. People became less nomadic as they developed dependable sources of food, and the people that inhabited the lands that became Egypt, Greece, and Babylon all were among the first Neolithic farmers.

Scientists have traced wheat and barley farming in the Middle East as far back as B.C. 8000 and sheep farming in Iraq, anciently known as Sumer and Babylon, as far back as B.C. 9000. The Sumerians dug canals and developed irrigation.

The Art of Weaponry:
From Clubs to Catapults

The evolution of weapons follows a quite logical sequence. First, pre-Paleolithic man discovered that hitting enemies with sticks and bones did more damage than hitting them with fists. Next, he discovered that clubs worked better than simple sticks.

Paleolithic man then discovered that clubs lined with sharp rocks did more damage than clubs without rocks, which led to the development of several ways to deliver blows with rocks. You could hit people with small rocks by throwing them with a sling, and you could hit people with sharp rocks by launching them on spears. (All of this is, of course, pure speculation since the people responsible for these inventions were too busy killing each other with sticks and stones to document their invention process.)

Apparently, knives and swords came from sharp rock weapons. Neolithic man decided that lining clubs with sharp flint chips was not as clever as grinding rocks down and making a stronger and more polished blade. These blades ended up on prehistoric scythes that were used to thresh wild wheat, and they also ended up on prehistoric knives that were used to thresh wild neighbors. They also discovered that spears could be reduced, balanced, and fired from bows.

Metal weapons began to appear about B.C. 3000, as the first Neolithic societies began to enter the Bronze Age. Several ancient Middle Eastern nations led this evolution. They used bronze to manufacture maces, swords, bows, arrows, axes, spears, and armor.

When it came to delivering rocks, the greatest weapon was the catapult. The first examples of these devastating weapons were really enormous crossbows called ballistas. These "double-armed" catapults fired darts three feet long. The Greeks and Romans improved upon this technology by creating stone-throwing catapults capable of hurling 10-pound rocks.

Religion: Something to Believe

Only an unenlightened fool would try to explain the influence of religion on the history of man in a few short paragraphs. So here goes:

Menes, the unifier of Ancient Egypt and arguably the world's first great ruler, convinced his followers that he was the son of a god. It was a good strategy because being the son of a god has a number of advantages. People join your army when you are the son of a god, your father presumably there (in spirit) helping your men win battles. And, of course, any battle you choose to fight even for the pettiest of reasons, becomes a holy war.

Having gods as parents also offers peacetime dividends. It means that your laws are inspired and your justice is divine. As the pharaohs discovered, it also means that your subjects will work slavishly to make you great monuments.

Egyptian and Sumerian rulers continued to claim divinity for centuries, but later rulers were not so bold. This did not mean, however, that they abandoned religion as a means of unifying their people. Many ancient kings said they were selected by the gods to be kings.

Being selected by the gods has many great advantages. Clearly, the gods favor your authority and will support you in times of battle. Conversely, your enemies are not favored of the gods (except in battles such as Greece vs. Troy, in which some gods liked the Greeks and others preferred the Trojans).

The advantages of having the gods on your side has not escaped modern leaders. Abraham Lincoln quickly discovered that more people were interested in fighting a holy war to end slavery than fighting a pragmatic war to preserve the Union; and the Japanese were willing to sacrifice themselves in combat during World War II because of the belief that their Emperor was divine.

Creating Alliances

In his book Leviathan: or the Matter, Form, and Power of a Commonwealth, Ecclesiastical and Civil, Thomas Hobbes described the natural state of humans as "nasty, brutish, and short." He argued that big people picked on little people, who in turn picked on anyone they could terrorize.

According to Hobbes, the only way for mankind to preserve itself was to create the "Leviathan," a monster bigger than anything that got in its way. The Leviathan was society—small men formed alliances that made them more powerful than big men.

Hobbes' theory should not be overlooked when considering the history of diplomacy. Take, for instance, the Yamato Clan of Ancient Japan. The Yamato were in and of themselves no more powerful than any of their neighbors. What made them special was their ability to forge alliances.

The leader of the Yamato Clan might form alliances with Clans A, B, C, and D while intentionally keeping these clans from forming alliances among themselves. These alliances were predicated on the notion that if anyone attacks one of the clans in the alliance, the other one will protect it. Hence, if Colony E attacked Colony D, the Yamato would come to D's defense.

Colony E would be foolish to attack Colony D because if the Yamato came to defend D, Colonies A, B, and C would come to defend the Yamato. This also served as a warning to Colony D not to break the alliance. In the end, the Yamato made so many alliances that they were able to steamroll any clans not wanting to join their league.

Forging allies was not always advantageous. Having allies during the terrifying reign of Ancient Assyria sometimes meant that you had to join your friends in a losing campaign against a nearly undefeatable nation. Fighting against Assyria meant that you would lose most of your army. Losing to Assyria meant pain and death.

Chapter Two

ROME AND A FEW OF HER ENEMIES

Thy Naiad airs have brought me home,
To the glory that was Greece
And the grandeur that was Rome.

—Edgar Allan Poe

In some ways, Rome did not fall. It evaporated into the fabric of modern society. Roman ideas and words have crept into nearly every facet of our modern world. We get bored in forums, watch athletic contests in coliseums, and despise our senators in the same manner as the Romans of old. The Russians, who considered their country an extension of Byzantine Rome, called their emperor a tsar—a derivation of the Roman word Caesar. (The Germans borrowed from the Romans, too, calling their leader Kaiser.)

The similarities go deeper, however. Roman society—derived from Greek culture—influenced western education and military science. Recordkeeping, an everyday function in modern western society, comes from the Romans, who were meticulous chroniclers of records and histories.

To understand Rome's power, influence, and historical significance, let's look more closely at this great empire, its allies, and its enemies (as seen from the Roman point of view).

Rome: Cruel Conqueror, Benevolent Occupier

Would that the Roman people had but one neck.

—Caligula

If you accept the legends—and some legends deserve acceptance—Rome was founded by twin brothers named Romulus and Remus.

Their story begins with Aeneas, a Trojan refugee looking for a safe haven from the Greeks after his people lost the Trojan War. Legend says that Aeneas found his way to the Tiber River, where he won the favor of King Latinus, and married his daughter.

Generations later, one of Aeneas' descendants gave birth to the twins. Their father was Mars, the god of war. The cruel-hearted villain in this story was Amulius, who usurped Aeneas' throne and tried to kill his descendants. He made one mistake, however. Instead of killing the boys himself, he gave them to a servant who simply left them along a riverbank. There, Remus and Romulus were discovered by a she-wolf who nursed them, eventually leaving them with a shepherd who raised them to manhood.

When the boys were of age to avenge their family, they killed Amulius and reclaimed their city. But now things really got ugly. Since they were both the same age, neither Remus nor Romulus could claim a birthright, so they had equal claim to the throne. Both wanting to rule, they decided to see whom the gods desired to be king.

On a particular morning, they went to see who could find the most birds—birds being a sign of divine approval—the winner being the one who observed the greatest number. Remus found the first bird, but only a moment later Romulus saw a flock and was declared the winner.

Unhappy with these results, Remus taunted his brother and leaped over the wall of the city. This angered Romulus, who slew his twin, declaring that all who leaped its walls would die.

Rome takes its name from Romulus—the man who tradition says founded the city and became its first king.

While the story about the wolf-boys is great fun, it is, um...a bit unlikely. Modern historians believe that at least two of the early kings of Rome were Etruscans—the people who inhabited the area before it became Rome.

Rome was embattled from its infancy as three tribes frequently raided the fledgling nation. A resolute people, the Romans survived these tribal skirmishes only to be sacked hard by marauders from Gaul (the area now known as France, Belgium, and part of Germany) in B.C. 390.

Rome sent an army to meet the Gauls, but the fierce appearance of these strange warriors confounded the Romans, and they were defeated, leaving their barbaric enemies to enter the city. According to Titus Livius, a Roman historian who wrote a 142-book set on the history of Rome, the only people left in Rome when the Gauls arrived were a garrison of soldiers and members of the senate.

Those who held the highest positions wished to die wearing the insignia of their rank or their decorations for distinguished service. So they put on the robes of civic dignitaries or of conquering generals and sat down on magisterial chairs in their courtyards.

Livius goes on to say that the Roman leaders were butchered in their chairs and that the people of Rome finally paid the Gauls 450 kilograms of gold to leave.

Rome recovered, however, and entered a series of wars with its neighbors. After defeating the Etruscans in B.C. 351, Rome set its eye on consolidating the Italian peninsula. As the great Macedonian army led by Alexander the Great tore through Asia Minor and the Middle East, Rome emerged as the greatest power on the peninsula. The Romans finished off the last of their neighbors around the time that Alexander died in B.C. 323. Though they would not become world conquerors for nearly 200 years, the Romans quickly began engineering strategic alliances to undermine the shaky empire Alexander had bequeathed his generals.

Macedonia:
The World's First Great Conqueror

Macedonia's rule was brief, vanishing after only two generations, but it propelled Greece into world domination.

In 359 B.C., Philip II became king of Macedonia, a small nation just north of Greece. Philip, who spent part of his youth as a prisoner in Thebes, had learned the Theban war technique of the phalanx—a formation consisting of two rows of eight men with overlapping shields and long pikes. Philip used this technique to win some impressive skirmishes with Greek city-states, and then used it again to punish a combined Athenian-Theban army in the Battle of Chaeronea in B.C. 338.

This last victory left Philip II the undisputed leader of Greece, but he did not have long to enjoy it. In B.C. 336, as he was preparing to invade Persia, he was assassinated.

Philip's son, Alexander, took over for his father and raised the empire's war efforts to new heights. He conquered Persia and Tyre. The Egyptians welcomed him and freely submitted to his authority. He established the city of Alexandria.

Alexander's world tour continued. He made his way through Asia Minor and even attacked regions of India before he finally died of natural causes in B.C. 323 at the age of 33.

Since Alexander did not leave heirs, his generals carved up his empire into three regions: Palestine, Egypt, and Syria.

Rome Ascends

As Alexander was ruling the world, the Romans were developing their own brand of military science. They established an all-volunteer army with enlistment terms that were both severe and generous.

Though joining the Roman army was a career move, few soldiers ever re-enlisted. To join, soldiers had to agree to a 25-year commitment. And Roman recruiting officers wouldn't take just anyone. To join, you had to be at least five-foot-eight, in good health, and a Roman citizen. (Up until the rule of Caesar, much later, only land-owning citizens could join.)

Soldiers were forbidden to marry, though this rule was not strictly enforced. After joining, they were sent to a rigorous boot camp with training in the use of the short sword and the javelin. Recruits were worked rigorously for conditioning. They were also drilled relentlessly on tactics and formations until they were honed in the skills of war.

This training proved invaluable when they faced tribal armies such as the Gauls, who were larger and stronger individually but completely disorganized in battle. Even the army of Alexander the Great was disorganized when compared with these disciplined forces.

But Rome could not muster a large enough army to conquer and occupy the world on its own. More than half of Rome's soldiers were mercenaries from conquered lands who joined "auxiliary" units in exchange for meager pay and citizenship. (Of course, the Romans, wise to testing their conscripts' loyalties, never used auxiliary mercenaries in campaigns against their homelands.)

Rome began its world domination tour by conquering the nations along the shores of the Mediterranean Sea. In B.C. 197, the Romans took Greece and started south. But not all of their conquests came through war. The leaders of several nations, including Egypt, decided they would rather be Rome's confederates than her enemies.

One people that did not submit were the Phoenicians.

Carthage: The Thorn in Rome's Side

Weigh Hannibal: how many pounds will you find in that great general?

—Justinian

Rome's aggressive movement around the Mediterranean was on a collision course. The Phoenicians, a seafaring people, would not bow to Rome's might. In B.C. 264, the unyielding Phoenicians and the unstoppable Romans went to war.

The fulcrum for the first Punic (Latin for Phoenician) War was the island of Sicily. The Romans wanted it, and so did the people of Carthage—a wealthy Phoenician city along what is now the Tunisian coast. Fully aware of the powerful Carthaginian fleet, the Romans were forced to build a navy using a captured Carthaginian vessel as a model for their new ships. With a navy finally assembled, war broke out. Two huge Roman fleets were lost, and only the third—propelled by enormous determination and courage—won the final victory.

Rome's sea-battle strategy was based on ramming other ships and capturing them by boarding. Roman galleys carried huge wooden bridges, or "gangways," with spiked legs that they would slam into enemy decks. The spikes would dig into the wood, securing their hold, and then soldiers would rush across and make the fight a hand-to-hand battle.

By taking control of the sea from the Carthaginians, the Romans were able to annex Sicily. They also took Sardinia. And they created an implacable enemy whose anger would one day bring the battle to the very gates of Rome— Hamilcar Barca.

The conflict with Rome meant desperate measures for Carthage. Its trade-based economy was crippled during the war. Losing its island colonies and suffering the cost of waging a 23-year war left Carthage unable to pay the mercenaries it had hired to help fight Rome. Having barely survived Rome, the Carthaginians now found themselves being attacked by the soldiers they had hired.

Carthage might have become a small footnote in history execpt for a great general named Hamilcar Barca. This stalwart leader rallied the Carthaginian army and defeated the traitorous enemy. In Hamilcar Barca's mind, however, the real enemy was Rome. He instilled this hatred for the northern empire in his

son, Hannibal, whose goal in life was to punish the accursed enemy. Hannibal was throughly indoctrinated and promised vengeance. And Hannibal was good to his word.

As a young man, Hannibal moved with his father to New Carthage (now Cartagena in Spain), a Carthaginian colony on the Iberian Peninsula. There, Hamilcar Barca tutored the boy on the finer points of military science. He also reminded him of his vow of hatred so that Hannibal, like Remus, might one day leap the walls of Rome.

At the age of 26, Hannibal took over his father's army. The second Punic War was about to begin, and this time the Romans would have to meet the enemy in their own backyard.

By now the Romans had conquered most of Iberia, establishing it as a sort of demilitarized zone between the Carthaginians and their homeland. The boundary between their lands was the Ebro River. A treaty between Rome and Carthage stated that crossing the river would be a declaration of war. The treaty was upheld. When Hannibal crossed the Ebro and entered Iberia, 69,000 infantryman, 12,000 cavalrymen, and 37 elephants arrived with him.

Hannibal's plan was extraordinary. He planned to bypass Roman outposts and attack the city unannounced. To accomplish this, he took the high road. Instead of traveling along the balmy Mediterranean coast, he led his men across the Pyrenees Mountains into France, then across the Alps and on to Rome. This route meant that he had to hack his way through the Celtic tribes of Gaul, the very people who had once brought Rome to her knees.

While some of the tribes let Hannibal's army pass unchallenged, others attacked as his men made their way along mountainous gorges on narrow ledges. Hannibal lost men and animals to these ambushes and still pressed on into the Alps, where he crossed rugged peaks of rock and snow. Of the 80,000 soldiers that began the march, only 50,000 now survived—and they still had the main event on the horizon.

With Hannibal at the helm, the Carthaginian army outflanked the Romans at every turn. Outnumbered in their first battle, Hannibal's men led the Romans into an ambush that cost the Romans 30,000 men and the Romans lost another 15,000 in their next meeting. By collapsing his lines around the enemy, he killed another 50,000 Roman soldiers in Cannae.

His best move, however, was purely defensive. Once, when confronted by a numerically superior adversary, Hannibal and his men retreated into a valley. As evening arrived, the Romans decided that the Carthaginians were trapped and that there would be no advantage in attacking at night.

As the night wore on, Roman watchmen spotted torches moving quietly along one side of the valley and warned their leaders that Hannibal was attempting to escape. The Romans followed, hoping to trap him, but they had fallen for a prank. Hannibal's men had tied torches to the horns of oxen and sent them packing. As the Romans converged upon an army of cattle, the Carthaginians escaped.

Hannibal's battle tactics were impeccable, but his overall strategy was flawed. Having dealt the Romans two crushing blows, he could have charged toward Rome with a psychological advantage. Instead, he spent the next several months dodging around the countryside, letting his men catch their breath and giving his enemies an opportunity to recover and cut off his supplies. The Romans even sacked New Carthage, Hannibal's Iberian home.

In B.C. 211, he got as far as the gates of Rome. He camped, threw a javelin into a sealed gate, but never attacked. His forces were too weak. From that time on, Hannibal was in retreat.

New Carthage fell to Rome in B.C. 210, and five years later Hannibal's army was on the run. By B.C. 202, the Romans took the war to Carthage, and Hannibal and his men abandoned any hope of conquering as they returned to save their homeland.

In B.C. 183, after spending time helping other enemies of Rome, Hannibal felt the tightening of the Roman noose. There was no more chance to escape. He'd heard of Roman enemies being paraded before the people then summarily executed, and that fate did not appeal to him. Instead, Hannibal Barca, the man who had taken an army across the Alps, poisoned himself and died.

Nearly 40 years later, in B.C. 146, the Romans destroyed Carthage once and for all. They burned the city, plowed the ashes into the ground, then poured salt over the ashes so that nothing would ever grow in its place.

The Rise of Caesar

Veni, vidi, vici
(I came, I saw, I conquered)

—Gaius Julius Caesar

Julius Caesar was a remarkable man, not simply because he proved to be a great general with a sound military mind, and not just because he repelled

Rome's worst enemies (and then turned around and conquered Rome itself)—but because he turned out to be an excellent dictator. Once in power, Caesar was good for Rome. He was born to a fairly wealthy family around B.C. 100. His uncle was a famous and respected general named Gaius Marius.

Rome was in turmoil during the days of Caesar's youth. The Senate, jealous of the power and popularity of its great generals, tried to keep the army busy fighting in other lands. Marius challenged the Senate and paid with his life.

After a stint as a junior officer in the army, Caesar was elected to the Senate at the age of 26. By B.C. 59, around the age of 41, his popularity—due in great part to his personal charisma—made him one of the most powerful men in Rome. It was just such charisma that cost Caesar's uncle his life.

To protect himself, Caesar allied himself with two of his greatest rivals—Gnaeus Pompey, who many considered the greatest military leader at the time, and Marcus Crassus, a Roman businessman whose wealth made him a target of Senate jealousy. This uneasy but powerful alliance gave its members safety from the Senate. Though the Senate might have challenged them separately, they were too strong as a group.

With Pompey and Crassus watching his back, Caesar became governor of three Roman provinces. One of these was Narbonese, which bordered Gaul, the land of Rome's ancient enemy.

Caesar used his post as governor to take command of an army. Though he wanted the army for protection, he also had to lead it into battle for the good of the Empire. But he did not realize was that he was about to enter a protracted war.

His first battles were with the Helvetii, a tribe of Germanic people who wanted to migrate across Narbonese. Caesar gave their enormous caravan permission to cross Narbonese, but then attacked them—effecting the wholesale slaughter of 80,000 Helvetii. His rational for the slaughter, according to Plutarch's Life of Caesar was, "The Germans were quite intolerable neighbors...."

To that point in history, most of Rome's frontier provinces were coastal lands around the Mediterranean. Caesar now took his armies north and west, through the lands we now know as France, Belgium, and Germany. Amazingly, he even nibbled at England. As he won one battle after another, his army grew and so did his prestige in Rome. He was, after all, fighting a holy battle with the nations that had once terrorized Rome.

As Caesar finished his conquest of Gaul, his wealthy ally, Crassus, led an army into Iraq. Unprepared for desert warfare, Crassus' army was massacred and he was murdered while meeting under a flag of truce.

With Crassus dead, the Senate now played Pompey against Caesar. Believing their man to be the better general, they increased Pompey's army and ordered Caesar to give up his command. Realizing that he would have no protection if he yielded his army, Caesar refused and marched on Rome. It took him less than a year to defeat Pompey, and in B.C. 45, he had himself declared supreme dictator of Rome.

He was murdered the following year, on March 15—the infamous Ides of March. (Interestingly, like Kennedy and Lincoln, Caesar received a warning shortly before his assassination at the hands of several senators. As he walked to the Senate that morning, someone handed him a note warning of a plan to kill him and providing the names of the perpetrators. He never read it.)

During his short tenure as supreme leader of Rome, Caesar made several momentous decisions. He began programs to restore the beauty of Rome. Because so much attention was focused on conquering new territories, the Senate had allowed the city to fall into disrepair. His urban renewal plan included improved housing and expanding the city. And as an act of good will, he left his riverside estate to the people.

In many ways, Caesar initiated the golden age of Rome. His nephew Octavius, later known as Augustus Caesar, continued along the paths laid by Julius Caesar. Rome flourished.

Over the next two centuries, the Romans would adopt for their army lighter, stronger armor offering better protection and more mobility. New generals would renew Caesar's invasion of England and win. And Rome would become an economic marvel as well as a military phenomenon.

Palmyra: Zenobia's Rebellion

She claimed her descent from the Macedonian kings of Egypt, equaled in beauty her ancestor Cleopatra, and far surpassed that princess in chastity and valor.

Maintaining safe trade routes and easy mobility between the Middle East and Europe became a critical issue as Rome turned its eye to commerce. With this in mind, the smarter emperors tried to accommodate cities positioned on

important crossroads. One such city was Palmyra, an ancient Syrian city-state that sat halfway between the Euphrates River and the Mediterranean Sea.

Thanks to its location, Palmyra was a wealthy city receiving a great deal of lenience from Rome. Emperor Hadrian made it a free city in 129 A.D., and Emperor Caracalla (who began his reign by murdering his younger brother) made Palmyra a colony and exempted it from taxes.

Around 254 A.D., Shapur I of Persia began an extraordinary campaign to take the Middle East away from Rome and keep it for himself. His forces captured 37 cities in the area and closed the area to Roman and Palmyrian trade. When Valerian, the Roman emperor at that time, met with him to discuss making peace, Shapur took him hostage. Valerian died a prisoner in Persia.

Valerian had an ally that Shapur had underestimated. Septimus Odenathus, a member of Palmyra's ruling family, was powerful and fierce. He assembled an army, struck back at the Persians, recapturing cities and avenging Valerian, and dealt a nearly crippling blow to the Persians. Naturally, he won the undying respect of Rome. Already a citizen of Rome due to his noble birth, Odenathus was named "Governor of all the East," by Gallienus, Valerian's son and co-emperor.

Shortly upon his return from a victorious battle with the Persians, a band of assassins led by a young relative murdered both Odenathus and his eldest son. But Odenathus' murderous nephew, and later Rome, did not take into account the strength and courage of Zenobia, the widow of Odenathus. She killed the assassins who had murdered her husband. She then placed herself on the throne by declaring her young son to be king and made herself his regent.

Unlike her husband, Zenobia had no interest in an alliance with Rome. Instead, she declared Palmyra independent, dubbed herself "Queen of the East," and set off to capture her ancestral home of Egypt. While Rome was distracted with other threats, she took Egypt and extended her reign into Asia Minor. Then the Romans came to visit.

Zenobia may have been a tough, well-educated woman, but she was no match for Aurelian—a hardened general bent on restoring Roman order. Some cities simply submitted when they heard whom Rome had sent. Others, such as Tyana, put up a fight but soon submitted to the unstoppable force.

The Palmyrian army, with Zenobia giving commands, met the Romans near Antioch—Rome's Asian capital. The Palmyrian army, composed mainly of light archers and heavy cavalry dressed in steel armor, overpowered the

Romans at first blush. Their cavalry broke through the Roman lines and forced a retreat.

But the Romans had a method behind their assault. After the Palmyrian archers used up their arrows as the Romans cavalry retreated, the archers were left undefended and unarmed. Aurelian's veteran troops closed in and eliminated the archers with ease, then turned on the cavalry.

They fought again near a town called Emesa, with the same results. Her army destroyed, Zenobia fled to Palmyra, her last refuge. She retired within the walls of her capital, made every preparation for a vigorous resistance, and declared, with the intrepidity of a heroine, that the last moment of her reign and her life should be the same.

Zenobia hoped that she could wait out Aurelian's siege, that her Arab neighbors would bring her food and supplies as the hot sun weakened the Romans. What she didn't count on was the Romans intercepting supplies as they arrived. When she heard that Rome had retaken Egypt, she attempted to flee with her son, but the Romans caught her.

Aurelian was exceptionally kind when Palmyra surrendered. He placed the city in the care of an appointed governor and left only 600 archers in the garrison guarding the city. His kindness may have been a token of his esteem for the fallen Odenathus, but it was misplaced.

As he returned to Europe, Aurelian was informed that the people of Palmyra had destroyed the garrison, killed the archers, and murdered the governor. He immediately turned his army and revisited the city he had dismissed so lightly.

Antioch was alarmed by his rapid approach, and the helpless city of Palmyra felt the full weight of his resentment. Aurelian himself wrote that old men, women, children, and peasants were victims of a terrible retribution.

Zenobia's punishment was cruel and unusual. Aurelian brought her to Rome, where she married a senator who kept her in his villa near the Tiber.

Two Romes

The Roman emperors who ruled the world came from many lands—Syria, Spain, Illyria, and Germany, as well as the Italian homeland. We often remember them for their eccentricities: Tiberius, who deserted his capital and ruled from a villa in Capri, consulting the stars with an astrologer; Caligula, who in his madness proposed his horse for consul; the miser Vespasian,

skeptical of his future divinity, who on his deathbed quipped, "I think I am becoming a god."

When the Praetorian Guard, elite protectors of the imperial city, assassinated Caligula, they pulled his uncle from behind a curtain and named him emperor. Claudius proved a good ruler but an unlucky lover. His third wife plotted against him with her paramour. But probably it was his fourth, Agrippina, who poisoned him. She enthroned her son Nero, then fought him for power. Nero had her thrown into the sea—when she swam ashore, his troops caught and killed her. Henceforth, as if to drown his guilt, he pursued pleasure above all else. He competed as a chariot racer, harpist, and actor—not surprisingly, he won every event he entered, even some he did not. At last, when everyone turned against him, he ordered a retainer to kill him, crying: "What an artist the world is losing!"

In Nebuchadnezzar's dream, he prophetically saw Rome as the legs of a great idol. Interestingly, Rome did split into two separate empires. Western Rome lasted until 476 A.D., when a young ruler (ironically bearing the same name as the fabled founder of Rome) was deposed. Detractors called him "Momyllus," meaning little disgrace.

Young Romulus, however, was hardly the first Western Roman leader to face ridicule and defeat. The tides of fortune had long turned on Rome, and the once-great empire barely stumbled through the fourth century.

In 306 A.D., Emperor Constantine turned his eyes eastward and resettled his nation's capital in Byzantium (now Istanbul). The empire remained united for another 90 years, but with the death of Theodosius I, in 395 A.D., the Roman Empire became two nations.

The Eastern nation survived another thousand years before fading into history.

Other Nations

Rome had more than its fair share of enemies. Here are some you'll be dealing with.

Babylon

Out of the chaos and struggle for power in the ancient world, a man of order arose—Hammurabi. This leader, who established the first Babylonian Empire and whose reign lasted from B.C. 1792-1750, created a special code of law that was inscribed on huge stone tablets. The laws were fierce and clear cut. Thieves, surgeons charged with malpractice, and boys who hit their parents had their hands cut off—innkeepers who overcharged for drinks were drowned.

Over the next 500 years, the Assyrians, Babylon's once docile neighbors, emerged as a great power. Few leaders had the nerve to willingly challenge them. The Assyrian army had mighty weapons such as enormous battering rams for destroying city walls and mobile towers manned with archers. If you fought against this massive force and lost, your entire army (and sometimes your entire population) could be subject to torture and death. The following is an excerpt from a letter written by an Assyrian leader:

"Many captives from among them I burned with fire, and many I took as living captives. From some I cut off their noses, their ears and their fingers, of many I put out the eyes. I made one pillar of the living and another of heads, and I bound their heads to tree trunks round about the city. Their young men and maidens I burned in fire."

Nineveh, the capital of Assyria, fell in B.C. 612. Once Assyria fell, the Chaldeans raised Babylon to new splendor. Under the leadership of Nebuchadnezzer II, the heir to the Chaldean throne, Babylon returned to world-power status, sacking nations and building a splendid fortified city.

This new Babylon was strong and beautiful. The largest city in the world in its day (2500 acres), Babylon was built on both sides of the Euphrates River and had walls so thick that it was said a four-horsed chariot could drive along the top. In the center of the city were two magnificent structures, a 250-foot ziggurat that featured three staircases and the palace of Nebuchadnezzer II.

Despite its might and thick walls, the city of Babylon was captured in a single night. During the reign of Nabonidus, Nebuchadnezzer's son, King Cyrus, the man who united the Medes and Persians, attacked the great city on a Babylonian High Holiday.

Rather than alert the Babylonians to his arrival by breaching the city's thick walls, Cyrus had his army reroute the Euphrates River so that they could wade through its bogs. The Persians quietly entered the city without disturbing the Babylonian celebration. Cyrus' men quickly murdered the few citizens who did see the army enter the city. When the Babylonians shouted for help, Cyrus' men "joined in the shout with them, as if they were revelers themselves," then killed them when no one was watching.

Egypt

Egypt is older than human history as we know it. It has existed in one form or another since approximately 3200 B.C., and was nearly 4700 years old when Columbus sailed over the edge of the Earth and found the other side. When the United States proudly celebrated its 200th birthday, Egypt was nearly 5200 years old.

Menes was Egypt's first king, but not the first pharaoh (meaning "he of the great house"). He and his immediate successors formed the first dynasty. The Egyptians did not start calling their kings pharaohs until the New Kingdom period—1700 years and 17 dynasties after Menes' reign.

Though it was certainly the world's greatest superpower in its time, early Egypt did not have a standing army. From the days of Menes all the way into the Old Kingdom period (2700 B.C., the third-sixth dynasties), the king of Egypt called his men to arms during times of war, then allowed them to return to their farms in times of peace.

Egypt did not emerge as a world-threatening imperial power for several generations. It flourished culturally in its Old Kingdom period (B.C. 2755-2255), emerged from a period of disunity lasting from B.C. 2255-2134, and began its Middle Kingdom Period, only to be conquered by Hyksos in B.C. 1700.

Described as an Asiatic Semitic people also known as the "Shepherd-Kings," the Hyksos army deployed a new weapon for which Egypt was unprepared—the chariot. The Hyksos chariot was a sturdy unit with heavy construction and four-spoked wheels.

During their years of captivity, a group of Egyptian princes in Thebes modified this design to fit the arid Egyptian landscape. After 120 years of occupation, an Egyptian army led by men in lightweight chariots with six-spoked wheels defeated the Hyksos army.

The royal power of Egypt suddenly centered around Theban princes, and the very imperial eighteenth dynasty began. During this reign, the dynamic Hatshepsut, Egypt's greatest ruling queen, usurped power from Thutmose III, who was both her nephew and son-in-law (the son of her husband's concubine who married Hateshepsut's daughter), and ruled Egypt.

After 20 years of unwillingly sharing the throne with Hatshepsut, Thutmose III got the last laugh after her death. He had Hatshepsut's name removed from all of the temples and monuments she had built.

Egypt used two kinds of fighting units—chariots and foot soldiers armed with bows, clubs, shields, and axes or spears. Two soldiers usually drove chariots—one whose job was solely to drive and another who assaulted enemies with arrows and javelins. Contrary to the Hollywood image of a line of chariots following swarms of foot soldiers into battle, it was the charioteers who usually led the way.

During the twentieth dynasty (approximately B.C. 1180), Egypt added a third weapon to its arsenal—fighting ships. After suffering from an attack by a group called the Sea People (possibly the Minoans), the Egyptians developed a navy and fought back, eventually defeating the invaders.

Greece

Between B.C. 800 and 650, the small autonomous city-states of which Greece was composed saw the rise of the "tyrants" (the word referred to the aristocrats who overthrew the existing monarchies). Though the term has come to refer to abusive leaders, the original tyrants, all too aware of their tenuous situations, were generally popular with their subjects.

In B.C. 546, Cyrus, the destroyer of Babylon, took his conquering act to Greece and captured most of the country in the name of Persia. After Athens and Eritrea revolted in B.C. 499, Cyrus destroyed an entire Greek town and demanded complete obeisance by all Greeks.

When Sparta and Athens revolted in B.C. 490, Cyrus sent a huge army to teach them a lesson. Unfortunately for Athens, Sparta was too busy with a religious ceremony to help in the war when the Persian army arrived. That left Athens to attend to Cyrus alone. Amazingly, the Athenian army defeated the Persians and earned independence without Spartan help.

In B.C. 480, Xerxes I, the son of Cyrus, deciding it was time to deal with the Greeks once and for all, sent one of the largest fighting forces ever assembled to that time. Severely outnumbered but Spartan to the core, the leader of the Spartan army met the Persians with a much smaller force in a narrow pass. Because of his choice of battlefields, the Persian's numbers were nullified. Only a limited number of men could attack the Greeks because the narrowness of the pass admitted only a few men at a time.

The plan might have worked, but a traitor showed Xerxes' forces the back door. To give most of his men time to withdraw, the heroic Spartan general and 1000 men held off the Persians as long as possible. They fought heroically to the last man and perished.

The Persians were not so successful in their naval assault. As Xerxes watched from a safe mountain location overlooking the battle, the 1200-ship Persian navy took on a 400-ship Grecian armada and lost.

The Assyrians

The most feared army of its time, the Assyrian army included chariots, archers, slingmen, spearsmen, battering rams, mobile towers, and spies.

As high priests to the god Ashur, Assyrian kings were assigned the task of enlarging their lord's holdings. Thus the Assyrian expansion was, to them, a holy war.

Unlike Greece and Babylon, Assyria was not a gracious master. Nations that did not surrender to Assyrian expansion were massacred. Those that gave up without a fight were required to pay huge tributes and submit to military service.

The Hittites

No one knows who the Hittites were or where they came from. Because they spoke an Indo-European language, many scholars speculate that they came from somewhere north of the Black Sea.

The Hittites, known to be fierce warriors with superior iron weapons, were the first civilization in their region to domesticate horses, and they had chariots before most of their neighbors.

A lengthy feud broke out between the Hittites and the Egyptians when the bereaved widow of the pharaoh Tutankhamun asked the Hittite leader King Suppiluliuma I to send one of his sons for a husband. The king reluctantly agreed, but the boy never reached Egypt. The queen fell from power and the young man was murdered in transit.

The feud erupted into an enormous battle in B.C. 1286 in which the Hittites used a stratagem to surprise the Egyptians. Egyptian reinforcements arrived, however, and both sides went on to claim victory.

Around B.C. 1200, Hittite civilization disappeared as mysteriously as it began. The Mediterranean "Sea People" defeated and destroyed the Hittite city of Hattusa. Shortly thereafter the Hittites disappeared.

The Persians

Ancient Persia was located in what is now Iran. Under the leadership of Cyrus, the Persians and Medes banned together and conquered the known world— from the Indus River to the Euphrates Valley to the Aegean Coast. To maintain this empire, Cyrus' descendants set up an elite 15,000-man royal guard who managed a much larger regular army that included recruits from conquered nations.

The Yamato Dynasty: The Clan that Would Be King

The Yamato Clan, named after the Yamato prefect on the main Japanese island of Honshu, rose to power sometime in the third century A.D. according to many historians.

Pre-Yamato Japan was a quagmire ruled by an estimated 100 rival tribes. The Yamato emperor, called a "Kimi," created a power-base by setting up strategic alliances with other tribes. As he grew more powerful, his partners slowly found themselves in subservient positions. He further promoted his position by promoting a Shinto religion in which the highest deity was a sun goddess of whom he claimed to be an heir.

Having unified much of Japan, the Yamato leaders then expanded into the Korean peninsula, where they set up an alliance with the kingdom of Paekche in their battle against the Silla—a Korean state allied with the Northern Chinese. The Paekche were weaker than their enemies and constantly needing help. In the end, the Silla defeated the Paekche and helped the Northern Chinese send the Yamato forces packing.

While the Yamato expansion into Korea was eventually frustrated by the Silla and their Chinese allies, it led to the introduction of new technologies and of Buddhism into Japan.

Little is known about Yamato battle techniques. What is known, however, is that the Yamato prized warriors and warrior skills. (It should be noted that the Yamato disappeared long before the Samurais and Shoguns rose to power.)

The defeat in Korea signaled the beginning of the end for the Yamato clan. Despite a brief return to power around 600 A.D., the Yamato Clan was unable to maintain its hold over the islands of Japan.

The Paekche

The Paekche were a third-century Korean people who established diplomatic relations with both Japan and China in a vain effort to establish themselves against more militaristic Korean kingdoms. It was through the Paekche that Japan was first introduced to Buddhism.

The Silla

Silla was a highly warlike third-century Korean kingdom that, in conjunction with the Chinese Shang (or Tang) Dynasty, ran the Yamato Clan out of Korea. With the Yamato no longer there to protect them, the Paekche and Koguryo kingdoms fell to the Silla, and by 668 A.D. the nation was unified.

References

Charles-Picard, Gilber. *The World of Hannibal; Greece and Rome: Builders of Our World*. Washington, D.C.: National Geographic Society, 1968.

Cottrell, Leonard. *Life Under the Pharaohs*. New York: Holt Rinehart and Winston, 1960.

Gibbons, Edward. *Decline and Fall of the Roman Empire*. New York: Harcourt, Brace and Company, 1960.

Grimal, Pierre. *The World of Caesar; Greece and Rome: Builders of Our World*. Washington, D.C.: National Geographic Society, 1968.

Hutchinson, Warner. *Ancient Egypt: Three Thousand Years of Splendor*. New York: Grosset & Dunlop, 1978.

Mellersh, H.E.L. *Sumer and Babylon*. New York: Thomas Y. Crowell Company, 1964.

Tingay, G.I.F. and Baddock, J. *These Were the Romans*. Pennsylvania: Dufour Editions, Inc., Chester Springs, 1972.

Chapter Three

WAR MECHANICS (SINGLE-PLAYER)

Julius Caesar made an amazing discovery while invading Gaul. He discovered that soldiers need to eat.

Before Caesar's campaign in Gaul, armies ate only the food they carried and anything they found along the way. This was fine for lightning attacks and quick-and-dirty campaigns, but when armies dug into towns and fortresses for months at a time, it was imperative that food had been stockpiled.

Caesar's response to feeding his well-traveled army was to set up supply trains that replenished food on a regular basis. Being governor of three neighboring provinces, Caesar had no problem arranging the logistics. Suddenly his army had a long-term advantage during sieges. He could wait out the enemy, and his soldiers were the ones with plenty of food.

This obvious requirement to arrange food supplies for an army is an especially important facet of real-time strategy games. The single-player activities in Microsoft's Age of Empires are not simply races to put together an army and invade the enemy—they require that players collect and allocate materials wisely. Developing a dependable system of immediate responses to feeding soldiers during battles and repairing damaged ships, walls, and towers during attacks is an important element in winning strategies.

Age of Empires and Microsoft's Rise of Rome are real-time strategy games (a euphemism for ulcer-causing challenges requiring nonstop decisions and action). These games are typically divided into missions or scenarios in which you are presented with goals and a force that, at the start, is inadequate to accomplish them.

Building Blocks

You begin most missions in Rise of Rome with a couple of villagers and a town center. Town centers are all-purpose buildings that can store wood, food, stone, and gold, as well as create new villagers.

AGE
of
EMPIRES

One of the defining elements in many real-time strategy games is the requirement to gather food and resources for building civilizations and armies. As you start your missions, have your villagers collect wood so that they can build barracks, houses, and other structures. Also have them build farms or forage for berries so that you can create more villagers or train soldiers.

You must also learn how to budget your resources. If it costs 50 units of food to create a villager and only 30 units of food plus 20 units of wood to train an archer, you may be tempted to go with the archer because he's cheaper. That's not a bad choice if your city is under attack and you want to place someone behind walls to protect against invaders. Archers are little use, however, if you need to gather wood or hunt for food.

Another defining element of many real-time strategy games is the style of combat. As you look at your screen during the game, you will notice that large portions of the playing map are blacked out. This is called the "fog of war"—you see only areas that your men have explored—and it creates problems for every player. Just because you can't see enemies hiding in the fog of war doesn't mean they can't see you. The only way to defog the map is to explore it, and the safest time to explore enemy territory is early in the game—before your enemies have archers and towers. Once you explore an area, it remains defogged on your map.

Of course, the sword cuts both ways. Once your enemies have explored your area, they'll see your buildings. Also, some units have longer lines of sight than others. Catapults, archers, and priests can see much farther than such nearsighted ninnies as axemen, clubmen, and villagers. There will be moments in the game when you think your villager is standing alone and undetected, while, in truth, a catapult is preparing to splatter him.

As you build your civilization, you'll need to send armies to explore uncharted areas in search of enemy cities. Naturally, this exposes your armies to all kinds of ambushes and other dirty tricks.

Another element of real-time strategy games (and this one is in marked contrast to traditional combat simulations) is that you do not take turns. In traditional war simulations—Risk, for example, or even checkers or chess—each side takes a turn striking at the enemy or making defensive arrangements. In real-time strategy games, both sides fight without pausing.

Real-time strategy games evoke emotional responses—laughter, joy, frustration, and anger. You spend time developing strategies only to discover that they don't work, or you thoughtfully develop an entire civilization only to

have a herd of mongrels
crush it into dust. You
scream, cuss, and rail—but
you love it!

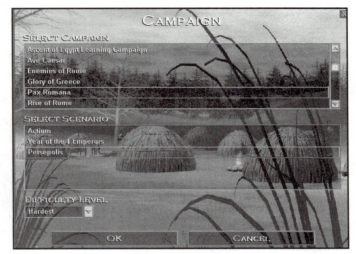

Scenarios
and Campaigns

The campaigns in Rise of
Rome compose an interactive
story. Think of a campaign as
a book with eight interactive
chapters called scenarios.

The scenarios are
missions based on historical
models. Each scenario begins
with a description of who
you will fight and why, and

*Use this screen to select your campaign and enter
the missions.*

present a set of objectives. Win the war, and the game gives you an explanation
of what actually happened in history. (If you're good, you may even help the
Romans or Palmyrans win battles that they actually lost.)

Before you can play a campaign, you need an identity so that your
computer can record your victories. To start a campaign, select the single-player
option from the opening screen, then select Campaigns. A window will open,
asking you to type in your name for a new campaign or to select your name
from a list if you are continuing one.

There are three windows inside the campaign selection screen. The first
lists the nations included in the campaigns—Rome, Carthage, Macedonia, and
Palmyra. The next window lists available scenarios. Bruce Shelley, one of the
evil geniuses who created Rise of Rome, wanted the game to contain scenarios
with factual story lines. With this in mind, he designed all of the scenarios
around pivotal historical junctures and worked to immortalize these historical
Kodak moments as challenging missions.

The third window sets the difficulty level for each scenario. Do not take
this decision lightly. On the easier settings, Rise of Rome lets you cruise along,
building your civilization and attacking your enemies whenever you feel ready.

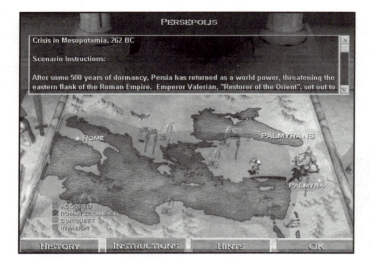

Each scenario is introduced by a set of circumstances and objectives.

You'll face the same number of enemies as in the harder levels, but they won't be as aggressive and they may even seem mysteriously nearsighted.

On the hardest settings, the game sends enemies at you on a regular basis. Enemy nations build their cities and armies faster—and enemy priests, siege weapons, and towers have better ranges of vision.

Logically, beginning players should not attempt the hardest levels, and experienced gamers should avoid the easier levels. Once you've selected your campaign, mission, and difficulty level, click OK to launch your mission.

Rise of Rome provides access to more than historical circumstances and mission objectives at the beginning of each scenario. A hints screen, available by clicking the button on the bottom of the screen, offers subtle suggestions.

Once you understand your objectives and want to begin the battle, click OK.

Campaign Differences

If you have just purchased Age of Empires and Rise of Rome, try playing Age of Empires' Egyptian campaign first. This campaign is a tutorial starting you off with easy missions, such as establishing towns, building farms, and slaughtering an underwhelming civilization. They get tougher as you go, but you won't face any real danger in Egypt until you get to the seventh mission.

Unlike the campaigns in Age of Empires, which cover a variety of civilizations, most of the campaigns in Rise of Rome follow a single nation—Rome. There is one exception—the scenarios in Ave Caesar are seen through

the eyes of Roman enemies Hannibal, Zenobia, and Spartacus (the latter a runaway slave who led a nearly successful revolt against Rome in B.C. 71).

This exception plays out in the first campaign. Ave Caesar follows certain events in Julius Caesar's life as he establishes himself as the most powerful man in Rome. The first scenario is based on an event in his early life. The next two are based on his battles in Gaul, where he proved himself to be a forceful general. The final scenario follows Caesar as he crosses the Rubicon Line. The Rubicon, a river in central Italy, was the boundary between Rome and the Cisalpine territories that Caesar had been sent to govern. Crossing the river was a declaration of war—and in this scenario, Caesar gets all the war he can handle.

The action in Enemies of Rome, the second campaign, has no real theme (except, of course, combat). In the first scenario, you control a primitive Carthaginian civilization as it prepares to attack Iron Age Romans while fighting their nasty Tool Age allies. From here you go to scenarios that involve building civilizations and a particularly vexing mission in which you must lead a powerful army through a deadly gauntlet.

In Pax Romana, you have to deal with the problems of running an established empire. The Palmyrans are unhappy, and the Assyrians are on the rise. These missions are among the toughest in the game. Expect to find yourself outgunned and outnumbered at every turn.

The final campaign—alphabetically though not chronologically—is the eponymous Rise of Rome. This set of scenarios lets you build, destroy, and defend wonders, and forces you to find ways to crack into a couple of cities with very puzzling designs.

The Original Campaigns

You need to own Age of Empires to play Rise of Rome. Here's a brief summary of the campaigns you'll tackle in Age of Empires.

Egyptian: This campaign is a tutorial. Very easy at first, it gradually becomes more challenging, but never gets difficult until the seventh mission.

Greek: This campaign begins with defensive missions and transforms into an offensive game. You go from helping the Athenians struggle against other Greek city-states to joining Alexander the Great as he conquers the world. The later missions are characterized by large freewheeling battles sometimes fought against multiple enemies.

Babylonian: This campaign is quite similar to the Greek campaign, except that more scenarios are defensive in nature. Much of your Babylonian experience will be about defending your territory rather than trying to expand it.

Yamato: This campaign is about revenge. In one mission, you send assassins to kill the leader of a clan who has challenged your allies. In two other missions, you go out to find and reclaim treasures stolen from your leaders.

Single-Player Death Match Basics

Rise of Rome has several play options available for those who have completed the campaigns or who do not relish the goal-oriented gaming style of the campaigns. The simplest of these options is the death match—a king-of-the-hill kind of battle in which you take on as many as seven computer-controlled nations in a fight for survival. You don't have to worry about guarding ruins or collecting artifacts—this is strictly a life-and-death situation.

The first thing you may notice in a death match is that all other nations appear to be ganging up on you. You can change that. By accessing an options window before your match, you can adjust settings. Here are several:

Number of Civilizations: You can have up to eight nations battling at once. This makes the second half of the game more difficult and considerably lengthy as you must clear as many as seven civilizations off the map for a victory.

Teams: You can form teams in death matches so that other civilizations join you in the battle as allies.

Starting Age: Most death matches begin with Tool Age civilizations racing to advance. The first nation to hit the Bronze Age usually takes the offense while others burrow in. (Some players actually prefer playing defensively in hopes of their opponents using up resources.) If you prefer to jump right into the battle, you can start your match in the Tool, Bronze, or Iron Age. This option generally leads to quicker matches.

Map Size: Changing the size of the map has a profound effect on the game. death matches on Large or Huge maps tend to be Iron Age battles. Since there is lots of space, nations tend to spread out and evolve before going to war. The "Small" and "Tiny" map options usually lead to Tool Age gang fights in which herds of clubmen kill villagers and swarm buildings.

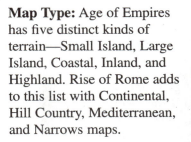

Map Type: Age of Empires has five distinct kinds of terrain—Small Island, Large Island, Coastal, Inland, and Highland. Rise of Rome adds to this list with Continental, Hill Country, Mediterranean, and Narrows maps.

Since you can select the kind of terrain on which the death match will be fought, it's important to know the characteristics of each map type. It's usually easier to beat the computer on maps with large bodies of water—though the computer does quite well in naval battles on

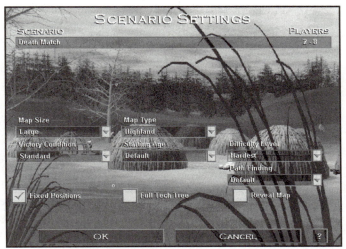

Using this screen, you can configure your death match in many ways.

the Hard and Hardest difficulty settings. Even so, the computer is slow to create a good fishing fleet, and you can often control large portions of the map by producing a strong fleet as quickly as possible.

Continental maps: Here all civilizations are located on a large island. While you can nibble away at the outskirts of your enemies' cities with triremes and juggernauts, the bulk of these wars are won with land troops.

Mediterranean maps: These are the opposite of Continental maps—they have a large body of water surrounded by land. You can seal off sections of these maps with a strong navy (think of your ships as mobile towers). You can use your ships to protect your army as you start invasions, and you should be able to find abundant fish supplies on these maps.

Small and Large Island maps: These are, of course, water-based maps with islands of various sizes. Battles on these maps are won and lost by controlling the waterways. If your enemies land their transports, your island will likely be overrun. If you can seal off your island and sink enemy ships as they approach, you will cost your enemy precious resources. You can destroy large sections of your enemies' cities with triremes and juggernauts on these maps.

Coastal maps: These feature a large body of water along one edge. Ships play a mostly defensive role in coastal battles. You can use them like towers to protect your city if you are low on stone, but they will not play a decisive role in any invasion plans.

Inland and Narrows maps: These each feature significant rivers. Narrows maps have large bodies of water on two sides and Inland maps usually have one large body and many rivers. You can use war galleys and scout ships to your advantage in the Tool Age and Bronze Age portions of these battles, but ships are generally useless later on. They will not have enough room to avoid catapult, tower, or archer fire—and enemy priests will have an easy time converting them. Left alone, your ships may even beach themselves while attacking and be destroyed by land forces. While you can establish a steady food supply with a fishing fleet in a Narrows battle, you shouldn't invest too heavily in a large navy.

Highland maps: These are land-based maps that usually include a couple of bodies of water. It's fine to build a couple of ships to use like towers in highland battles, and you might want to do some fishing—but don't count on major naval battles. Of all the terrain options, only the Hill Country map lacks bodies of water.

You begin death matches with three villagers, a town center, 20,000 units of wood and food, 10,000 units of gold, and 5000 units of stone. These initial supplies are more than sufficient for a fast battle; but should the match devolve into a war of attrition, you will need more supplies to continue.

A quick word to Palmyra fans. One of the drawbacks with Palmyra is the expense of its villagers. Each costs 75 units of food—meaning you will have a longer start-up time in most situations. Since you have 20,000 units of food from the opening bell, this problem is neutralized in death matches.

The first point of order in a death match is to get your city ready. You will need houses so that you can build a large population. Assuming your match starts in the Stone Age, you'll need a granary and a storage pit for upgrading your forces. You may even want to build several storage pits so that you can make multiple upgrades quickly. This comes in handy if you get invaded before your army is ready to fight.

Death matches are races in which the first person with a standing army wins. Don't just build one or two barracks, stables and archery pits—build as many as ten so that you can crank units out. You don't get points for economizing—so think big.

Random Map Basics

Random Map battles are almost exactly like death matches. The main difference is Random Match's allowance of one additional, and very important, option—you can select three different victory conditions. The Standard setting allows you to win by holding all artifacts or ruins for 2000 years, wiping your opponents off the map, or building a wonder. Ironically, perhaps, the Standard victory setting offers the most challenge.

The other difference between death matches and Random Map games is the amount of resources allocated in the beginning. But this is no minor change.

You begin Random Map matches with three villagers, a town center, 200 units of food, 200 units of wood, and 150 units of stone. (You can opt to start with extra resources—1000 units of wood and food and 750 units of stone.)

Having to scramble for food and wood from the start slows the pace of the game. Instead of simply getting to build, build, build—you now have to forage and hunt. Many players put together armies of clubmen and attempt to annihilate some of their neighbors. Such a move would be a wasted effort in a death match. With 20,000 units of wood and food, you can simply replace your buildings and people.

Chapter Four

WHAT EVERY EMPEROR SHOULD KNOW

There is no *best* weapon in Microsoft's Rise of Rome. Clubmen may be able to kill villagers, but they are no match for axemen, who in turn cannot stand up to cavalry, who are vulnerable to towers, which are helpless against heavy catapults.

Every unit has its own strengths and weaknesses. Play the strengths and you put together an unbeatable army. The trick is coming up with the right combinations of units and keeping them organized for peak performance.

A number of excellent changes has been made in the game since the original Microsoft's Age of Empires release in 1997. Age of Empires was a best-selling title and one of the most popular choices on Microsoft's Internet Gaming Zone. The result of so many players competing online is a dynamic cross-fertilization of new ideas. The best players learned from each other, and some developed uses for certain units that surprised even the game's developers.

In fact, there's been an interesting evolution in Age of Empires strategic thinking. One of the first strategies of choice was the "archer rush," in which players took civilizations with strong bowmen such as the Assyrians, and tried for the early knockout. The archer rush gave way, however, to the "Bronze Age Invasion," a strategy that encouraged players to rush to the Bronze Age, put together a cavalry posse, and try to overwhelm opponents. Other strategies have also come and gone.

To date, no strategy has proven unbeatable, yet some styles and tactics remain formidable. One strategic component that's common to top players is good personnel management.

Remember as you play this game that everything under your command is expendable. Whether it's a war elephant, a priest, a tower, or an entire town, you may come to a point when you must sacrifice it. And this brings us to the key of the gods—the Delete key.

Right click on any man, beast, or building under your control, then click Delete and it will die. This is essential to remember. The same wall that kept

your enemies out during their spoiled invasion may prevent your army from leaving your city to begin your attack. Delete it.

Perhaps, toward the end of a mission, you've reached your maximum population. You can look for fishing boats and villagers, units with little offensive value, and delete them. In the world of Age of Empires, Delete is the key to personnel management.

To understand more about the units you'll be managing, let's look at specifics. What follows is a summary of the kinds of units you can train, beginning with those you can train in the Stone Age and ending with units unique to the Iron Age.

Stone Age Forces

The Stone Age phase is generally considered to be a foot race to the Tool Age. It is a good time to explore the map. Since your enemies are unlikely to have anything more powerful than clubmen, the greatest dangers you'll likely encounter during the Stone Age are a few lions.

The Stone Age, however, is the time when you stake your claim on the map. You should send villagers to find berry bushes, stone, gold, and wood—then build storage pits and granaries beside them to dig in and grab supplies. You will have to defend these claims in later eras—so do not spread yourself too thin.

You need villagers to construct buildings, cut wood, hunt gazelles, and forage for food.

Villagers: The Basic Building Blocks of Society

Villagers are both your most basic unit and your most valuable unit. You need villagers to erect buildings, to gather food, to mine stone and gold, to repair buildings and walls, to fix ships after and during battles, to tend farms, and to hunt. In a pinch, you can even throw them into battle.

Your society stagnates when you run out of villagers and no longer have the means to create more of them. Conversely, you can build an entire city with one villager and 120 units of wood to build a storage pit; but once you lose all of your villagers, all you can do is hold on until your resources give out.

Points of Interest

- Purchasing woodcutting, gold mining, and stone mining upgrades from your market speeds your villagers by enabling them to carry more materials at one time.
- You can upgrade your villagers' strength and speed once your society enters the Iron Age. The Jihad upgrade, available in most Iron Age temples, increases your villagers' speed, strength, and hit points. The siegecraft upgrade, offered in Iron Age markets, increases their ability to attack walls and towers.
- Because they are both fast and cheap, Jihad and siegecraft villagers are the perfect tool for destroying catapults. Once you place a villager—or anyone else—directly in front of a catapult, it stops firing.

Clubmen

You can train only one kind of soldier in a Stone Age village: the clubman, a big-hearted troglodyte who tends to stand around and smack other clubmen like a kid in a pillow fight. (Historically, clubmen used tree limbs with shells and sharp stones embedded in the wood—not pillows.)

Clubmen are the only combat units available for Stone Age battles. They are slow and not particularly powerful, and it doesn't take much to wipe them out since they can't sustain much damage. In other words, unless you're planning a Stone Age assault, you should probably use your food for villagers since they can gather resources and erect buildings between battles (and fight nearly as well as clubmen).

Points of Interest

- The best feature of clubmen is their automatic conversion into axemen after you purchase the upgrade in the Tool Age.
- Once you enter the Tool Age, you can increase the attack rating of your clubmen and axemen by researching toolworking.

Clubmen: They're slow, they're weak, and they can't take much of a punch—but they're the only Stone Age warriors in the game. Purchase the upgrade in Tool Age, and Clubmen convert to Axemen.

Researching metalworking in the Bronze Age, and metallurgy in the Iron Age, also increases their attack rating.

- You can increase their ability to withstand attacks by researching leather armor (Tool Age), scale armor (Bronze Age), and chain-mail armor (Iron Age).
- You can make your clubmen and axemen more resistant to damage from bowmen, archers, towers, and ships (other than catapult triremes, fire galleys, and juggernauts) by researching bronze, iron, and tower shields.
- A lowly axeman can destroy a watchtower with the upgrades described above.
- If you enter the Tool Age before a nearby enemy, here's one way to obliterate them. Choose the axemen upgrade in your barracks, and then send a war party of at least six clubmen to attack them. (You should also first research toolworking or leather armor in your storage pit.) Your upgrades should take effect as the battle begins. While your Tool Age axemen will have little problem cutting through their population, you may want to send some reinforcements as the battle continues.

Fishing Boats

Who says you have to spend food to make food?

You've got a Stone Age village and you need to store up to 1300 units of food to get to the Bronze Age quickly. Should you train 15 villagers at 50 units of food a piece? Ask your enemies to give you food and extra time so that you can put together a better army? Or create a large fleet of fishing boats and start gathering food instead of spending it?

Fishing is the best way to accumulate food quickly.

At a cost of 50 units of wood, fishing boats are a bargain—assuming you have access to a body of water with at least one school of fish.

Points of Interest

- You can use fishing boats to block and trap enemy transports for your galleys and triremes.

- Fishing boats make great scouts for clearing the fog of war from Mediterranean, coastal, continental, and island maps.
- Fishing boats count against your population limits. When you have caught all available fish, use the Delete key to destroy your fishing boats so that you can build other units.

The only way to stop merchants from trading is to sink them.

- Do *not* destroy enemy fishing boats once all of the fish are gone. Each existing boat is a place holder that could later be filled with a war elephant or a juggernaut.
- You can upgrade your fishing boats into fishing ships after entering the Bronze Age.

Trade Boats

Trade boats are small, unarmed ships that do nothing but ferry wood, food, or stone from your dock and exchange it for gold with other nations. This can be very important if, for instance, your city is in a forest with lots of wood and no gold. Since you need 800 units of gold to enter the Iron Age, you will likely need to trade wood for gold with a wealthy nation.

While trade boats are faster than fishing boats—making them good for scouting expeditions early in the game—they are utterly useless unless other nations on the map have docks.

Points of Interest

- You can use trade boats to slow the supply of your enemies' resources and harass them. There are only three ways to stop trading boats from taking your gold: chase them away, sink them, or destroy your dock.
- If your opponent has a limited supply of gold, you may be able to keep him from entering the Iron Age, or from building priests and siege weapons, by sending a steady stream of trade boats.

The antidote to Tool Age bowmen, slingers help you round out your forces without having to erect additional buildings.

- You can upgrade your trade boats into merchant ships after entering the Bronze Age. This enables you to raid your enemies' gold at an even faster rate!

Tool Age Forces

The way in which you develop your Tool Age society can determine your strategy for an entire game. If you want to wage a defensive battle, assign villagers to mine stone and build walls and towers. Archers make excellent defensive units in the early stages, too.

Just remember, the goal of most Tool Age civilizations is to enter the Bronze Age, and to do so requires 800 units of food. Do not waste food researching leather armor for your bowmen if you have not even built an archery range. You may want to spend food on armor for the units you have trained—but more often than not, the real battles start in the Bronze Age.

Slingers

Rise of Rome introduces several new units, one of which is the slinger.

Slingers are soldiers who throw small rocks at their enemies. They are slower than bowmen, have less range, and don't cause all that much damage—but they come with shielding against missile weapons, and a lone slinger can kill a lone bowman without taking too much damage. Axemen, on the other hand, can hack right through them in tight spaces. Like bowmen, slingers are faster than axemen and will continually fire and retreat until they run out of space.

The most advantageous quality of slingers: They enable you to place protective units along a wall so that you're not forced to spend precious resources building an archery range. With this strategy, you can begin to invest in the training of soldiers instead of spending 150 units of wood on a building, and then waiting until you get more wood to start the training process.

Points of Interest

- If you place slingers near your towers, the towers will spot the enemy first and begin firing—the slingers will automatically investigate and join the fight.

- Slingers are champions at destroying towers. Though one will die before the battle is over, it takes only two basic slingers to destroy a watch tower.
- There are no improved or composite slinger units. You can make them tougher and more aggressive—but slingers, like axemen, become completely obsolete in subsequent ages.
- Once you enter the Tool Age, you can increase your slingers' attack rating by researching toolworking. Researching metalworking in the Bronze Age, and metallurgy in the Iron Age, also increases their attack.
- You can increase their ability to withstand attacks by researching leather armor (Tool Age), scale armor (Bronze Age), and chain-mail armor (Iron Age).
- You can make your slingers more resistant to damage from bowmen, archers, towers, and ships (but not catapult triremes, fire galleys, and juggernauts) by researching bronze, iron, and tower shields.

Bowmen

Bowmen may seem useless at first glance, but even those of the basic variety can be used quite effectively in certain situations, and upgraded archers are among the most effective soldiers in the game.

You cannot build an archery range and train bowmen until you advance into the Tool Age, and then you get only basic bowmen with an attack rating of 3 (a lower rating than the lowly clubmen). It is useless to send bowmen to attack enemies. They don't have the firepower to kill anything fiercer than a gazelle, and they can't withstand much more damage than a villager.

They do, however, work well in packs. Have four or five bowmen attack the same clubman, and they'll kill him quickly. Bowmen are also effective at attacking enemies from cliffs or from behind walls. It may take them a while to kill their enemies, but they'll get the job done if they have a barrier to protect them.

Points of Interest

- To build an archery range, you must have built barracks and entered the Tool Age.
- You can use bowmen to lure axemen out of position before launching assaults.

- A bowman must shoot a scout ship 40 times to sink it.
- Bowmen have the same range as watch towers and scout ships.
- You can increase your bowmen's range by researching woodworking, artisanship, and craftsmanship in your market.
- Be aware that you can later increase your bowmen's attack rating by researching ballistics and alchemy in your Iron Age government center.
- You make bowmen slightly more durable by researching leather, scale, and chain-mail armor in your storage pit.

Scouts

Scouts are as fast as any unit in the game, and faster than everything else in the Tool Age. They can absorb a fair amount of punishment (they die after 60 hit points). On the other hand, these horseback riders don't hit any harder than standard villagers.

Points of Interest

- Scouts are invaluable when it comes to locating ruins and artifacts in the Tool Age. They fly past towers so quickly that they barely take damage, and nothing can catch them.
- This proper employment of Scouts can save you from humiliating losses. You automatically lose if your enemies find and control all ruins or artifacts for 2000 virtual years. You can usually reset the clock by sending a couple of scouts to find a ruin or artifact. The scouts may not be able to hold on to that ruin with their weak attack, but they can reset the clock until you can get a stronger force to the scene to finish the fight.
- Scouts are a good Tool Age weapon for killing priests. Scouts can get to priests quickly, and they're not particularly dangerous foes should the priest convert them.
- You can upgrade your scouts' attack considerably by researching toolworking, metalworking, and metallurgy at your storage pit. Upgrade them enough, and they become as dangerous as standard heavy cavalry units—and you don't have to spend your gold.

Bowmen don't pack much punch, but they can be a major nuisance.

- You can make your scouts more durable by researching leather, scale, and chain-mail armor for cavalry in your storage pit.
- Researching nobility at your government center also makes scouts more durable.

Light Transports

Light transports are small boats that can carry five land units across bodies of water. They are too small to carry invasion forces and have no offensive abilities, but they can sustain considerable damage before sinking.

Points of Interest

- One way to hold on to an artifact is to load it onto a light transport and send it into deep water—where the only recourse your enemies have is to try sinking your ship.
- Build light transports as quickly as possible when playing on small island and large island maps. You may need to get villagers to other islands to find wood, gold, or stone.
- Light transports can be used to block or trap enemy transports.
- In later rounds, try to have your priests convert enemy transports. You can thwart an entire invasion by converting the boats, and then sinking them.
- You can upgrade your transports to heavy transports after reaching the Iron Age. Heavy transports carry up to ten passengers and are slightly faster than light transports.

Scout ships are the only Tool Age units that can hold their own in the Bronze Age.

Scout Ships

Many people believe that the key to winning in chess is taking and controlling the center of the board. The same can be said about certain maps in Rise of Rome. With small and large island maps, the player who controls the

waterways has a decided upper hand. The key to nabbing the waterways is to make a dominant fleet of scout ships and to hunt enemy docks.

Scout ships are floating mobile towers. They have the same basic range as towers and archers, but they do nearly twice as much damage with every shot. They move as fast as scouts, and they can absorb heavy damage before sinking. Best of all, they are easy to repair. Simply click a nearby villager, then left click a damaged ship and the villager will repair it.

Points of Interest

- If you can seize the oceans, you can destroy your enemies' docks before they launch ships, prevent enemies from sending transports with soldiers into your territory, limit their resources, pick away at their men and buildings, and horde all of the fishing rights for yourself.
- Villagers can repair ships through walls. Just get the villager and the ship right next to each other, and the villager will repair it by osmosis.
- Scout ships are basically stupid. If you don't keep an eye on them, they will be lured too close to shore and destroyed by land units.
- You can increase your scout ship's range by researching woodworking, artisanship, and craftsmanship in your market.
- If, for some odd reason, you still have scout ships in the Iron Age, you can increase the accuracy of their arrows by researching ballistics in your market. You can also increase the power of their attacks by researching alchemy in your market. And, if you still have scout ships during the Iron Age, pour a lot of research into land units because your navy is as good as dead!
- You can upgrade scout ships into war galleys during the Bronze Age. War galleys have a slightly better attack range, do nearly twice as much damage with every arrow, and can absorb one-third more punishment than scout ships.
- You can upgrade your war galleys to triremes in the Iron Age. While triremes have only a slightly better attack range and rating than war galleys, they look and sound much cooler. Triremes are armed with ballistas that batter anything in their way.
- Because they are armed with ballistas instead of catapults, triremes are safer to use when establishing a beachhead in enemy territory. Your ships and armies will not be hurt if they are hit by friendly fire from triremes and ballistas. Catapult fire from catapult triremes and juggernauts (see

Iron Age Forces later in this chapter) will mash them to bits.

- Triremes are better in sea battles than catapult triremes because they can batter the bigger ships with their steady stream of ballista fire while avoiding slow-moving catapult projectiles.

Bronze Age Forces

Priests are harmless, innocuous, and one of the most diabolical weapons in the game.

The Bronze Age is the time when you either begin your invasions or are invaded. Armed with cavalry, priests, and catapults, a single wave of Bronze Age invaders can inflict more damage than an entire Tool Age civilization could ever hope to. It should be noted that in the Bronze and Iron Ages, the quantum evolutionary leaps are in military technology, not resource gathering.

Priests

For a mere 125 units of gold, training priests is a rare bargain!

Since priests can heal your army, they pay for themselves every time they save just two cavalry units. If you have priests nearby, you can send your cavalry to rush towers, then heal them as soon as the work is done. It certainly pays to group your forces between battles so that your priests can restore their health.

Priests can also convert enemy units, though you will want to be selective about what you attempt to convert. Do not try to convert chariots or chariot archers—they will simply charge straight up to your priest and kill him. Bowmen and cavalry are more receptive to conversion—but they, too, are likely to kill your priest before being converted.

Points of Interest

- You must build a temple to train priests.
- Station priests near walls to protect your city. Priests have long-range vision, so having them near walls will help you spot invaders quickly. Their conversion range is also farther than most units' attack ranges, so you can start making converts early. (After entering the Iron Age, you can increase your priests' conversion range by researching afterlife at your temple.)

- It takes priests 50 seconds to rejuvenate their faith between conversions. They can still heal your units while rejuvenating, but they cannot perform conversions during that time. (Once in the Iron Age, you can cut that time in half by researching fanaticism at your temple.)
- One of the easiest and best units to convert during Iron Age battles is the war elephant. This unit is so slow that it never gets to your priests before changing faiths and sides, and it can do extensive damage to your enemies once it converts.
- There are two new upgrades for priests in Rise of Rome—martyrdom, an upgrade that automatically converts any unit that kills your priest (great for multiplayer shenanigans), and medicine, which allows your priest to heal units more quickly.
- Priests are best used in small groups so that they can heal each other. It takes very little damage to kill priests, so watch their health points carefully. (You can double their hit points by researching mysticism in your temple. You can also make your priests move faster by researching polytheism.)
- The only way to create new units once you've reached your population limit is to convert enemies.
- While your priests have a better range of vision than enemy troops, they become visible to the enemy while trying to convert their troops.
- After entering the Iron Age, you can research monotheism and give your priest the ability to convert enemy priests and buildings. (The problem with converting buildings is that your priest must get right beside them— a truly vulnerable position—to perform the conversion.)
- While you won't be able to convert enemy town centers, you will be able to convert towers—assuming the tower is distracted and don't end your priest's sermon ahead of time.
- In later rounds, try to have your priests convert enemy transports. You can stop an entire invasion by converting the boat it is traveling on, then sinking it. Better yet, you can keep the boat alive and affect your enemies' population level with useless units.
- Once you enter the Iron Age, you can make your villagers faster, stronger, and more efficient by researching Jihad in your temple.

Swordsmen

While axemen are completely unequipped to compete with the towers, archers, and soldiers of the Bronze Age, basic short swordsmen are not all that much better prepared. They have slightly higher attack and hit ratings—and that's it. They move at the same speed as axemen and have the same range of vision.

Purchased with food and gold, short and broad swordsmen both inflict and absorb more punishment than axemen.

Points of Interest

- In theory, a short swordsman can destroy a standard Tool Age tower. The tower would require 30 seconds to kill the swordsman. Assuming the swordsman manages to approach the tower without getting shot, he should demolish it in 23 seconds and leave with nearly one-third of his health. (A standard broad swordsman can demolish a Tool Age tower in 18 seconds.) This scenario fails to consider upgraded towers, clusters of towers, and towers with nearby repairmen. It also overlooks armor and metallurgy upgrades.
- Since they cost only 35 units of food and 15 units of gold, swordsmen work out to be fairly inexpensive if you have a good supply of gold.
- Swordsmen make a good second wave during Bronze Age invasions. Once you've penetrated your enemy's walls, you can send in a troop of swordsmen to destroy houses and buildings as your catapults demolish towers and your cavalry attack priests and archers.
- You can upgrade your short swordsmen for broad swordsmen during the Bronze Age, improving their hit and attack ratings for a one-time cost of 140 units of food and 50 units of gold.
- You can improve your swordsmen's attack ratings by researching toolworking, metalworking, and metallurgy.
- You can improve your swordsmen's hit ratings by researching leather, scale, and chain-mail armor. You can also protect them from archers, towers, ships, and ballistas by researching bronze and iron shields.

Roman Improved Bowman
40/40

Roman Composite Bowman
45/45

A line of bowmen behind a wall can even stop a wave of cavalry.

Roman Chariot Archer
70/70

What chariot archers lack in punch they make up for in speed.

• Once you enter the Iron Age, you can upgrade your broad swordsmen to be long swordsmen and legionnaires. While the upgrade to legionnaires costs 1400 units of food and 600 units of gold, it enables you to train very good attack units for very little money. Legionnaires cost only 35 units of food and 15 units of gold to train, once you buy the upgrade.

Improved and Composite Bowmen

With increased range and one-third more power in every shot, improved bowmen and composite bowmen make great defenders. Place five or six behind a short wall, and they will cut down your enemy's cavalry before they can break through walls. They cost a little more than swordsmen, but they are much more effective at spearheading and stopping invasions.

Points of Interest

• Researching improved bowmen costs 140 units of food and 80 units of wood. Upgrading to composite bowmen costs another 180 units of food and 100 units of wood.
• You can upgrade a composite bowman's range to match that of priests and catapults by researching woodworking, artisanship, and craftsmanship.

Chariot Archers

Chariot archers have two purposes in life: defending walls and killing priests. They're especially good at defending walls because they are fast and can shift from one trouble spot to the next more quickly than any other Bronze Age archer.

Also, chariot archers are the atheists of the Bronze Age—they are resistant to conversion by priests, and their arrows are particularly effective at killing these holy men. A good chariot archer can show a standard priest the truth about the afterlife in less than five seconds.

Points of Interest

- You must research wheels in your market before you can train chariots archers. (Who wants a chariot without wheels?)
- You can improve chariot archers with all the standard armor and craftsmanship upgrades, and you can add to their durability by researching nobility at your government center.

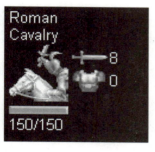

Cavalry is the first truly effective invasion unit you get in the game.

Cavalry

Fast, powerful, and able to absorb a great deal of damage, basic cavalry are possibly the most powerful forces in Rise of Rome. If you beat your opponent to the Bronze Age and manage to send several of these units into his Tool Age town, you can end the game.

Points of Interest

- Cavalry are expensive to build—70 units of food and 80 units of gold. Don't waste them.
- You do not have to research technologies to train cavalry. If you have multiple stables and enough gold, you can crank them out as soon as you enter the Bronze Age to get a jump on your enemies.
- When they ride into clusters of enemy towers, lone cavalry units tend to become indecisive about which tower to attack. They generally charge around for a few seconds, eventually pick a target, and die having done very little damage.
- If your opponent needs gold or wood, send a couple of cavalry units to his resource area, where they'll deal swiftly with all defenseless villagers.
- Once they enter a town, your cavalry can slaughter civilians and infantrymen alike. Your cavalry's attack rating nearly doubles against infantrymen.
- One-on-one, cavalry units and Bronze Age guard towers are evenly matched. Both take approximately 38 seconds to kill each other.
- You can upgrade your cavalry's attack by researching toolworking, metalworking, and metallurgy at your storage pit. Researching leather, scale, and chain-mail armor for cavalry in your storage pit increases their hit value.

Chariots are specialists for killing priests, villagers, and catapults.

- Researching nobility at your government center improves cavalry's hit points.
- You can upgrade your cavalry into heavy cavalry and cataphracts in the Iron Age. While the upgrade to heavy cavalry is not particularly expensive, the jump to cataphracts costs 2000 units of food and 850 units of gold. This is not a bad investment if you have unlimited supplies of food and gold, but you don't want to make this upgrade if you're on a budget.

Chariots

Just as chariot archers are good at protecting your city from within its walls, chariots are good at getting to invaders and harming them. They can destroy approaching catapults and priests better than cavalry, and they cost a lot less.

Points of Interest

- You must research wheels in your market before you can train chariots.
- Chariots, though less expensive than cavalry, are not as effective in invasions. But they are equally effective in defending *against* invasions.
- Like chariot archers, chariots are conversion-resistant and their attack rating increases while attacking priests.
- You can upgrade chariots' attacks with toolworking, metalworking, metallurgy, and nobility. You can improve their hit points by researching leather, scale, and chain-mail armor for cavalry.
- Once you enter the Iron Age, you can upgrade your chariots to scythe chariots. Created for Rise of Rome, scythe chariots are faster and far more deadly than regular chariots. They strike with such force that they can injure several attackers with a single blow. (The upgrade to scythe chariots is extremely expensive.)

Camel Riders

Another new unit in the Age of Empires universe is the camel rider.

Camel riders have one overriding purpose: to wreak havoc on enemy cavalry.

These units are not particularly fast, nor do they have an impressive attack rating. They exist for the single purpose of attacking and defeating cavalry. Not only are camel riders able to defeat cavalry in one-on-one battles, but they also cost a lot less.

Points of Interest

- Like chariots, camel riders are relatively ineffective in invasions.
- A standard camel rider can kill a heavy cavalry unit in a one-on-one battle.
- You can upgrade the attack strength of camel riders with toolworking, metalworking, metallurgy, and nobility. You can improve their hit points by researching leather, scale, and chain-mail armor for cavalry.

Stone Throwers

Stone throwers are small catapults. They are slow, but they have a longer range than archers, towers, and war galleys. They are effective in destroying towers and walls to open the way for an invasion. You can also use them to kill priests—assuming the priest does not see them coming—but they are too slow to kill soldiers.

You can upgrade your stone throwers to catapults and heavy catapults after entering the Iron Age.

Points of Interest

- Stone throwers, catapults, and heavy catapults (and catapult-armed ships) are the most stupid units in the game and can turn a surefire victory into a humiliating defeat. When catapult weapons see enemy units, they instantly fire at them. They will fire at the enemy even if your cavalry is swarming nearby, and you'd better believe that your men will take serious damage. The best way to prevent this: Change your enemy to neutral in your diplomatic settings so that your stone throwers and catapults will fire only when fired upon, or at targets you select.

Stone throwers, catapults, and heavy catapults offer great firepower.

Roman
Hoplite

+ — 17

5

120/120

Roman
Phalanx

+ — 20

7

120/120

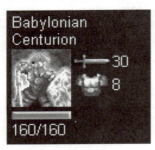

Babylonian
Centurion

+ — 30

8

160/160

Hoplites and other academy units are incredibly powerful, but painfully slow.

- The catapult weapon will stupidly meander toward enemy buildings or units, even when it is unsafe to do so. Changing your diplomatic settings will prevent this from happening.
- Catapult weapons have the best range of vision and attack range in Rise of Rome—but like priests, they (ballistas, too) become visible to enemies once they fire.
- All catapults and ballistas have a minimum attack range and cannot defend themselves when enemy units stand in front of them.
- Once you enter the Iron Age, you can make your catapult weapons more accurate by researching alchemy at your government center, and increase their attack ratings. If your catapult is under attack from a group of archers or pirates, aim for their center.

Hoplites and Academy Units

The supreme warrior of the Bronze Age is the hoplite. This slow-moving human tank inflicts more than twice as much damage per second than cavalry and costs a lot less. The only problem is that hoplites move so slowly they have trouble catching up to anything but buildings.

Points of Interest

- You must build stables and an academy to train hoplites.
- Hoplites can destroy two Bronze Age watch towers and survive. (It's a close call, however, if the towers are close enough together for both to shoot your hoplite simultaneously.)
- Hoplites are especially effective at defending towns.
- You can upgrade your hoplites to phalanxes and centurions after entering the Iron Age. While an upgrade of hoplite to phalanx costs only 300 units of food and 100 units of gold, it does not increase your hoplites' hit rating. It simply increments their attack strength.
- The upgrade to centurions costs 1800 units of food and 700 units of gold, but it yields an infantryman with a very lethal attack. (Centurions, though, are no faster than hoplites.)

- You can increase your academy units' attack rating by researching toolworking, metalworking, and metallurgy.
- You can increase your academy units' hit points by researching leather, scale, and chain-mail armor.
- Researching bronze and iron shields increases hoplite hit points when attacked by ballistas, towers, bowmen, war galleys, and triremes.
- Researching aristocracy makes academy units move a little faster, but it won't qualify them for the Olympics.

Iron Age Forces

The real battle begins in the Iron Age. That's when each civilization's specialties come out. It's when the nations with the strongest priests start their wholesale conversions, and when the nations with the toughest ships seize control of the waters and terrorize the coasts.

The Iron Age is also the time when the tower becomes a non-issue. A single stone thrower can knock out a city of towers—so do not depend on towers to pull you through the final stages of your battle.

The way to win an Iron Age war is to choose a couple of super-weapons and use them to dominate. While most of the top units cost no more than their lowly Bronze Age counterparts, they cost a fortune to research. Do not let up on your food gathering and gold mining now! You will need food, gold, and wood to research and build an army with decisive power.

Elephant Archers

There is a sort of irony about the elephant archer. This huge, ponderous mobile mountain carries only a bow and arrow. But the arrows from this unit are extremely potent. Upgrade your elephant archers' attack rating by researching ballistics and alchemy, and he will pack a solid punch. Since this archer is attached to an elephant, he will be able to take his firing act into well-fortified places.

Mobile tower or prehistoric tank, elephant archers are a sure-footed way to get your arrows behind enemy lines.

Points of Interest
- Elephant archers are great for crowd control—send them into a group of villagers or infantrymen, and they can create a surprisingly high number of casualties.

Roman
Heavy Horse Archer

8
0
2
7

90/90

Roman
Horse Archer

7
0
2
7

60/60

Horse archers are extremely fast and relatively durable, but lack the powerful attack of cavalry units.

- You can upgrade your elephant archers' range by researching woodworking, artisanship, and craftsmanship.
- Increase your elephant archers' attack and accuracy by researching alchemy and ballistics in your government center.

Horse Archers

Horse archers and heavy horse archers are the fastest units in the Age of Empires pantheon. This makes them excellent defensive units. They can get to trouble spots quickly, and they move so quickly that they render catapults and ballistas ineffective. (Helepolises, with their rapid fire, can annihilate horse archers.)

Points of Interest

- Horse archers are great for ambushing siege weapons. When you hear a catapult or a ballista fire, send your horse archers to the scene and they'll be able to overwhelm it before it can fire on them.
- You can upgrade your composite horse archers' range by researching woodworking, artisanship, and craftsmanship.
- Increase your horse archers' attack and accuracy by researching alchemy and ballistics in your government center.
- You can upgrade your horse archers' durability by researching leather armor, scale armor, chain-mail armor, and nobility.
- You can upgrade your horse archers to be heavy horse archers, but the incremental increases you get in speed, attack rating, and durability do not necessarily justify the cost (1750 units of food and 800 units of gold) of the upgrade.

War Elephants

War elephants are one of the best all-around offensive units in Age of Empires. They create such force when they attack that they can kill several defenders at once, or destroy buildings and kill repairmen at the same time.

When Age of Empires was first introduced, few players recognized just how valuable war elephants could be. It seemed like a ponderous unit that did little more than bulldoze previously cleared towns. Then the multiplayer gaming crowd discovered their value. Now war elephants are coveted invaders, recognized for their powerful attacks and good follow-through.

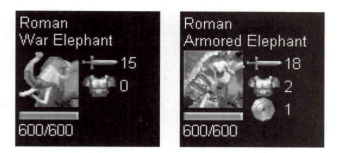

War elephants are slow and vulnerable to priests, but they can clear out a city or destroy a Wonder of the World in no time flat.

Points of Interest

- War elephants are excellent at destroying Wonders. If you are busily engaged in other battles when your enemy erects a Wonder, send a herd of war elephants to demolish it. They may not come back alive, but they will at least attempt to bash their way to it, and barring significant fortification, they will succeed.
- You can upgrade war elephants to armored elephants, a new unit created for Rise of Rome.
- An armored elephant can kill a standard war elephant, then destroy a sentry tower, and survive.

Catapult Triremes

Catapult triremes and juggernauts may be the most powerful weapons on the Age of Empires seas, but they have a huge limitation. It takes catapult weapons five seconds to shoot. Smaller ships can fire an arrow, move, and fire another arrow during that time. Controlled by a reasonably skillful player, triremes will generally defeat

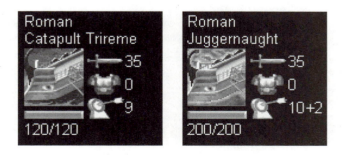

Catapult triremes and juggernauts don't just clear the beach for your landing—they pulverize it.

catapult triremes in battle. In fact, it's not uncommon for a lone trireme to beat two catapult triremes.

Traveling in fleets, catapult triremes and juggernauts can usually clear out enemies. They are especially effective in fleet-to-fleet battles because fleets of ships are generally too slow moving to dodge catapult fire.

Points of Interest

- Catapult triremes and juggernauts are fast ships, but standard fishing ships, triremes, and merchant ships are slightly faster.
- Triremes can absorb more punishment than catapult triremes. Watch your health bar when being attacked by smaller ships or bowmen.
- You can use catapult triremes and juggernauts to clear towers and buildings before invasions.
- Since they move much faster than regular catapults, catapult triremes can usually outmaneuver and defeat land catapults.
- Catapult triremes are completely vulnerable to ballista attacks.
- You can upgrade your catapult triremes to juggernauts. It's an expensive upgrade that nearly doubles your hit points and gives each shot you fire a larger radius.
- You can upgrade your catapult triremes' and juggernauts' fire power by researching alchemy and engineering.
- Researching ballistics increases your ships' weapons accuracy, a big plus when you are trying to squish some pesky priest before he converts your ship.

Carthaginian Fire Galley
24+6
0
1
200/200

Fire galleys are useless in land battles, but they are perfect for special uses, especially in defense.

Fire Galleys

Fire galleys are galley-sized ships that serve as the counter-punchers of the Age of Empires sea. A new unit to Rise of Rome, these ships are designed to protect your shores rather than attack your enemy's coastline.

Fire galleys may be small, but they have a potent weapon—short-range, flame-throwing billows that torch and incinerate enemy ships. This mighty weapon would make fire galleys nearly invincible titans except that they cannot even begin throwing flames until they touch their target.

Points of Interest

- Fire galleys are unmatched at preventing invasions. They trap and destroy fast-moving transports much more easily than triremes or catapult triremes.
- Fire galleys are designed to counter-punch triremes. They take some damage fighting their way in, but they can sink a trireme in seconds as they blow flames down their hulls.
- Catapult triremes and juggernauts destroy fire galleys easily. Use standard triremes to fight catapult-armed ships. The fire galley's speed is its best asset against catapults.
- Fleets of four or more triremes will sink fire galleys as they move in for the attack.
- Fire galleys are excellent at destroying docks, but they cannot destroy inland targets.

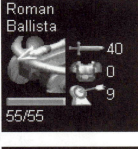

Though ballistas are not as powerful as catapults, they fire faster and offer some excellent advantages.

Ballistas

Ballistas, a cross between catapults and bowmen, are enormous bows that shoot tree-sized arrows. Though they do not do as much damage as catapults and they have only two-thirds of the attack range, ballistas shoot faster. Unlike catapults, ballistas do not harm your men with their fire.

Points of Interest

- Ballistas have better range than ballista towers.
- You can place ballistas behind walls to protect cities. They are excellent at fighting off invaders, but are vulnerable to catapults and priests.
- Helepolises—upgraded ballistas—are no more powerful than regular ballistas and have only slightly better range, but they have twice the firing speed. Ballistas fire once every three seconds, and helepolises fire twice in that time.
- By researching engineering, you can upgrade your ballistas' and helepolises' range by 20 percent.
- By researching alchemy, you can upgrade your ballistas' and helepolises' attack rating.

- By researching ballistics, you can upgrade your ballistas' and helepolises' accuracy.

Buildings

There are no new buildings in Rise of Rome, but there has been a major alteration, and it's amazing how one small change can affect a game.

With the buildings in Age of Empires, you could only order and train one unit at a time, so you had to build multiple barracks or keep clicking your barracks if you wanted to train more than one clubman or swordsman. In Rise of Rome, you can place orders for multiple units.

To order five slingers, for instance, click five times on the Slinger icon in your barracks. Your barracks will begin training the first slinger. Once he is trained and presented, work will begin on your next one.

This is an important change! It means that you can now trust·your barracks, stables, academies, siege workshops, and archery ranges to train your second wave of invaders as you take your first wave to launch an attack.

Some things have not changed, however. Whether you choose to enter battles as Rome or one of her enemies, your empire's abilities will be determined by the buildings you erect. This will determine how quickly you can build forces, whether you wage an offensive or a defensive battle, the strength of your units, and the speed and size of your army.

There is an economy to many of the missions in Rise of Rome that does not necessarily apply to the multiplayer and random map games. You start out with huge resources in death matches, and most random map games have abundant supplies of food, gold, wood, and stone—but these items are often harder to locate in the campaigns. When playing the campaigns, you may want to build more slowly than in death matches.

Following is a list of buildings and the advantages each kind offers you.

Civilian Buildings

While you will not have to worry about getting food to your soldiers, you cannot train new units until you have sufficient food and housing available.

Houses

You have to have a sufficient number of houses for your troops before you can train them. You are allowed 50 men in the campaigns (you can set various

population limits in multiplayer games), so plan on building 12 to 13 houses in every mission. Press F11 to keep population info displayed at the top of your screen. Your barracks, stables, archery ranges, docks, temples, and other buildings will simply stop training new units until you have sufficient housing.

Once you build houses, they don't serve any truly significant purpose. You can use them as barriers to keep enemies from entering your cities—but houses do not offer any kinds of upgrades and are very easily destroyed.

Your enemies have the same city planning problems that you have—they, too, can only train soldiers if they have houses to put them in. Destroying your enemies' houses may temporarily stall them from training new troops, but it is only a temporary fix since houses are cheap and easy to build.

You may want to spread your houses out slightly. Though the original strategy was to build a small, tight suburb, the multiplayer experience proved that invaders will aim catapults at these neighborhoods, destroying three houses at a time.

Granaries

Granaries are buildings that hold food. Placing granaries beside bushes and farms speeds up your villagers' production speed by reducing the distance they have to travel to deposit food.

You also need granaries to build guard towers, walls, and a market.

Storage Pits

Storage pits are similar to granaries, except that they are used for storing stone, gold, and wood. Hunters can also store gazelle, elephant, alligator, and lion meat there. Placing storage pits near woods and stone and gold deposits will speed up material gathering in the same way that placing granaries near bushes speeds up food gathering.

Storage pits hold combat and armor upgrades for your soldiers, cavalry, and archers.

With the exception of town centers and houses, storage pits are the first buildings you should erect in most situations.

Town Centers

Town centers have three purposes: building villagers, storing food and resources like granaries and storage pits, and advancing to new ages. Once you construct two Stone Age buildings and acquire 500 units of food, you can use

600/600

Most scenarios will begin with this scene—a group of villagers standing around a town center waiting for orders.

50/50

Farms can provide a steady source of food long after you have picked all of the berries, killed all of the animals, and harvested all of the fish on your map.

350/350

You can purchase upgrades for your city's production capabilities through markets.

your town center to upgrade to the Tool Age. With 800 units of food and two Tool Age buildings, you can upgrade to the Bronze Age, and with 1000 units of food, 800 units of gold, and two Bronze Age buildings, you can upgrade to the Iron Age.

While your town center is durable and can absorb a lot of abuse, it can be destroyed—so protect it. Once it is destroyed, the progress of your civilization is effectively stymied unless you have entered the Iron Age and can build more—in which case you would need your town center solely for training villagers.

One last point of strategy: It costs 200 units of wood to build a town center (80 units more than it costs to build a storage pit or a granary), but town centers do the work of granaries and storage pits. Build town centers when you set up new colonies and you'll save yourself some wood.

Farms

Farms provide a stable food source for your cities. Unlike fishing, hunting, and foraging, which require food and produce on the hoof, you do not have to depend upon nature to farm (at least not in this game). You only need land and wood.

You need a market to build and upgrade farms. A new production upgrade is offered with every Age.

Markets

Markets have upgrades for all of your city's economic activities. You cannot build farms until you have a market, and once you have a market you can use it to upgrade your farms' productions.

Markets also have upgrades for woodcutting (which also improves your missile-weapon range), gold mining, stone mining, and your villagers' siege

abilities. You also need to research wheels at your market to build chariots.

Under normal circumstances, markets should be the first building you construct when you enter the Tool Age.

Civic and Government Buildings

Some buildings have neither a direct military purpose nor an economic or agricultural purpose, yet these buildings can play immensely important roles during your missions, so don't take them lightly.

Temples

Priests can be one of your most effective weapons. You can count how many priests you can squish with a catapult, but you can't count how many catapults you can squish with a priest. Seriously, priests even help you cheat in this game.

The safest way to use priests is to place them near walls and barriers so that they can convert units that cannot readily fight back. Priests are great at converting catapults, cataphracts, heavy cavalrymen, centurions, phalanxes, long swordsmen, transports, war elephants, and villagers. They have trouble communicating with chariots and chariot archers. Archer units are also a problem.

But the bottom line is this: you need temples to train and upgrade priests.

Docks

You need to erect a dock to build ships. Fishing boats place their fish in docks for storage, so you can improve their production by placing docks near good fishing spots to cut travel time. You can also improve your trade production by building docks along trade routes. The further apart your docks are, the more gold you'll get.

Government Centers

Government centers are Bronze Age buildings that offer nothing but upgrades, but some of those upgrades are extremely valuable. During the Bronze Age, the only upgrades they offer are three peace-loving technologies: nobility, which

You need to build temples to train and upgrade your priests—essential units for success.

You need docks to build ships and receive fish from fishing boats and gold trade boats.

Government centers
have the upgrades to
turn your siege weapons
into genuine tools
of destruction.

improves your cavalry, chariot, and horse archer hit points; writing, which lets you see previously fogged parts of the map that your allies have explored; and architecture, which lets you erect buildings 33 percent faster and makes walls and buildings 20 percent more durable.

During the Iron Age, your government center will offer more aggressive upgrades—engineering, which improves the range of your triremes, ballistas, helepolises, and catapult weapons; aristocracy, which makes your hoplites, phalanxes, and centurions 25 percent faster; logistics, which lets you exceed your population cap by training barracks units; alchemy, which increases the attack ratings of your missile-firing weapons (catapults, towers, archers, bowman, ballistas, and ships); and ballistics, which increases the range of your missile-firing weapons.

Military Buildings

There are five buildings for training soldiers—barracks, archery ranges, stables, academies, and siege workshops. They don't teach dance in hoplite academies, and the stables in Rise of Rome don't teach chariot racing.

Barracks

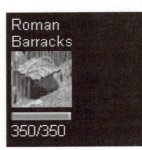

With the addition of
slingers, barracks now
play a bigger role in Tool
Age strategy.

You get but one kind of military building and one kind of soldier during the Stone Age—barracks with clubmen. During the Tool Age, you can upgrade your barracks to train axemen. You can also train slingers. By the time you get to the Iron Age, however, you will have the opportunity to train broad swordsmen, long swordsmen, and legions.

Archery Ranges

Bowman may not do much damage on their own, but put a group behind a wall, and they can stop an invasion. Even more importantly, bowmen come in all kinds of shapes and sizes.

There are basic bowmen who are cheap to train and painless to replace. There are chariot archers, horse archers, and heavy horse archers who are extremely fast and can get to trouble spots quickly and defend shores and walls against invasions. There are even industrial composite bowmen with long-range weapons, and elephant archers who are slow and lumbering but can bash their way behind enemy lines.

Bowmen are decisive units in multiplayer games, and many top players have built their entire strategy around getting them.

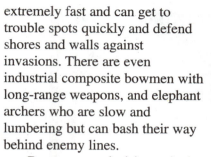

Bowmen are one of the key units in many multiplayer strategies.

Having stables allows you to train fast close-combat units with powerful attacks.

Stables

Stables create a line of fast-moving units with fierce close combat attacks. Bronze Age cavalry are the key to launching effective invasions. In Rise of Rome, you also train camel riders, the antidote to cavalry attacks, in your stables.

Stables are your training grounds for chariots, which can fight priests and war elephants to create all forms of havoc. (You also need to research wheels in your market before you can make chariots.)

Siege Workshops

You need siege workshops to build the big weapons of war—catapults, ballistas, and their upgraded versions. These are the weapons you will need to breach walls and destroy towers without sacrificing armies of men.

The only weapon offered by siege workshops during the Bronze Age is the stone thrower, but they offer several additional weapons during the Iron Age.

The weapons manufactured in siege workshops are great for finishing missions. They were designed to shatter walls and remove towers, and are especially good at destroying wonders.

Academies

Academies are specialized training centers that produce soldiers with lances. These soldiers move at an irritatingly slow gait when sent to stop an invasion, but they are especially fierce fighters who can take a beating.

You need an academy to train hoplites, phalanxes, and centurions.

These sacred ruins look like Stonehenge, but few will believe there were Celts in Ancient Egypt.

Who says "wonders never cease"? A few catapult shots and this wonder ceased to exist.

Additional Buildings

Throughout the missions and in some styles of death matches, you will discover sacred ruins from long-extinct civilizations. Find and control these ruins for 2000 years, and you win your match automatically.

Wonders of the World

Wonders of the World are the sure signs of success in Rise of Rome. To build one, you need 1000 units of gold, wood, and food. You also need a lot of builders and time. Building and maintaining a wonder for 2000 years automatically wins a death match or random map game. (Remember that researching architecture is a must!)

The greatest and most satisfying achievement for players in Rise of Rome is to destroy their enemies' wonders.

Chapter Five

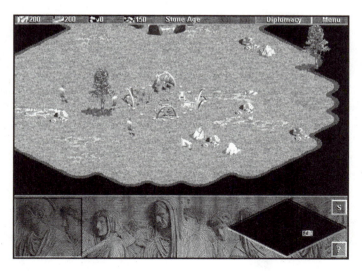

CIVILIZATION BUILDING

When most players think about Microsoft's Age of Empires, it's the battles that come to mind. But what's nearly as important as the ability to fight in this game is the development of good civilization-building skills.

With the exception of the few short scenarios in which you must lead an army from point A to point B, every mission in Microsoft's Rise of Rome is about building an army first and attacking later. More often than not, you will begin in the Stone Age with little more than a town center and a few villagers. Indeed, the competitor who builds civilizations the fastest generally gets the early advantage. Holding on to that advantage, however, requires a different set of skills.

There's an art to building strong cities that can stand up to invasions and provide enough food and resources to build and support a venerable army. The trick is to find the right equilibrium—the exact number of villagers to erect buildings, harvest food, mine minerals, and explore the map. Granted, the more villagers you train, the faster they can accomplish each task—but train too many villagers and you use up your resources with the undesirable result of a prosperous society helpless to defend itself.

Though there's room for variation, most random map games, death matches, and scenarios begin with this scene: a few villagers and a town center.

Because their villagers cost only 35 units of food, the Shang have an early advantage (unless you are playing a death match and starting out with abundant resources).

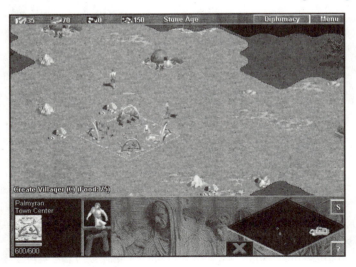

Palmyran villagers cost 75 units instead of the usual 50, but they work at a slightly faster pace.

On the other hand, if you commit too many resources to building an army, you will have a civilization that languishes in the Stone or Tool Age, unable to defend itself against Iron Age assaults.

Building in the Stone Age

Though the cosmetics often vary, you will begin most games with the same basic building blocks—a town center, 200 units of food, enough wood to build some houses and a storage pit, and a few villagers. According to Microsoft game tester Robert Howg, who holds an extremely impressive record on Kali, you need to advance your civilization from the Stone Age to the Bronze Age within 12-13 minutes.

Before you do anything else, start training new villagers to get the ball rolling. In the early going, it's important to establish a large work force so that you can gather materials and build quickly.

Strategy Point

- In Age of Empires, you could dictate that your town center train one villager at a time. In Rise of Rome, take advantage of the ability to order several villagers trained at a time.

Every civilization in Rise of Rome has strengths and weaknesses, but one of the Shang's strengths becomes apparent at the very start. While most villagers cost 50 units of food, it costs a mere 35 units to train Shang villagers. Since the default setting begins most matches with 200 units of food, this means the Shang get an extra villager from the start.

Palmyran villagers, on the other hand, cost 75 units of food but work faster than other villagers. You can create only two villagers from default resources, placing you at a distinct disadvantage if you choose Palmyra as your civilization. It's a short-lived disadvantage. Once you've overcome the initial deficit, the speed with which Palmyran villagers gather resources becomes a great benefit.

Strategy Point

- Players begin death matches with 20,000 units of food and wood. With those kinds of resources, you won't notice the additional costs of training Palmyran villagers.

Don't worry about stone or gold in the early going—Stone Age civilizations have no use for either. The first concern is gathering food to train villagers and wood to build houses, granaries, storage pits, and a dock. A good rule for the opening minutes of any match: train the villagers to gather food and wood, and use the wood to build houses for training more villagers.

Also, assign three or four villagers to mine stone. You generally start off with 200 units of stone, which may sound like a good supply. It disappears quickly, however, when you start building towers.

You don't get bonus points for economizing, so train a large work force— somewhere between 25 and 30 villagers. One of the benefits of having many villagers is the elimination of the need to micro-manage your workers. With 15 or 20 villagers, you must spend precious time ensuring that villagers jump from one job to the next.

Strategy Points

- Build a substantial army of villagers—as many as 30 if your landscape has the resources.
- Assign more than one villager to erect buildings. Two villagers can create a storage pit and start gathering resources more quickly than one.
- Do not build houses in tight groupings. Enticing as it may be to develop your own virtual subdivisions, heavy catapults can destroy several houses at a time if they're clustered.

The next strategic step in building your city quickly is to cut down travel time. Carrying wood and rock to a crowded storage pit eats into your time. By building storage pits alongside gold and stone deposits and heavily wooded areas you will save valuable time.

Finally, while you don't need to build barracks to progress to the Tool Age, you'll need them to get to the Bronze Age. There is little advantage to building multiple barracks unless you plan to train axemen, slingers, or swordsmen, but you should build at least one barracks during the Stone Age.

It is also important to avoid congestion. Too many players build one dock to service an entire fleet of fishing boats. As the game wears on, these docks get tied up as you produce more fishing boats and scout ships.

Strategy Points

- Move your military ships away from your docks as you build them. The only value in having scout ships, war galleys, and triremes is in battle— so move your ships out to form a blockade or look for targets. They're of little value floating near your dock.

Building in the Tool Age

During the Tool Age, you have the opportunity to begin fine-tuning your civilization in preparation for war. While most players see the Tool Age as little

Build farms in groups around granaries and town centers so that your farmers don't have to waste time walking back and forth.

more than the brief sliver of time between the slow-paced Stone Age and the moment when the drama really begins, other players try to grab an early lead in the Tool Age with mass attacks.

Decide in the Tool Age how you plan to feed your civilization. If you have access to a large body of water with lots of fish, you may want to concentrate on building a sizable fishing fleet. If, on the other hand,

you are playing a more land-locked scenario, research farming upgrades and build additional granaries.

You can procrastinate about building barracks and training clubmen in the Stone Age, but wait too long to start building armies and defenses in the Tool Age and you're headed for disaster. Unless you are planning an all-out assault, you'll probably want to begin this age by researching and building towers and walls. The research option is in your granary.

Strategy Point

- Be sure to take advantage of natural barriers such as cliffs, bodies of water, and woods when building.

Incorporate natural barriers into your walls as much as possible. Instead of blocking off wooded areas with walls, for instance, walls placed in gaps between trees keep enemies out. The only Bronze Age units that can damage natural barriers such as trees and stone deposits are villagers.

One benefit of sending villagers and clubmen to explore the map early in the game is that it helps you determine your enemies' locations and what invasion paths they are likely to take. This information can help you block their invasions as effectively and economically as possible.

Of all the kinds of maps in Rise of Rome, Mediterranean maps offer the best strategic advantages for defensive players—assuming they are keeping pace developing their civilizations. Mediterranean maps, maps with a single body of water surrounded by a ring of land, almost always have narrow strips of land. These areas are easily walled off and protected with towers, bowmen, and scout ships. Even if you are still in the Tool Age, you will have little trouble defending your border against a Bronze Age rush if you have bowmen, slingers, towers, and a villager to repair your walls and towers.

In the meantime, use the Tool Age to turn your city into a military processing assembly line. Too many novice players build one of each of the military buildings and call it quits. Having one barracks makes sense only if your opponent attacks you with one soldier at a time.

If you like to close your games with heavy horse archers or chariot archers, build five or six archery ranges. If you favor a cavalry rush, build multiple stables. But don't build them only in the heart of your city—build them near

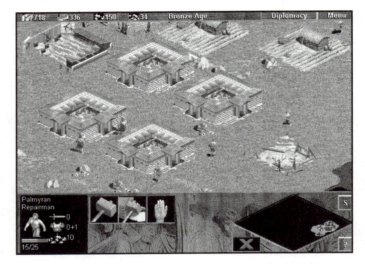

Erecting multiple barracks, stables, and archery ranges enables you to pump out fighting units as needed.

the edge of your claimed territory so that you can train and send them to the front quickly.

Also, make sure you have access to multiple sources of stone and gold. Some players like to create satellite locations around gold or stone deposits by having a couple of villagers build a storage pit and a couple of towers, and then building a wall around the area.

You must build two Tool Age buildings to advance to the Bronze Age. That generally means a market and either stables or an archery range.

Building in the Bronze Age

If you are planning to play from a defensive posture, the Bronze Age is your last opportunity to fortify your defenses before the action begins. If they haven't attempted an invasion already, your enemies will come calling during the Iron Age, so you'd better prepare your reception in the Bronze Age.

Of all of the buildings in the Bronze Age, government centers are the most defense oriented. Offense-minded players may not care about researching architecture to strengthen buildings against attacks, but this technology may save your civilization if your enemies are preparing to invade. On the other hand, you can also research logistics and create a sea of broad swordsmen to invade your enemies.

Whether you decide to play from an offensive or defensive tact, you will need to construct two Bronze Age buildings to advance to the Iron Age. (In truth, you will likely need more than two of these valuable buildings to survive to the Iron Age.) Defensive players should probably choose government centers

and temples as their first Bronze Age edifices. As noted previously, having a government center will let you research architecture to shore up your buildings. Having a temple lets you train priests who can heal your wounded units and, when stationed around your walls, convert enemy units. Offense-minded players may prefer to build academies and siege workshops as their first Bronze Age buildings.

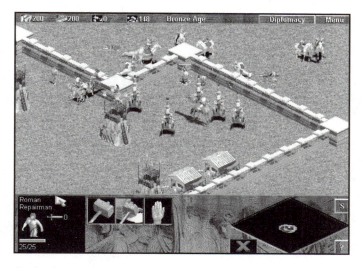

Barbarians at your gates? Build chariots and chariot archers instead of composite bowmen and broad swordsmen or you may find yourself short on gold when you try to advance to the Iron Age.

Hoplites are the only academy units you can train during the Bronze Age. While slow to move, hoplites have high hit points and inflict great damage on anything they attack. Send a wave of 20 hoplites into an unsuspecting Tool or Bronze Age foe, and you're almost assured a victory.

Along with erecting two Bronze Age buildings, you will need 1000 units of food and 800 units of gold to advance to the Iron Age. If you are already fending off an invasion, you may want to use that food to train chariots and chariot archers. Using gold to train hoplites, priests, and composite bowman, on the other hand, is another story.

While trees cover the landscape of most maps, gold is a much more limited commodity. Throw too much gold into broad swordsmen and you may find yourself short of gold when you need ballistas, priests, and juggernauts in the Iron Age. Even worse, go crazy creating defenders and you may indeed find yourself locked in the Bronze Age for the rest of the game.

Strategy Point

- If you find yourself in trouble in the Bronze Age, use your easily renewable resources—wood and food—to train chariots and chariot

archers. These fast units may lack the power of hoplites and swordsmen, but they can get to the fight quickly and will slow the enemy down.

Building in the Iron Age

The Iron Age involves very costly upgrades for extremely powerful units. Heavy horse archers are fast, and a swarm of them can tear through enemies quickly, but it costs 1750 units of food and 800 units of gold to upgrade from horse archers to heavy horse archers. The upgrade from heavy cavalry to cataphracts costs 2000 units of food and 850 units of gold. Upgrading from catapult triremes to juggernauts costs even more.

Strategy Points

- You can research martyrdom, a technology that allows you to convert any enemy by sacrificing a priest. To do this, select an enemy with great strategic value, then send a priest to convert him. As soon as the priest begins chanting, left click on him with your mouse, then click Delete. Your enemy will instantly switch sides.
- Martyrdom is great for converting towers and siege weapons in key locations, but it costs 600 units of gold.

While all of these upgrades are attractive, you need to be selective about which ones you purchase. You can invest 900 units of gold into upgrading from catapult triremes to juggernauts, or you can combine that gold with 2100 units of food and train 60 legions. If you are playing on a Continental or Hill Country map, 60 legions are far more valuable than juggernauts. On Small Island maps, on the other hand, juggernauts are the ultimate weapon.

Whatever upgrades you select, you should build multiple facilities for training your favorite units by the time you reach the Iron Age. You should also have reasonable fortifications to provide warning—if not protection—when enemies cross your borders. Finally, you should still have at least 15 villagers gathering food and other resources so that you can be training back-up waves of units while deploying your initial units in combat.

With the exception of wonders, there are no buildings in the Iron Age that you could not construct in the Bronze Age. (Of course, building a wonder changes the entire tenor of a game.)

One way to win matches against human competitors is to build a wonder and protect it for 2000 years. While many players disapprove of victories achieved with wonders, you should consciously consider that option before spending too much stone and gold. (You need 1000 units of wood, stone, and gold to create a wonder.)

Town centers make excellent walls.

You can conserve gold by training chariots and chariot archers instead of cavalry and horse archers in the Iron Age. While horse archers are more powerful than chariot archers, you cannot train them without gold. With wood being the most common commodity, you can always build farms and produce food, but gold is harder to come by.

Since wood is more common than stone, you can save stone for building towers using wooden buildings for fortifications. You can make great walls by building town centers. While these walls cost 200 units of wood per town center, they stand up to catapults better than standard walls.

Should you decide to create a wonder, here are a few things to keep in mind. Since wonders are easily destroyed, build them in a corner of the map (experienced players are often successful with this strategy). Positioned in this manner, enemies can attack from only two directions.

Strategy Point

- Never build wonders near water. It takes but a few shots from a juggernaut to turn wonders into distant memories.

You need to build a strong defense network before you build a wonder. Most players prefer to surround their wonders with concentric rings of walls and towers lined with archers, siege weapons, and priests. Building these defenses is a huge investment of military might and manpower. Expect to spend almost as many resources building your perimeter as you spent on the wonder itself.

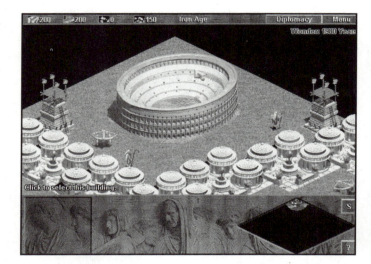

Building wonders in a corner of the map cuts your enemies'
attack options in half.

Be sure that you have cavalry, swordsmen, or academy units near your catapults. One of the preferred ways of destroying wonders is to use priests to convert siege weapons, then turn those weapons on the wonder they were recently protecting.

Once you start construction on your wonder, the game will announce your project and its location to all of your enemies. Expect a lot of drop-in traffic. Just be sure that you have horse archers or chariots to rush any siege weapons your enemies throw at your towers. Because of its enormous range, one heavy catapult will bash its way through the most elaborate defenses unless you send fast-moving and powerful units to destroy it.

Chapter Six

BATTLE: A TACTICAL GUIDE

Knowing the finer points of civilization building is important, but the real excitement in Microsoft's Rise of Rome is in the battles. This chapter contains a sampling of battle tactics—disjointed maneuvers, tricks, and techniques that can be used in both single-player and multiplayer games.

Since every single-player scenario offers a unique goal, the strategies for achieving these goals are included in the individual scenario walkthroughs in Chapters 7-10.

Misusing the Scenario Builder and Other Abuses

These key tips will go a long way toward enabling you to thrive and survive.

Chemistry Lessons

Know how different units match up against each other—this is the most important tactical knowledge you can possess in this game. Fire Galleys, for instance, were designed to be Trireme-killers. Slingers were designed to stop archers and hurt towers, but they don't stand up to abuse from swordsmen.

Learning to fight is easy. It's learning how to win that's tough.

Select the Scenario Builder from the opening screen.

If you're really serious about learning how units match up, you can find out by using the Scenario Builder.

Select the Scenario Builder from the opening menu, and then choose the Create a Scenario option on the next screen. Since you're more interested in testing units than creating a scenario, don't bother tweaking the map. (If you want to test naval units, switch the terrain to Water or Deep Water.)

Next, define the opponents in your contest by clicking Players at the top of the screen. Remember, in order to do battle, opponents must belong to different civilizations. Scenario Builder automatically places two civilizations in each scenario—if you want to add more, click Number of Players along the left side of the screen. You can place anywhere from two to eight civilizations in your scenario.

Each civilization offers units with special strengths: Roman legions attack 33 percent faster than other legions, and Choson legions have the highest number of hit points, for example. If you want to test civilization-specific units, be sure to define the nations using the Civilization field in the bottom left corner of the screen.

Don't bother setting ages, resources, or other options. They won't impact your test. You can place cataphracts in Stone Age battles when you design your own scenarios.

The next step is placing your combatants. Click Units at the top of the screen. Now select the units you want to test from the menu along the left side of the screen. Once

The player options in the Scenario Builder allow you to customize every side of every battle.

you have placed one army, click Players field below the Units Menu, and begin placing units for the other army. Place both sides in front of each other so that they do not have to look for each other before fighting.

Once you have built both sides, click Menu in the top left corner of the screen, and then click the "test" option. Your computer will configure the information, and then show you the battle.

The scenario builder is not only a great test laboratory for matching units against each other, but it also gives you the opportunity to practice certain battle techniques, such as dodging ballista fire with cavalry and horse archers. You can use it to practice such skills as attacking ballistas without getting hit and tricking enemy catapults into killing each other with a villager.

Hot Keys

It's hard to keep track of multiple units in the heat of battle. Cavalry frequently goes chasing some enemy villager and leaves its position undefended. You sometimes lose track of units by forgetting where you sent them last. Then, when you really need them, you have to search the entire map to find them.

There's an answer. You can group units together and assign them a hot key on your keyboard. Then, whenever you press that key, you automatically select them (assuming they're still alive).

To assign a key to one unit, place your pointer over the unit and press your mouse's left button. (To assign a key to a group of units, hold the button down and draw a box surrounding all units you wish to select.) Now press Control (Ctrl) and any of the number keys (1-9) along the top of your keyboard.

Once assigned, you will access those units with the corresponding number key. You can also use this trick to organize your army during battle.

Misusing Diplomacy

Despite their enormous destructive power, many serious Age of Empires players do not use catapults because they are so hard to control. When catapults see enemy units attacking your soldiers, they fire at them—indiscriminately

The little number on the left shows that units have been grouped and assigned a hot key.

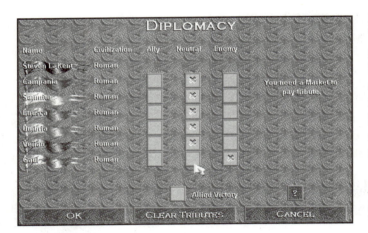

Setting your diplomacy to neutral will help reign in your siege weapons and reduce your friendly-fire casualties.

killing everyone in the area. When they see enemies attacking your walls and buildings, they kill the enemies—and damage your fortifications. (Ballista and helepolis' fire is the exception. The only damage suffered is by the enemy.)

Catapult triremes and juggernauts have the same problem. There's nothing wrong with sending them to clear a beachhead for your transports, but you had better send them far away before sending your transports.

There is a somewhat satisfactory solution to this dilemma. Go into your diplomacy settings by clicking Diplomacy in the top right corner of the screen. Change the Relations settings from enemy to neutral, and your troops will no longer initiate attacks on enemy units. This is not a perfect solution. With your diplomacy set to neutral, your units will generally let your enemies attack before responding—but it will help protect your forces from friendly fire. (We prefer ballistas and triremes to catapults and juggernauts—but the best attack is a varied one combining catapults to take out towers and to finish buildings, and ballistas to kill enemy units.)

Spying with Achievements

Rise of Rome does not have a telepathy setting to reveal your enemies' thoughts, but it does offer a small window to give you an idea about their resources.

Click Menu in the top right corner of the screen, then click Achievements on that menu. You can gain small pieces of intelligence information by clicking each of the bars in Achievements Summary.

Click the Military Achievements bar, and you will see a graph displaying which civilization has the largest army and who has the most kills. If you are in

an every-civilization-for-itself match with three or more nations, you may want to monitor your opponents' losses. If somebody takes a big dip, you might consider riding into his town to finish the job.

Clicking the Economic Achievements bar will bring up a graph showing who has the most gold and how much they've accumulated. It also shows tributes paid, which can help you uncover secret alliances.

The Time Line reveals which Age your opponents

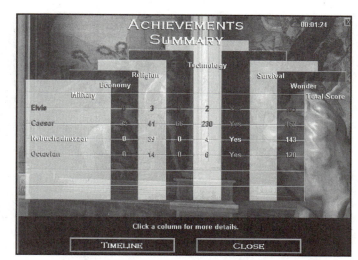

You can get small glimpses of your opponent's economic and military strength by using the Achievements menu.

are in—valuable information since they will often begin attacking after reaching the Bronze Age. At the very least, it will let you know if you are keeping up with their pace.

Reusable Numbers

The Babylonians have built a wonder, and you have 2000 years to crush it. This is no time for civility or sentiment. You need to crank out battle units and send them into the meat grinder—rows of Babylonian ballista towers—and hope that a few survive to clear the way for your next wave of victims.

You cue-up your barracks, stables, siege workshops, archery ranges, and academies so that they keep pumping out men and beasts.

If you hot-key your men as they appear, you can send these waves in a fairly organized fashion and check on their progress as they bore their way toward the enemy wonder. This is an especially important tactic if you're forced to launch your invasion from one corner of the map to attack a target in an opposite corner. You won't have to spend time micro-managing each wave as it makes its way across the map because now you'll be able to easily locate them.

Rushing straight into a row of watchtowers, these slingers are mowed down having destroyed only two towers.

Fun with Towers

Towers can make or break you in many missions. Here's a look at tips for both offensive and defensive play.

One at a Time

A lone slinger cannot destroy a watch tower under the best of circumstances, but clustered slingers can destroy towers in a tight formation by concentrating their fire on one tower at a time. If the towers are in a well-designed formation, two and possibly three towers will be able to hit your slingers before they get in range—and you will sustain casualties. But the concentrated force of ten slingers can bring down a tower before it kills any of your slingers.

This is an important point in situations where you are sending heavy catapults to clear the way for your infantry during Iron Age invasions. Look for corners before attacking walls and towers. If you move along walls systematically and you will get more mileage out of your heavy weapons.

Tower Formations

Build towers in tight groups of three or four so that they are within range of each other. The obvious benefit of building towers in square or triangular

formations is that they can defend each other—but there are fringe benefits, too.

Left to their own artificial intelligence, invaders tend to become confused when attacked from multiple directions. When lone cavalry units ride into these formations, they try to attack whatever hits them. When hit by one tower after another, these units ride back and forth without pausing to hit any particular tower.

Make sure that more than one of your towers is concentrating on that unit. Do not allow your towers to be distracted by a passing axeman while more dangerous units— such as cavalry—ride through unmolested.

Tower Attacks

Killing villagers and destroying houses are very important offensive "musts" early in the game. The old adage in boxing is "Kill the body and the head must die." The same is true in Rise of Rome. Kill enough villagers and destroy enough houses to cripple opponents, and you can wipe them off the map.

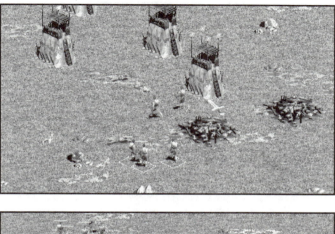

By moving in from an angle and isolating each target, all ten towers are destroyed—and four slingers get to walk away from the battle.

Cavalry become disoriented when riding through tower formations.

On the carnage-to-cost scale, building towers near enemy gold and stone mines scores quite well.

The best way to slaughter villagers is to find areas where they congregate and are only lightly guarded. The biggest concentration of unprotected villagers can usually be found around stone and gold deposits.

If you locate your opponents' gold and stone mines during the Tool Age, send two villagers to the supplies and build a watch tower. More often than not, the enemy villagers will attempt to swarm and destroy the tower. Have your villagers repair the tower during the attack. (If you are playing against a human opponent, he will probably notice your villagers and kill them. If you are playing against the computer, your villagers will likely not be hurt.)

If you're really lucky, you may kill off an entire wave of villagers and have time to build a second tower before reinforcements arrive. Either way, you will slow your opponents' advancement into the Bronze Age and kill several of his villagers with a very small investment.

Towering Opponents

One of the benefits of sending villagers to explore the map from the game's start is that you can erect buildings wherever you've explored.

Some players in a death match game (pretty much the only scenario in which you start out with enough stone to do this), will explore the map quickly—then place dozens of towers all over their enemies' territories and send villagers to build them. Your enemies will locate most of these towers and destroy them—but all it takes is a few strategic towers to turn the tide of a game.

The best defense against this strategy is to use the overview map on the bottom of your screen. Colored squares will appear to indicate your opponents' construction sites. If you see squares in your territory, send a reception squad and destroy them. With any luck, you kill villagers and yet-to-be-started towers—costing your opponent stone, men, and possibly the game.

Think Numbers

Paying attention to some simple math will help your game strategies—and help you keep your sanity.

Flood of Two Ages

You can build government centers and broad swordsmen in the Bronze Age, meaning that if you have the gold, the food, and the aggression, you can research nobility to double the barracks allowance and invade your enemies.

Cavalry units are more powerful than broad swordsmen in a one-on-one battle, but in quantities, your swordsmen will attack like a colony of ants. They will swarm towers and beat them into dust. They will pour through cities destroying villagers and tearing down buildings. Of course, they'll take casualties, but a force of 50 or 60 broad swordsmen will eventually catch and demolish any Bronze Age challenges set before it.

Matters change, however, in the Iron Age. The best way to stop a mass attack is to counter with a force combining strength and speed. A pack of ten heavy horse archers can wear down an army of swordsmen as they invade, especially if you have researched alchemy. By always staying out of reach, horse archers can reduce enemy armies without a single casualty.

Priests and catapults are fairly useless against mass attacks, but ballistas and helepolises can destroy the first lines of enemy units before they reach your city limits. Use walls to slow your enemies or bottleneck their attack routes, then hit

Even without walls, a barrier of towers and war elephants can stop a barracks unit invasion. It's vulnerable, however, to heavy catapult and priest attacks.

them with bowmen and towers. Ballista towers and war elephants also make a great defensive deterrent. The elephants can crush the swordsmen as they try to make their way through your towers.

Ballistas are Social, Catapults are Not

It takes a ballista four shots or 12 seconds to kill heavy cavalry. It takes five shots to kill a cataphract and two shots or six seconds to kill a scout. To make matters worse, ballistas cannot fire at units right beside or in front of them—they need space to defend themselves. In other words, lone ballistas or helepolises are vulnerable to attack. They are far more effective in groups of five or ten. Raining tree-sized arrows on their attackers, a group of ballistas can wear down armored elephants and cut down cataphracts before they are close enough to strike back. (Even so, keep cavalry or chariots nearby to help defend them.)

Titan or Titanic?

War on the water is a defacto component in Rise of Rome. Here are several tactical observations and tips that will help.

Waging War from an Island Fortress

The safest way to wage island warfare is to wall off your island until you are ready to fight. This will not stop scout ships and war galleys from shooting from off shore, but it will prevent transports from landing.

One important tip to remember is that you can repair injured ships through walls. Just bring the ship as close to the wall as possible, and then assign a villager to repair it. The villager will kneel in front of the wall and start pounding his hammer, and your ship will be healed!

Kamikaze Fishing Fleets

Fishing ships are fast, and juggernauts are stupid—it's an equation that leads to a lot of fun. Not only do juggernauts and catapult triremes show a certain lack of judgment about firing at enemy ships close to their own, but they also have a five-second downtime between shots.

A well-steered fishing boat can therefore lead catapult triremes and juggernauts into all kinds of mischief. You can weave a fishing boat in and out of enemy fleets to cause their ships to hit each other, or you can lead an enemy fleet on a wild-goose chase away from your territory while your docks pump out ships.

A word of caution, however. Tricks that work on slow-moving catapult

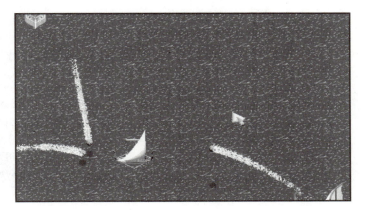

A lone fishing boat can easily outmaneuver an entire fleet of juggernauts.

triremes do not work when applied to regular triremes. More importantly, fire galleys are the only boats in Rise of Rome that move as quickly as fishing ships. Play around with fire galleys, and you're going to get burned.

Setting Traps

Beware of invasions from the sea. After finding a nice supply of stone and starting to build your city, it almost never fails that some John Paul Jones

wannabe storms your island with cavalry and archers.

Light transports are slow, but they absorb a lot of damage without sinking. They'll take 24 arrows from scout ships before sinking. Even war galleys need 15 shots or 30 seconds to destroy them. In that time, the transports will have reached you, turned off their "fasten safety belt" sign, and unloaded their deadly cargo.

It takes practice, but being able to trap and destroy enemy transports can save you serious grief in battles on Island maps.

The best way to destroy transports is with fire galleys. They are slightly faster than heavy transports, much faster than light transports, and they inflict a great deal of damage very quickly. Unfortunately, you cannot build fire galleys in the Tool Age.

To kill transports in the Tool Age, and in later ages if needed, trap them with merchant or fishing boats, and then finish them with war ships.

Here's the best way to set a trap. Send a trapping boat across the transport's bow, and then close in behind it with two galleys or scout ships. You will probably have to repeat this procedure several times to sink a transport—but if there are only a few areas to land on your coastline, you should be able to finish the job before the transport unloads.

Wonders with Wonders

They might be the bane of many online gamers, but wonders can assure victory with a resounding finality.

The Wonder Lure

Okay, multiplayer purists, here's a way to use wonders that will meet your approval.

Now, you should not employ this tactic until you have amassed more than 2500 units of every resource and maximized your population limit with as many chariots and cavalry units as possible. Once you have saved up this fortune, begin building a town in a remote corner of the map, away from your main city. Seal 10 or 15 villagers in a fortification with thick walls and several towers, and then launch a feinting attack to distract your opponent as you begin constructing a wonder in your new city.

Do not commit too many units to this attack—you simply want to test your opponent's resolve. (This will cause your enemy to expend resources and use precious minutes before going after your wonder.) Five or six horse archers or a band of chariots attacking villagers should be enough to get the job done.

Now the fun begins. More likely than not, your opponents will throw everything they have into demolishing your satellite town and wonder. They will send vast armies toward that corner of the map, and while they will not

suffer many casualties destroying poorly defended walls and towers, it will take them a few minutes to finish the job.

While they are thus occupied, you need to cue your barracks, academy, and stables so that they'll replace the villagers who built your wonder, then send your army to attack your opponent's city. This invasion needs to be fast and powerful—cataphracts are the best unit because of their speed and hefty number of attack points. Your goal is to destroy your enemy's priests, villagers, temples, houses, and town center. Clean out these buildings, and you will leave your opponent unable to renew his army. (Be sure to get the priests and temples because it only takes one converted villager for an enemy to rebuild his entire empire.)

One last thing: use Delete to kill all of the villagers around your wonder once you begin your attack. Your barracks and stables will begin training units to replace the villagers. That way you will have an army to defend your city in case your enemy tries to attack it after destroying the wonder.

Is There A Wonder in the House?

You're busy building your army when the computer plays that familiar gong and announces that your enemy has begun building a wonder. Here's a long-shot solution that involves no risk—build a house beside it.

You don't even have to build the house, really. The computer automatically illuminates areas in which wonders are being built. Click that area, find an open spot, and place a house there.

The computer automatically displays sites in which wonders are being built. Place a house beside the construction, and nearby catapults may mark that wonder for dismemberment.

With any luck, you enemy will have heavy catapults defending the wonder. The catapults will immediately turn and begin firing at the house, and you know how heavy catapult fire destroys everything in the adjoining area. Not only do they smash the house you've started, but they'll also destroy the wonder and kill the villagers that were building it.

Chapter Seven

AVE CAESAR

Rendering unto Caesar that which is Caesar's would have been a full-time job. Here was a man whose future truly seemed written in the stars.

Emerging as one of the most powerful men in Rome, Caesar became governor of three outer territories, built an army, conquered untold territories in western Europe in which Rome had little hold, and then warred in Egypt before finally vanquishing Rome herself.

Mission 1: Caesar vs. Pirates

When Caesar was a young man just entering the military, while on tour in the Mediterranean, he had the misfortune of being captured and held for ransom by pirates. He swore he would avenge this humiliation, and they laughed, never realizing the depth of their young captive's determination.

When Caesar returned home, he used his family's money to hire mercenaries and made good on his promise. In Caesar vs. Pirates, you get to help young Caesar take his revenge. Your objectives are to destroy every pirate dock on the map and to keep Caesar alive. As any mercenary can tell you, it's always a good idea to keep the boss alive.

You begin the mission with young Caesar (represented as a heavy cavalry hero with 402 hit points and plenty of armor and attack points), 400 units of wood, 400 units of food, and 300 units of stone. You are on an island located along the western edge of the map. Your first task is to head north and find a friendly village that waits to join your cause.

There are several pirate axemen and slingers in the woods on this island. Charge head-on and kill them. If you don't, they'll attack your village as you expand. Don't worry about them hurting Caesar—he has an enormous number of hit points and a very powerful attack. (Even on the hardest level, you'll lose less than 200 hit points.) These guys still don't know who they're dealing with.

Charging into a pack of slingers may be suicidal for regular cavalry, but this is Caesar.

Once you make it past the pirates, you will find your friendly village—four villagers, a Stone Age town center, two waterfront sentry towers, and a dock. Assign the three villagers in the main part of your village to start chopping down the trees along the edge of the map, and then ride farther north to find your fourth villager. Have him build a storage pit beside the stone mine and start mining it.

It may not be long before the first pirate ships come to visit your shores. Even if they don't come immediately, they will harass your fishing ships. Build two galleys, and then upgrade to triremes. As you harvest more wood, make a blockade of triremes and claim your waters. You will eventually expand this blockade to claim the entire map.

In the meantime, build your workforce. Train ten new villagers to harvest the wood, stone, and gold on your island. Build a storage pit by the gold mine in your southeastern woods. Since you have a seemingly endless supply of wood, build a dock in the northwestern river (by your stone mine), ferry five villagers back and forth as they clear a construction spot beyond the river, and then build a town center there. Leave two villagers to chop wood in that area.

At this point you should probably do a little city planning. Priests are very helpful in this scenario, so you need to build a temple. Your priests' first task should be to heal Caesar. You'll probably tuck him away in a safe corner for the rest of this mission, and that's okay—you should not take any chances with him.

You'll spend most of this scenario involved in naval battles. Build a market and research craftsmanship. Also build a government center so that you can research engineering and ballistics. Once you do this, your triremes will be strong, have greater range, and shoot more accurately.

Don't bother building a siege workshop in your base. You'll need one, but you might as well build it closer to your enemies so that you spend less time transporting your weapons. There are three pirate civilizations in this scenario—one in the western corner of the map, one along the southeastern edge, and one in the southern corner. (The one along the southeastern edge has several smaller branches throughout the map.)

With the exception of the southern pirates' main dock,

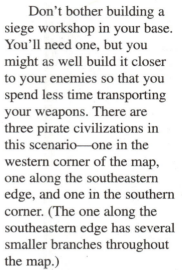

Your first town is an economic base. Build docks, a market, a government center, a temple, and lots of houses.

you'll have little trouble clearing your enemies and destroying their docks with a large naval force. Build ten triremes and five juggernauts and three corners of the map are yours.

Once you have your fleet, it's time to expand—clear the smaller pirate settlements out of the islands to the south and build your fishing area.

The settlements in the islands consist of docks, watch towers, slingers, bowmen, and few houses. The pirates will send fleets of scout ships and galleys, but your triremes will have no problem sinking them. The real danger is fire galleys, which are faster than triremes. Their armor is trireme-resistant, and one fire galley can burn its way through a fleet of triremes. They are vulnerable to catapults and catapult triremes. If you can get them to come near land, they make easy and profitable converts for your priests. (You should also massacre the brown pirates along the southeastern edge of the map as you destroy the island colonies. Get to them early enough, and then you can stop them from mining their gold.)

Your enemies will try to invade your base as you expand. Their main interest will be invading the spit of land on which you found your first town center. Fortify that shore with a row of towers and leave a couple of triremes to guard it—the pirates will not be able to make a meaningful landing. Make sure

You'll run into some resistance as you clear out the islands.
There is safety in numbers, so be sure to send at least five
triremes in every fleet.

The pirate civilization along the southeastern edge of the
map is the least developed of the pirate nations.

to choke off routes to your eastern shores in the meantime. You do not want the pirates to get a foothold on your island.

As you clear out the islands, you'll find stone and gold deposits. Since you will be mainly on the offensive in this scenario, you won't need much stone. Gold, on the other hand, will help a lot. Send villagers to mine gold deposits whenever you find them. Head west and clear out the yellow pirates once you have enough gold to build an armada with four juggernauts and eight triremes.

The biggest problem with attacking the yellow pirates is sorting the challenges that require triremes from the problems best handled by juggernauts. Have your triremes destroy the pirates' galleys and your juggernauts clear the towers out of the way. If the galleys attack your juggernauts while they are battering towers, have your juggernauts fall back until your triremes have cleared the waters.

The yellow pirates have several catapults and will try to lure your triremes into range and sink them. Destroy the juggernauts with your catapults, and then have your triremes destroy all that remains. Destroy the docks, the town center, the houses, and the villagers—but don't worry about the cavalry or military buildings. Once the villagers are dead and the town center destroyed, the yellow pirates will not be able to rebuild.

The last pirate civilization has combined horse archers, ballistas, and towers to make a solid defense.

Now it is time to repair your ships and prepare to invade the brown pirates in the south.

The brown pirates are the ones with the fire galleys. If you have eradicated fire galleys while clearing the islands, you will sail into fairly empty harbors when raiding these pirates. If you've seen only a few fire galleys so far, rest assured that more will be waiting for you in the harbor. If this is the case, your best bet is to mount a combination land and sea assault.

These pirates have set up a potent defense of ballistas, horse archers, and towers. If you're making a land invasion, approach their harbor from the west and land a force of three priests and six ballistas outside the wall guarding their harbor. Use your ballistas to clear away any horse archers in the area, and then have your invasion party wade around the wall on the land bridge and head up the road leading to the beach. From there you can use your priests to convert some of the fire galleys and have your ballistas fire at others.

Now launch your final assault. Have your juggernauts destroy towers and clear the way for your triremes. Have your triremes protect your juggernauts from horse archers, and have your juggernauts finish the mission by destroying the docks located in this harbor.

Ways to Lose

The easiest way to fulfill both of this scenario's objectives would be to put Caesar on a transport. Remember, he must stay alive.

The pirates are a crafty bunch. They will send merchant ships to lure your triremes away from your fishing ships, and then send scout ships and galleys to attack your fishing boats. They may even go after your juggernauts.

Additional Hints

Don't bother building barracks. As long as you sink the pirates' transports before they land, you will have no need of ground troops.

Use priests to convert fire galleys if at all possible. One fire galley can easily clear a harbor of regular galleys, and they do well against triremes.

Place villagers on an island near sea battles so they can repair your ships quickly.

Mission 2: Britain

As the governor of Rome's western territories, Julius Caesar did more conquering than governing. The tribes that inhabit Britain have come to the aid of the Gauls, Caesar's current enemies, and Caesar has decided to cross the English Channel and punish them. To complete this scenario, capture the ruins in Britain and keep Caesar alive.

You begin this mission with a large army that includes Caesar, centurions, legions, improved bowmen, two catapults, two ballistas, two priests, heavy transports, and a fleet of juggernauts.

This is not a one-on-one battle, however. The Veneti, a civilization to the east, want to join in against the Romans—and they have fire galleys. You can conquer Britain without bothering with the Veneti, but they will sink your navy while you fight on land if you don't sink their fleet and destroy their dock.

Three Veneti fire galleys will close in on your navy the moment the scenario starts, so select all of your ships and sink the fire galleys before they do too much damage. You must also guard against Veneti transports until you've neutralized their threat.

Despite the fact that you're not trying to colonize Britain, you're going to want to have a few villagers to collect food and wood for training new troops—and to repair your ships. Despite the civilizations on the British Isle, the Veneti

pose a larger threat in the beginning. Take five of your juggernauts over to their island to wipe out their towers, harbors, bowmen, and military buildings. Kill everything except a few villagers and a storage pit. Converting villagers will be of no benefit unless you convert a building for them to put wood in—and priests cannot convert town centers.

Once the island is sufficiently pulverized, have your priests convert the remaining villagers and the storage pit. Then rebuild the island for yourself. You'll

The Veneti don't plan to stand by and watch the fireworks between you and Britain. Destroy their docks and covert their villagers.

need to build lots of houses. Remember, your population includes the large army with which you started the mission.

Converting Veneti and taking over their island will not give you access to a full technology tree. You will not be able to build barracks, docks, stables, temples, or siege workshops. You will be able to build towers, but there is no stone on their island. You will also be able to build farms, town centers and academies. The ability to build academies and train centurions on Britain will give you a big leg up in this scenario.

Your next step is to destroy the towers guarding Britain's craggy coastline. Watch out for catapults and chariot archers. They will sneak up and fire down at your from the tops of cliffs. Once you've smashed the towers and any unfortunate units that meandered within your range, send two juggernauts up the river that divides Britain in half, and kill every villager, chariot, and slinger that comes by.

If you follow the river to its top, you will come to a plateau. There is a temple and two towers at the top of that plateau. You can't reach the second tower, but you will be able to destroy the temple and one tower. There are priests up there, too. Kill them the moment they show themselves. In fact, kill

Send juggernauts up the river to bombard everything that comes within range.

Begin your invasion at the mouth of the river.

everything that comes within range.

Now land your invasion at the mouth of the river. Sweep out the area and be sure to kill every chariot before landing your priests. You must protect them and your siege weapons—and don't bring Caesar along. You'll do fine without him.

Move north along the west side of the river. If you have converted the Veneti, bring a villager and have him make 10 or 15 academies, and then cue them all to produce centurions. That way, when you lose your first man, 10 or 15 new centurions will replace him.

There is a walled area with a tower and a catapult just west of the river. Destroy both with a heleopolis so that you don't have to worry about it distracting your army.

You'll see a hill at the top of the river. The path up that hill leads to two towns and two ruins. Use your centurions to destroy the watch towers guarding that path and massacre the

people. Now, there is a priest on a terrace overlooking the city. Your centurions can't reach him, so avoid him until you've killed everybody in the top corner of the map. Then send your heleopolis to teach him about the afterlife.

Once you've mopped up the area to make sure that no stragglers undo your work, send one of your men to each of the two ruins and prepare to invade the town to the west.

This is the moment when you will be glad you converted Veneti villagers and built up your army. The last town is almost directly west of the waterfall at the top of the river. It is a walled city with only one entrance, and here you'll find priests, catapults, chariot archers, and towers. You could try to fight your way in, but your goal is to take control of the ruin, and you accomplish that the moment your men reach it.

Group all of your centurions in one large battalion and have them march right in the front gate. Priests will convert one or two of them and catapults will kill a few, but the mission will end as soon as they pass through the gate and reach the ruin.

Ways to Lose

The surest way to lose is to ignore the Veneti. They will leave you landlocked on your first island if given the chance, and their fire galleys are skilled transport and juggernaut sinkers.

Losing your priests early in this scenario can also cause you to lose. Don't take foolish chances converting Veneti archers or cavalry. If you have a safe vantage point, it's fine to convert cavalry, but archers are always a danger to priests.

Additional Hints

Though your villagers cannot build archery ranges or stables, your priests can convert them. Convert the stables in the northern corner of the map and you can start training scythe chariots—an excellent weapon if you are saving gold to train centurions.

Mission 3: Alesia

This scenario is based on one of the most intriguing moments in Roman history—a moment in which Caesar the aggressor found himself under siege.

Caesar returned to Gaul to discover that the unorganized barbarians had formed a powerful army under the leadership of Vercingetorix. An imaginative general, Vercingetorix put Caesar on the defensive by having his army besiege Caesar, even as Caesar attacked the village of Alesia.

Your objective is to capture Vercingetorix, who is well protected in Alesia, the town in the center of the map. You must capture him and keep Caesar from harm to win.

As the scenario opens, you are between a rock and a hard place, with your forces sandwiched between the walls of Alesia and the walls they've erected to keep Vercingetorix's allies out of your camp. You have four villagers, four legions, and Caesar in part of your camp, and composite bowmen scattered throughout the area guarding the walls. There are breaches in your walls—but, fortunately, you start out with enough stone to fill the gaps.

Your first task is to repair gaps along the western side of your walls as quickly as possible to stop the barbarians from entering and overpowering your men. Once the walls are repaired, build a storage pit beside the stone mine near your western wall. You're going to need the stone.

The next trick is to attack the civilization to the east before it gets established. Send Caesar and your legions to massacre them and destroy their town center. Once they're dead, the mission becomes considerably easier.

Now that they are gone, send a villager to build a granary beside their berry bushes. Wall off their half of the map when you get the opportunity, and you'll have space and resources to assemble an overwhelming army.

The first five minutes of this mission are the most crucial. Once you have a solid workforce and a growing army, it won't take long before you can visit the civilization in the northeastern part of the map and annihilate them, too.

The final battle comes when you press Delete to destroy your own walls and charge in to get Vercingetorix. He is the white heavy cavalry unit trapped in a walled-off area in the center of town. There are horse archers in the pen with him, so don't march to the walls with a couple of phalanxes and expect to rush him. Your best bet is to build a pack of heleopolises so that you can take care of Vercingetorix and his guard from a distance.

You should send cavalry with your heleopolises, but if you've been killing his men as they approached the walls—especially his villagers—there is an excellent chance that Vercingetorix and his men will be the last living units inside his walls. Either way, the scenario ends the moment you kill him.

Ways to Lose

The biggest danger in this scenario is inactivity. Wipe out the nation to the east quickly, or the situation will be too tough to control. Once you have control of the entire eastern side of the map, wall it off and tap into its resources as quickly as possible. You'll need an army of villagers to prevent your walls from leaking Gauls.

Additional Hints

You shouldn't bother with the "rush in and catch 'em unaware" maneuver—Vercingetorix already has sentry towers and catapults.

Do not panic if one of your enemies manages to break into your compound. Send centurions, legions, or cavalry to defend the area and have a villager seal the wall as soon as the enemies are gone.

Build towers along every long stretch of wall. You will need these towers to hold off enemies until you can get a villager to the scene to repair the wall.

Build extra towers along the inside wall in the southwestern portion of your camp. The Gauls have gold mines there, and you'll be able to kill many villagers if you have bowmen or towers there.

Your best bet for keeping your walls whole is to hot-key groups of villagers and station them evenly throughout the camp. That way you won't have to search for them when a wall in their area is being breached. You can find them by clicking their hot-key and send them right to the trouble.

Mission 4: Caesar vs. Pompey

Scared and jealous of Caesar, the senate flattered a masterful general named Gnaeus Pompey into going to war with him. The senate promised Pompey that he could be emperor if he defeated Caesar. (It's doubtful that they would have fulfilled this promise—the reason they wanted to stop Caesar was their fear of his power.)

This is a very straightforward scenario: you must defeat Pompey and keep Caesar alive.

You begin with two hoplites, four legions, two catapults, and four villagers. Your first task is to build a town center and establish your city and army. One of the two nations that have risen against you, Afranius, is already well established with siege workshops, towers, and a large population.

The good news about this scenario is that it challenges you to maintain a war on two and possibly three fronts. The bad news is that if you fail to make a decisive strike early on, Caesar vs. Pompey turns into an ugly battle of attrition requiring you to launch wave after wave of invasions until you wear Pompey down.

The key to winning this mission in a reasonable amount of time is risking Caesar himself. Caesar has high attack and hit points, meaning he is a one-man army when it comes to dashing past towers and attacking villagers. Instead of keeping him cloistered in some safe corner in this mission, you're going to use his talents.

As the scenario begins, you will notice that Caesar is at the end of a road. Have him follow that road south and west across the river and through

Caesar has run ahead of his army. It's dangerous, but it's the only way to achieve a quick victory.

Afranius' town as quickly as possible. Towers will shoot at him, hoplites and chariots will chase him—but he must not stay and fight.

As you pass through Afranius' city, you will arrive at a clearing that serves as a crossroad. Turn left at this juncture and cross the river. You will then ride through a gauntlet of towers and take a little damage, but it's nothing that Caesar can't handle.

When you get past the towers, turn left and look for villagers. Kill everybody you

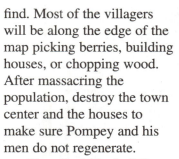

find. Most of the villagers will be along the edge of the map picking berries, building houses, or chopping wood. After massacring the population, destroy the town center and the houses to make sure Pompey and his men do not regenerate.

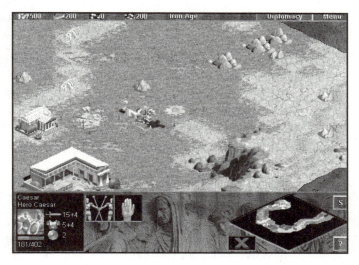

If Caesar can kill Pompey's villagers and destroy his town center, the mission is practically over.

You should be building your original base as Caesar clears Pompey's territory. Build a town center near your starting point and have your villagers forage for berries, chop wood, and build houses. Afranius has a large army and will send dozens of ballistas your way, so dig in. Build towers to distract his ballistas and chariots to attack them. Mine the tiny gold and stone deposits around your base and you'll have enough resources to finish this battle.

Your objective is to wipe out every trace of Pompey. Now that you control his land, don't worry about Afranius. Stall him until you've destroyed Pompey's buildings and you win.

That is where your two catapults come in. There are two slopes leading from your base territory to the lake dividing the map. Build a dock by the eastern slope, and then build a light transport—and send a villager and your two catapults to Caesar.

You are sending the villager as a backup. Pompey's land has far more resources than your original territory. If you're unable to get to Pompey's building before Afranius overruns your first base, you may have to seal off this area and make it your new home.

Have your catapults destroy all of Pompey's towers and buildings. They should start in the north and work their way south, ending up at the bridge Caesar used to cross from Afranius' land to Pompey's. Your last two targets will be the yellow towers on Afranius' side of the bridge. If you've destroyed the

rest of Pompey's buildings, the mission will end when those towers are destroyed.

Ways to Lose

This is an easy mission to lose or get bogged down in. Do not dawdle even for a moment as you lead Caesar past Afranius' men and against Pompey.

You are also vulnerable during the mop-up stage. Afranius is a formidable enemy with abundant siege weapons and resources.

Additional Hints

Build chariots. They are fast, powerful, and cheap. Throw them at ballistas in groups of three and you'll destroy them every time.

Wall off Pompey's land once you seize control of it. That way, if Afranius destroys your catapults before you can finish the towers and buildings, you'll have time to develop both of your cities.

Save your game the moment Caesar kills off the last of Pompey's villagers. If things go wrong with the catapults, you will be able to load your saved game rather than having to replay Caesar's attack.

If you cannot manage to kill all of Pompey's men with Caesar, restart the mission. Wearing Pompey and Afranius down in a battle of attrition could take hours.

Chapter Eight

ENEMIES OF ROME

The Romans were not the only history makers of their time. While Hannibal never had a salad named after him, he certainly holds a prominent spot in military history. Zenobia may not have a town named after her in Missouri, but she too is known by historians—and there is a town named Palmyra in New York.

You don't view the world as Roman in three of these missions, but rather as an enemy of Rome. And as such, true to history, you're waging battles as an underdog.

Mission 1: Crossing the Alps

Hannibal's crossing of the Alps is one of the most memorable moments in military history. This was a case of a powerfully willful man defying nature, fear, and mortal frailty to accomplish a feat so unthinkable that Rome was completely unprepared for it. Hannibal not only marched an enormous army across the Alps, but he did it with elephants.

Your objective in this mission is simply to get Hannibal and his army across the map. Obviously enemies and traps await. Ensemble's crack team of professional cartographers put in overtime on this mission. Try to take the shortest path between two points on this map, and you'll end up in dangerous cul-de-sacs, defending your elephants' derrieres.

You begin this scenario with a seemingly unbeatable army that includes elephants, cavalry, archers, and more. Hannibal, represented by an armored elephant, is at the head of your army. Above all, you must keep him safe.

If you look at the miniature map in the bottom corner of your screen, you will see several tiny illuminated areas. One area displays a cluster of yellow dots. This is the spot where your captured scouts are imprisoned. By clicking on that area of the map, you can see them and have them break through the walls of their jail. Then, when you reach them, they will be waiting.

These villagers are your missing scouts.

If you follow the flags and stay on the well-paved road, you're in a dead-end.

Having initiated their great escape, start your journey by heading straight along the road. You will pass a watch tower that shoots a few token arrows at you— get used to it. In very little time that watch tower will be one of your fonder memories from this mission.

Halfway up the northwestern edge of the map, you will come across two flags marking a road to the east. Don't take them— they lead to a dead end— literally. Continue heading north following the path you were on. A short way up, the plateau to your right will end, and you'll see a storage pit to your left. Go any farther north and you will run into an enemy city—so turn right and head east along the bottom of a grove of trees.

A plateau lines the right side of your path. Have your men stay as close to the plateau as possible to avoid enemy towers to the north. When you reach the end of the plateau, head south between the eastern ridge of the plateau and the forest.

You can follow this path south for only a short distance, and then your road will turn in a northeastern direction. Follow the path, but continue sticking close to the plateau. The path leads to an enemy town with sentry towers guarding its entrance. Take your army through the gap in the plateau to your right.

This will lead you to a fork in the road. The valley in which you are traveling forms a Y with one road heading northwest and the other southwest. Taking the

Since you have better, more durable archers than the Romans, this wall offers you protection-instead of them.

latter road means you must pass through a gauntlet of seven sentry towers, and then face some Bronze Age cavalry and swordsmen.

By heading north, you'll avoid those traps and have a brief stint of smooth sailing. You will eventually run into a wall guarded by bowmen. Of course, a wall is no problem for armored elephants, but it gives the bowmen lots of time to demonstrate the finer points of archery.

On the other hand, you have archers of your own. Have your elephant archers kill every enemy that comes within range, and then break the wall. Stay as far south as you can and head straight until you run into another wall. Break it. Continue heading straight—you'll find your missing scouts.

Continue west, hugging to the top of the stone ridge. You will come to another wall. Have your archers destroy the tower guarding the wall and the soldiers behind it, and then break through.

You will now march past several houses as you head west to yet another wall. Smash through this wall and head south along the road. Stay as close as you can to the rocky ledge to your right—you'll be passing guard towers. The road will lead you to a final gauntlet that cannot be avoided. Stay on the road heading south and east. When you reach the end of the road, you win.

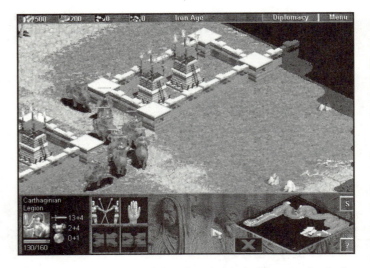

Tired of smashing walls? Passing through this gauntlet is the other option.

Ways to Lose

Despite all of the traps and pitfalls of this mission, the odds are squarely on your side. Avoid unnecessary battles and push ahead.

Additional Hints

You begin this mission with 500 units of wood and 200 units of food. Once your prisoners break free, have them build an archery range and train four bowmen. (You will have to build several houses before the range will begin training them.)

You can use these bowmen to thin the Romans guarding the western wall of their prison.

Remember to keep Hannibal safe. Do not use him to break walls guarded by towers.

Make sure to have your elephant archers lead the way as you approach walls.

Elephant archers have better firing range than sentry towers. Have them destroy towers from behind the safety of Roman walls.

Do not spend too much time clearing the path from behind walls, however, or the Romans will send a catapult after you.

Speed is of the essence in this mission. Don't fight enemies you can simply walk past.

When hit with arrows, your men may become distracted by towers. Be sure they keep pushing ahead.

Mission 2: Third Greek War

Once proud masters of the world, Macedonia never managed to recapture its splendor after the death of Alexander the Great. Part of this downward spiral was brought on by Rome's constant search for ways to nick their crumbling empire. In this scenario, the Macedonians are angry because the Romans have interfered with their plans to acquire a valuable economic waterway.

Don't even bother trying to raid this government center until you have a sophisticated Iron Age attack.

Your objective is to destroy Pergamum's government center—but before you can concentrate on that effort, you must build a strong civilization and take care of Rome's pesky allies.

You begin this mission with two slingers, two scouts, and 500 units of wood, food, gold, and stone. You have access to trees, berries, stone, and fish, but you are on a tiny finger of land—and the brown and yellow Roman camps located along Pergamum's walls have better resources. And then there is the Pergamum government center—a huge walled-off complex filled with phalanxes, heleopolises, resources, and farms.

Begin this mission by making the best of a bad situation. Build your town center near a stand of trees. There are two main entrances into your camp, an open area at the southwestern edge of your land and a land bridge to the north. Walling these areas off is not the solution—there are too many alternate routes for a determined enemy.

Build towers by these entrances and place slingers and axemen beside the towers. This will not keep your enemies out, but it will buy you enough time to build a strong army to defend yourself.

You will need to gather food by combining fishing and farming in this scenario. While the yellow Romans have a small fishing fleet, they will allow

Let the yellow Romans build a granary near your town, then attack it. They will send helpless villagers to repair the building.

you to have a pretty safe run along the southeastern river in the beginning of the scenario. Build a fleet of war galley or triremes, and they will never challenge your right to the river.

The fishing spots in the northern river are more spread out. Build fishing boats and war galleys to patrol it as soon as you advance to the Bronze Age—that will help protect against invasions from the brown Romans of the north.

Faithful to history, the waterways in this scenario have an important economic role. You've got trees. You need gold. Build a large fleet of merchant ships and keep your trade routes open. Remember to avoid destroying enemy docks when you raze their cities.

Once you have a good handle on your small lot of land, send a villager to the northern corner of the map to build a town center and cut wood. You'll need to wage a two-front war to beat the Pergamum army, and establishing a second city is the first step.

The yellow Roman civilization, your nearest neighbors, is primitive but extremely aggressive. You can throw an all-out assault in their land once you've advanced to the Bonze Age, but there are also ways to soften them up. Send your galleys and triremes along the outskirts of their town and kill their villagers to slow their production.

Also, they will try to build a granary by two berry bushes in the southern corner of your town. Attack the granary, but do not destroy it. They will send villager after villager to repair it. If you keep killing their villagers, they'll continue to send more—and you'll be depleting their resources.

If you've harassed the yellow Romans sufficiently, wiping out their civilization should be quite simple. You should be in the Bronze Age by this time, so send in your Tool Age axemen, slingers, and bowmen, and have them do the job.

Make sure they do not go near Pergamum's walls during their assault, however. Pergamum has ballista towers and heleopolises guarding its walls. Send your Tool Age army too close to a walled-off ballista tower and you will have a short-lived offensive.

You will run into towers when you reach the western end of the Romans' village. There is no need to destroy these towers. If you've killed their villagers, destroyed their houses and military buildings, and demolished their town center, they will not return.

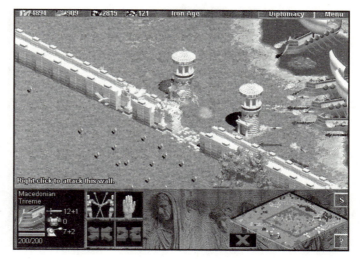

While one fleet of triremes lures the heavy fire power out of position with a raid in the north, a second fleet blasts its way through the walls surround Pergamum.

The next step is removing the brown Romans from the scenario. They have sentry towers, stone throwers, and priests—so they will not be as easily removed as their yellow cousins. If you have been accumulating food and trading wood for gold, you should have enough resources to upgrade your horse archers for heavy horse archers.

Send a stone thrower to destroy the first towers out of the way, and then send your heavy horse archers to kill everyone they see. As your horse archers clear the way, send your catapult to bring up the rear and mop up the Roman's buildings.

Eliminating the brown Romans opens the way for you to access additional resources—enabling you to build the enormous army you'll need to invade Pergamum on two fronts—both involving water.

Your first front is just below the eastern corner of Pergamum's walls. There is a small hole in the wall with a river running through it. Two ballista towers guard the gap. Send a villager up stream from the gap and have him construct two docks. Build four catapult triremes and send them to destroy the towers.

Use a huge company of heavy horse archers to destroy the town center. They can get to it faster than any of your other land units.

Don't be surprised if they are sunk before razing either tower—Macedonian siege weapons have very poor range.

Once the first wave of ships is destroyed, send in another, and keep sending in ships until you destroy the towers. Then build triremes and send them through the gap to kill any ground units that come to investigate.

It will not take long before several heleopolises come to protect the waterfront. They will massacre your ships as soon as they appear. Keep sending ships and trying to destroy a few of the heleopolises.

While you are doing this, assemble a huge army of heavy horse archers. Have them ready to rush in and attack the government center the moment the wall opens.

Have five triremes go down the river that ends by the western corner or Pergamum. Have them blast the wall of the city and create a gap for your heavy horse archers.

The moment the gap opens, have your horse archers charge straight in toward the center. The slow-moving heleopolises that would have repelled your attack will be up north, waiting for your next naval assault. If you've sent enough heavy horse archers, you will be able to destroy the government center before the Pergamum army is able to respond.

Ways to Lose

Don't be distracted by the Romans' early invasions. They will be short lived. Just slow their forces down, and their invasions will enable you to reach the Bronze and Iron Ages before they do. The easiest way to lose, however, is to go after Pergamum early.

Despite the resources inside Pergamum's walls, it is a fairly static civilization that starts and finishes the scenario with a lot of firepower.

Additional Hints

Be sure to research alchemy and ballistics before sending your horse archers into battle.

Once you control the map, you will have access to nearly unlimited wood and gold, and you can manufacture all the food you will need by making farms. Use this to your advantage by purchasing every imaginable upgrade.

Mission 3: Spartacus

Step into the world of Spartacus—slave, gladiator, leader of a rebellion that set the Roman Empire on its ear. The fact is, Rome showed the gladiators how to hate and taught them how to fight. When they escaped and joined an already existing rebellion, a new and unexpected torrent swept through Southern Italy.

You are Roman in this scenario. Your objective is to end the rebellion by killing the enemy, and you are not working alone. The largest civilization on the map is your ally—unfortunately it's not much of a military force, and the gladiator army has no problem beating its way through farmers.

You begin this scenario with nine villagers and a Bronze Age village. You also have a little time to build your forces since your helpless allies lie between you and the gladiators. Don't get too comfortable, however. With armored elephants, centurions, and heavy horse archers, it will not take the Slaves much time to tear through your agrarian friends.

From the outset, this scenario may look too tough to beat. The slaves have every imaginable upgraded super unit. They have heavy horse archers, armored elephants, and heleopolises. What they don't have is any way of renewing their forces. Every time you reduce their army by destroying one of their units, their army shrinks and stays shrunk.

The trick to winning this mission is to use the numerous stone and gold deposits around your land to make walls, towers, and priests. The walls will slow their armored elephants and centurions while your priests convert them. Train at least ten priests and scatter them along your walls.

Using the trees to the east of your camp as a natural extension of your wall, shore up your borders and fortify them with towers. Stretch your walls all the

The Slave army has no problem breaking through your walls.

The last slave unit, a catapult, flees as converted armored elephants attack it.

way to the lake at the bottom of the map, and build a dock in that lake—there are lots of fish. Build a fishing fleet and triremes to guard your dock.

Now that you have a solid food source to last you through the siege, train a couple of archers and cavalrymen to act as buffers—but put most of your efforts into training priests. As enemies come to your walls, have your priest convert them, and then Delete a section of your walls to let your new convert inside for a healing. After the convert enters, have a villager reseal the wall.

Do this, and the only real danger you will face will be from slave siege weapons, heavy horse archers, and priests. Slave priests are dangerous because they have excellent range, and their horse archers have the alchemy upgrade—but the real danger is a group of heleopolises traveling like a wall of death. With their long attack range and rapid-fire attack, they can atomize anything you throw at it.

Chariots are the solution for taking care of slave priests and catapults. Send three chariots after any of these threats. You may lose one or two of your chariots—but your units are renewable, theirs are not.

The best answer for the heleopolises is a wide row of towers. The heleopolises will likely destroy half of your towers, but it doesn't take much damage to destroy siege weapons. Your towers will prevail. You can hedge your bets, however, by having chariots or cavalry rush the heleopolises as they concentrate their fire on other targets.

Ways to Lose

Do not go out against the slaves in open battle. You would need a very significant army to fight those guys head on. They want to come to you—so let them.

Additional Hints

You will have a problem if the entire slave army comes pounding on your door all at once. Send a couple of villagers out and have them build towers around the map. The slaves will stop to destroy these towers when they see them, slowing down their progress.

Focus on converting heavy cavalry, armored elephants, and centurions. They are the safest units to convert.

Using two priests at once during conversions not only makes your conversions faster, it also confuses many attackers so they do not retaliate against your priests.

Be sure to research martyrdom. It may come in handy.

Mission 4: Odenathus vs. Persians

Harboring dreams of once again becoming a world power, the Persians are challenging Rome's authority in the region. Fortunately for Rome, Septimus Odenathus, prince of Palmyra, is willing to fight for Roman rule.

Your objective in this scenario is to destroy the Persians. You begin this scenario with a walled-off Bronze Age town composed of slingers, bowmen, and villagers. You also have two satellite towns in the frontier between you and Persia. One of these satellites consists of a tower, a granary, and a ton of berries. The other is similar except that has gold and a storage pit.

The Persians are going to take your outposts no matter what you do. You might as well take out a few Persians in return.

The Persians will overrun your outposts no matter what you do. Build walls and towers, and they will bring them down with catapults. Build stables or archers, and their swordsmen will bulldoze them. You simply do not have enough time to protect them.

On the other hand, these Persians are so intent on expanding their empire that they leave themselves unprotected. Their city is divided in half, with one part in the northern corner of the map and the other part in the eastern corner.

Their northern city is mostly houses and a priest. Their southern city contains their vital organ—the town center. Both parts of the town have numerous towers, but the north side also has a temple and priests.

As the scenario begins, build towers around your outposts. This will slow the Persians' advance toward your city. Since their first attack will be with standard bowmen, it will thin their ranks.

The Persians will attack your granary outpost first, so build an automatic defense around it with three sentry towers. Don't bother building a wall since the first units to attack it will be bowmen.

Your storage pit outpost will have a little more time. Build a wall between the trees in front of your pit and place towers behind the wall. If you work quickly, you'll be able to mine most of the stone from the pit. Do not worry about the gold. In this mission, gold is mostly a distraction.

While outposts get underway, you need to get to work in your main city. Build your workforce up to 20 villagers, with most of your workers cutting wood while a few pick berries and mine stone. Do not worry about advancing to the Bronze Age—your entire goal is to build waves of chariots and chariot archers.

Launch your first attack when you have a fleet of 15 to 20 units. You probably want to have two chariot archers to every chariot because chariot archers can attack buildings protected by towers. Use your regular chariots to attack catapults, priests, and unprotected buildings.

Since the Persians put a higher priority on your berry outpost than your storage pit, go after their northern city. That way you can destroy their villagers when they return to repair their buildings.

Start training the next wave of chariot archers before your first wave leaves. That way they can defend your walls. The Persians will actually be more interested in capturing your city than protecting their own. In a Bronze Age battle, a wall and a row of chariot archers is a potent defense.

Even though they are intent on conquering the entire map, the Persians will send some reinforcements to attack your chariots. It will probably take two or three waves of attacks to decide the scenario. Use your first invasion to slaughter villagers and houses. Head for their other city, located in the eastern corner of the map, in your second invasion. Concentrate all of your efforts on obliterating their town center, and then destroy more houses.

The rest of the mission will be a simple mop-up exercise. You may have the misfortune of running into a stray catapult or swordsman—but by mounting a flash attack, you will prevent them from acquiring such deadly Iron Age weapons as horse archers and armored elephants.

Ways to Lose

Sometimes the best remedy for a potent offense is a strong offense paired with a reasonable defense. There is no way you're going to out-expand these ancient Persians, so let them overextend themselves, and then stab for their heart.

Additional Hints

Upgrade your towers as quickly as possible. This will increase the damage the Persians take while attacking your outposts.

Research nobility and artisanship before launching your invasion and it will have more success.

Be prepared to spend time repairing walls and fixing towers in this scenario. The Persians will not go down without a fight.

Your chariot archers will have better range than the Persians' sentry towers once you research artisanship.

Once you've eliminated all enemy units, you can save time by building a siege workshop and catapults to finish the operation.

Chapter Nine

Pax Romana

Conquering the world is difficult, but maintaining your hold is even worse. As world dominators, the Romans faced intrigue and rebellion from many quarters. Rome tried to maintain order in its territory with a velvet fist, rewarding submissive nations with patience while viciously suppressing those who challenged the Empire. The term decimation came from the Roman practice of lining up entire villages and killing every tenth person as punishment for rebellion.

Mission 1: Actium

A romance between Marc Antony and Cleopatra developed after the death of Julius Caesar, but it was short-lived. Combining Alexandrian forces with his loyal troops, Marc Antony led an insurrection—trying to win freedom from Rome. It, too, was short-lived. Octavian, Caesar's nephew, smashed their rebellion.

In this mission, you control the Romans as they attempt to destroy Marc Antony's town center, and the town center of Alexandrai, Cleopatra's

One of your objectives is to sink Cleopatra's barge, the juggernaut in the middle of this large collection of juggernauts.

Use cavalry and chariots to attack Marc Antony's ships when they cross the sandbar to assault your walls.

home. Along with the town centers, you must destroy Cleopatra's barge (represented by a juggernaut with 500 hit points and 60 attack points).

You begin this scenario with an Iron Age city that is under attack. But don't worry, you have more than enough muscle to repel this offensive. What you don't have, unfortunately, is enough firepower to go after Marc Antony's base. He's located just south of you on the same piece of land, so you can expect lots of visits.

Even worse, he has a head start at establishing a stronghold. You're going to have to scramble to prepare for his next invasion.

To make matters worse, Cleopatra has a powerful navy with triremes and juggernauts blockading the waters east of your island. There will be a lot more than red tape involved in establishing control of the eastern seaboard in this mission.

Begin by beating Antony out of your territory, and then building your work force and resources so that you can turn the tables on him. From the start, be sure to equalize the pressure being exerted on your southern front. Antony's navy is going to send catapult triremes to bombard your towers and walls until you show that you're ready to sink his ships.

Once your cavalry and swordsmen have beaten Antony's first invasion back, assign your villagers to begin foraging the berries in the front of your city. Train more villagers and send them north to harvest the wood, gold, and stone. There's no need to build an enormous work force in the beginning of this scenario once you create a fishing fleet in the western sea. As to your land forces, an initial team of seven villagers chopping wood, three mining gold and two mining stone will do, but you may want two extra villagers to construct buildings and repair ships.

Should you decide to go after one of the civilizations in the early going, you might consider Alexandria. Located in the southern corner of the map, the Alexandrian island is poorly fortified as the mission starts. Send a trireme to kill the bowmen, catapult, and chariot archers guarding the island, and then send a chariot and a catapult to finish the job.

In truth, this is only mildly advantageous. Left to their own devices, this Alexandrian civilization will do little more than send

Use a row of heleopolises to smash through Marc Antony's towers and destroy his town center.

transports with chariot archers to your door. These incursions will be a minor nuisance. The real threat comes from Marc Antony and his catapults and catapult triremes. Use chariots to destroy his ships and siege weapons. His catapult triremes have to sail on to a sandbar to come within range of your city walls—speed out and set upon his ships while they're vulnerable on the sandbar. More often than not, both your chariot and the attacking catapult trireme will be destroyed, but it's a good trade. Chariots are far less expensive.

Marc Antony has a well fortified city with lots of long swordsmen and towers. The best way to counter his defenses is with a relentless strike that pulverizes everything in its path. Since resources are plenty in this scenario, your best bet is to use upgraded siege weapons. Make a brigade of approximately ten heleopolises and have them mow down everything between your town and Antony's gates.

Antony's town center is just a little distance past his gates. Have your heleopolises destroy the towers surrounding the center first, and then barrage the town center. Do not go too deep in the town, however. Cleopatra has built a ballista tower behind a wall in the southern end of the city. It has better range than your heleopolises.

Don't worry about Antony's swordsmen sneaking up on your heleopolises during your attack. Heleopolises have a great sense of self-preservation and automatically turn and fire when danger approaches. Just the same, keep an eye out for enemy units. The problem with siege weapons is that they are easily destroyed.

Once you've demolished Antony's town center, it's time to drop in on the Alexandrians—assuming you did not attack them early on. They will have a fleet of catapult triremes by now. It's amazing how easy it is to destroy two or even three catapult triremes with a regular trireme—all you have to do is stay at the edge of your firing range, continue moving erratically to make their slow-firing catapults miss, and shoot.

Once you've destroyed their fleet, send a trireme to clear a landing area on the southernmost point of the island. Be especially mindful to kill any chariot archers and bowmen—then send a landing force of one catapult, three chariots, and a priest. Have the catapult destroy any towers and smash its way into town. The Alexandrians may have priests, so send your chariots to end any sermons. Once they destroy Alexandria's town center, you will have completed the ground wars in this mission.

The final step is to sink Cleopatra's barge, a juggernaut with 500 hit points and a 60-attack point rating. (Juggernauts generally have 200 hit points and a 35-attack point rating.) Cleopatra has arrayed her navy in concentric semicircles, with her ship blocked off by a line of five juggernauts partially guarded by five triremes. To make matters worse, there are several sandbars around these ships, and Cleopatra has stationed composite bowmen.

After capturing Marc Antony's land, you'll have access to a seemingly endless supply of gold. You will be able to construct a huge fleet and steamroll Cleopatra should you desire. Since you can build a massive fleet at any point, you might want to try and finesse this battle. One way to do this would be to station your battalion of heleopolises along the southeastern point of your island so that they're facing Cleopatra's triremes. Once your heleopolises are in place, use a trireme to see if you can trick enemy ships into coming within your heleopolises' range.

Whether you simply flatten Cleopatra with a fleet of juggernauts or use more subtle methods, this mission ends when her ship sinks.

Ways to Lose

Cleopatra will sink your boats in the east, and the Alexandrians will occasionally send transports to compromise your shores—but in the end, it's Marc Antony who poses the real threat. Let him get solidly entrenched and you'll need more than a few heleopolises to unseat him.

Additional Hints

The Alexandrians have a Marc Antony heavy catapult on a ledge near their city. As long as you approach the city from the south and stay as far inland as possible, you'll remain out of the catapult's range.

You can use priests to harass Antony by converting his long swordsmen.

There is an island with large deposits of gold, stone, gazelles, and trees in the western corner of the map. If you need more resources, this uninhabited island would be the best place to go.

Mission 2: Year of the Four Emperors

Nero is dead and a battle has begun to see who shall become emperor. Let's see—Caesar was stabbed to death, Nero had to commit suicide before he was killed, Claudius was poisoned by his wife.... Roman emperors don't seem to die of natural causes, and here are four guys who actually want the job! In this case, you are Vespasian—the wannabe who triumphs.

You begin this scenario with a Stone Age town center, three villagers, 400 units of wood and food, 200 units of gold, and 300 units of stone. Your goal is to protect a wonder on the eastern side of the map while destroying a wonder located in the west. Once you've destroyed the western wonder, you are to build your own wonder in its place.

There are three civilizations working against you. There is a Macedonian town in the northern corner of the map, just across a river from the wonder you are to protect. The Greeks have an Iron Age city on an island near the wonder you are to destroy. They've evidently grown attached to the wonder—they will defend it and attack you when you come to destroy it. Finally, the Palmyran civilization is just north of you on the other side of a grove of trees. Like you, the Macedonians and Palmyrans begin the mission with a Stone Age civilization. Unlike you, however, none of these nations will have to wage a campaign on three fronts.

Palmyran villagers will horde berries and resources wherever they find them. Don't try to share with them— remember their villagers work 20 percent faster than yours. Send a chariot to the area and slaughter them instead.

Your first task will be to build two population centers. Send two villagers to your eastern wonder and have them build walls and towers to protect it. Your wonder is near the northeastern edge of the map—there is a stand of trees just north of it. Once you enter the Tool Age, you can fill the gap in the trees with a wall and your wonder will be safe on two sides.

Attacks on your wonder will come from the west. Macedonians and Palmyrans will cross the land bridge just west of the wonder as they attack, so build walls around the west and south to keep them out. You must rush to the Tool Age and build walls, towers, and an archery range. Place bowmen behind you walls to protect them.

Palmyra is more of a direct threat than Macedonia in this scenario. The Palmyrans will try to kill your civilization. All the Macedonians want to do is destroy your wonder. Even so, you should attack the Macedonians first, once you reach the Bronze Age.

Lose your wonder and you cannot fulfill your objective. Fortunately, the Macedonians have put more effort into attacking your wonder than building their city. Build a temple and two stables in the compound beside your wonder. Train three priests to convert cavalry as they attack your walls, and train five to eight chariots to attack the Macedonians.

If you make it to the Macedonian city before it turns Bronze, you will find a poorly defended town center. There will be a few watch towers along the eastern side of the city, but they will be too far away to save the town center and villagers from your chariots. Start your assault by attacking houses, then kill the villagers arriving to repair them. Work your way to the town center and destroy it. Once the houses, villagers, and town center are gone, you won't be worrying about any threat from Macedonia.

Attacking Palmyra will not be as easy. The Greeks will defend the Palmyrans, and they have catapults, ballistas, and phalanxes. They are stuck on an island in the lake to the west, however, and will only be able to attack by crossing three land bridges.

Your best bet for defeating the Palmyrans and destroying their wonder is to attack from the east with a decisive force then seal off the land bridges. Since you'll need long-range weapons to keep the Greeks on their island, heleopolises are probably your best bet.

The Macedonians will not ever wait to go Bronze before attacking your wonder. By committing resources to a Tool Age attack, they will leave themselves vulnerable to an aggressive Bronze Age retaliation.

Build multiple siege workshops, upgrade from ballistas to heleopolises, and construct ten heleopolises. Send them around the eastern side of the forest that separates you from Palmyra, and then begin your attack. Obviously, you need to kill military units first, then kill villagers, then destroy their houses and town center. Leave some houses and buildings partially destroyed to attract any villagers you may have missed, and work your way west.

Once the villagers, houses, and town center are gone, destroy the wonder. Next, divide your heleopolises into two groups and place them in front of the southern and central land bridges. This will effectively seal the Greeks in. They can cross on the northern bridge too, of course, but there are trees to the north that will partially block quick access to your troops.

Now that you have control of the area and have cleared away the enemy wonder, bring all of your men to Palmyra. Have your chariots, heleopolises, and priests guard the area as your villagers build their wonder. You win the moment they finish their work.

Ways to Lose

This is not supposed to be a drawn-out campaign. Macedonia and Palmyra are weak. Rush to the Bronze Age and destroy them. The danger is in delaying—wait too long and they will build their forces. And the Greeks will get involved.

The easiest way to lose, however, would be to attack Greece in the beginning. They'll beat you silly.

Additional Hints

Don't worry about conserving stone or gold. There are deposits all over the map.

There are two lakes teaming with fish, one in the northwest and the other in the southeast.

Mission 3: Ctesiphon

The Persians have really gone and done it this time! Not only have they attacked Roman held territory, challenged Roman authority, and established a healthy economic empire—they've also kidnapped Valerian, emperor of Rome.

Amazingly, the Romans decided to bargain with the Persians rather than fight them. Raiders have intercepted the ransom the Romans sent to pay for Valerian, and your objective is to deal with the raiders by destroying their stables, recover the stolen ransom (represented by three artifacts), and deliver it to the Persian wonder.

You begin this mission in utter chaos. Things are quiet in the eastern corner of the map, where you have a small army, but you can hear the sounds of a massacre happening elsewhere. That is the sound of the raiders slaughtering your wagon and stealing your treasure.

Your tiny army is no match for the powerful local forces that terrorize this vicinity, so you'll need to build your army to recover your treasure and avenge your humiliation. Fortunately, there is a group of non-aligned villagers just a little to the east. When you find them, they will instantly join your ranks.

To find them, head east, across the bridge, and follow the road north and west. You will pass a huge field of berries and a granary as you cross that first bridge. Send villagers back to claim it, and it's yours.

Speaking of going back, sending all but one of your villagers back to the granary is a good idea. The Parthian cavalry patrols the road by the village

regularly—if they spot your village they will attack. By sending your villagers back to the spot where they started, you'll hide them from the Parthians and place them in an area with a huge crop of berries, a large gold mine, a vast rock deposit, and trees.

Food, rock, gold, and trees in the same spot! A free granary! This is the best real-estate deal in the whole game.

Send your villagers back. Have them build a town center and rebuild their city while your army guards the entrance to the valley. With so many resources so centrally located and a fairly good supply of resources to begin with, you'll be able to develop a working Iron Age city with a temple and a siege workshop in a matter of minutes.

The next step is thinning the enemy. The easiest way to do this is with towers and priests. There are several gold and stone mines north of your abandoned village along the road. Send three priests and four villagers to open areas adjacent to the busiest mine, and have them build three towers. The moment the towers are up, the slaughter begins.

The Parthians will send cavalry and horse archers to destroy your towers, but that's where your priests come in. Convert and heal the cavalry while your towers deal with the horse archers. Before long, you'll have an army of cavalry, and the mine will be cluttered with the bones of your victims.

Don't stop with three towers. Continue towering up, and you'll destroy the majority of your resistance.

There may still be some Parthians in the neighborhood, so use your new converts to explore and kill everything they find.

You may have noticed a walled area with an artifact on the top of the hill. Don't get too close to that ridge. There is a heleopolis inside that pen that fires at anything within range. To make matters worse, there are three heavy horse archers and three ballista towers guarding the pen—and to add insult to injury,

Insisting on controlling this area, the Parthians will exhaust themselves trying to reclaim this mine from your towers.

they've all been upgraded with alchemy.

Taking care of the heleopolis and the towers is no big deal. You can knock them all off with a single catapult. The heavy horse archers are another story. The easiest way to lure them is to send two priests and a catapult near the ridge—but still out of range of the heleopolis. The horse archers will fire at your catapult. Have one priest convert the archer while the other heals the catapult. The heleopolis will immediately obliterate your converts, but you'll be able to dash the heleopolis once the horse archers are out of the picture. Once the towers, heavy horse archers, and heleopolis are destroyed, have your catapult raze one of the walls of the holding pen.

Freeing this artifact is less than half the battle. To claim it, you'll have to cross a small island populated by 11 lion kings and one alligator. You will also have to demolish several towers. It is while you are bashing your way to the first artifact that you will stumble into the second and third ones.

Take two catapults, a priest, and your convert cavalry, and head north along the road. Use your catapults to destroy any towers you see along the way. Follow the road across the bridge and continue destroying towers. Remember, one of your objectives is to destroy enemy stables, too.

You should discover the second artifact on a slope leading toward the northern corner of the map. The third artifact is up even further, in a holding pen at the top of the map. Use your catapults to destroy the towers around the artifacts and to break the second one free.

Now for the real fun. There is a small river running along the western edge of the map. Once you've destroyed the towers overlooking the city, send a

catapult to the wall near the river. You will see lots of lions and an alligator. Blast them, and then break a hole in the wall and send riders to claim the last artifact. (They will have to kill four alligators on the way to the artifact, but that should be no problem.)

You will also pass two stables on your way to the artifact. Destroy them—that is one of your assignments in this mission.

The final stage is delivering the artifacts to the

Deliver these artifacts to this door and victory is yours.

Sasanian wonder, which is located in the eastern corner of the map. The easiest way to do this is to build a dock in the river running across the northern portion of the map. By building a dock and a light transport, you will avoid having to deal with composite bowmen stationed along the road.

But not so fast—you're not through yet. There are seven heavy cavalrymen waiting for you across the river. You could build an army to fight them, but the quickest solution is to get them with your priests. Have the transport drop your priests on the spit of sand across the river. You will then see the cavalry, standing in a ring. Have both of your priests convert the closest rider, then have him flee to the river. Have your priests heal him, then use him as decoy to bring the other riders by the ledge. Convert three or four of them and kill the rest.

Now, bring your artifacts across the river, and have your new converts escort them. Head north toward the edge of the map. You will see a bunker with two towers, two heavy cavalry units, and a heleopolis. Don't worry, they're Sasanian—they're friendly. Follow the road south and east until you get to the gate leading to the Sasanian wonder. There you will encounter your final obstacle—four Persian composite bowmen. Have your heavy cavalry kill them and deliver your artifact to the wonder's door.

Ways to Lose

Do not let the heleopolis and heavy horse archers on that first mountain know of your presence. If they discover you, they'll end your mission, pronto! In fact, the first portion of this scenario depends on stealth. You must take great pains not to be discovered until you're strong enough.

Additional Hints

This is a mission in which martyrdom may come in handy. If the heleopolis or the heavy cavalry become too vexing, use martyrdom to circumvent killing them. Just remember to keep your finger on Delete and execute the moment your priest starts chanting.

The Palmyrans have triremes and catapult triremes in the waters. There's no need to fight them, just don't have your men linger near the shore.

Use farming as a means of gathering food once your berries run out.

It's important to learn how to catch horse archers and other fast units with foot soldiers. Once the archer has selected a target, have the target retreat past other foot soldiers, and then have the other soldiers attack as the horse archer rides past.

There will be priests and a temple on top of a hill overlooking the Parthian city. Be sure to have your catapult destroy them before anything else.

Mission 4: Queen Zenobia

Zenobia, widowed bride of Odenathus, is an intriguing character. Her husband allowed his native Palmyra to ally with Rome—but she would have nothing to do with the Romans. By all accounts she was a powerful, strong-willed woman who despised Rome, yet she ended her days as the wife of a senator.

In this mission, however, we see Zenobia as she battles Rome. You are now her enemy, and you are charged with defending the empire's borders and razing Palmyra. You begin with a Tool Age civilization that includes three villagers and 500 units of each resource.

There are three islands running in roughly parallel strips along this map. Interestingly, you begin this scenario with two town centers on the middle island, which is also possessed by a civilization known as the Alemanni. The Alemanni begin as a Bronze Age civilization. However, the only building in

their city is a town center. Train five or six villagers and send them north to build a couple of towers near the Alemanni town center. The Alemanni will throw everything they have into trying to destroy those towers, and they'll kill themselves off in the effort.

If you can get five or six villagers to the Alemanni quickly and build two towers near their town center, you will kill them off and get their island to yourself.

Your main base is located on the western island. You have good resources scattered around there and a few buildings, but you have aggressive neighbors to the north. (Your only granary is on that island, too. Remember to go to the granary and research towers as you send your villagers north to meet the Alemanni, or their offensive will be very short lived.)

The Goths, with whom you share the western island, begin this scenario as a Bronze Age civilization, and that's where you want them to end it. They are a very aggressive people, and you must use your resources to get a flying start in this mission. Train villagers as quickly as possible, and build a perimeter to keep the Goths out.

This may seem like a lot to do while you are still in mid-attack on the Alemanni—but consider this: if all goes well, you will possess two thirds of the map within the first 15 minutes of this scenario.

There is a forest between you and the Goths. Treat the forest as if it were a wall, and build clusters of three towers in the breaks in the forest. The Goths will send bowmen and short swordsmen to attack your towers, but their raids will have little effect.

You have a dock on the eastern shore of your island. Don't bother with it. The nearest fish are off the southern shore—so build a second dock to the south and send fishing boats from there. Build a market and research woodworking. Build stables, too. As soon as you have 800 units of food, upgrade to the

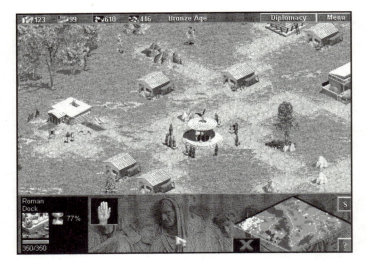

A quick glance at the Goths' city planning reveals that it is poorly fortified and ripe for attack.

Bronze Age, research wheels, and start pumping out chariots.

You should also erect a siege workshop the moment you hit Bronze. You need one stone thrower and an escort of bowmen and chariots as quickly as possible. It's time your western citizens had the island to themselves.

For all of their aggression and resources, the Goths have not made good use of their land. Their city is spread out with a few sentry towers for protection.

Overall, it's an easy sack. The Goths will send short swordsmen to stop your invasion, but you can neutralize them by having your bowmen soften them as they approach, and then let your chariots finish the job.

The most dangerous weapon of this invasion is your stone thrower. Keep it busy attacking sentry towers. If it sees Goth swordsmen, it will fire at them, even if it kills your chariots. Once you've destroyed the towers and town center, send your stone thrower back to your base. Your men will be much safer that way.

You have neither the need nor the time to kill every Goth building. Just be sure their men are all dead and that the town center is gone, then send villagers to take over the city. The Goths had great stores of gold and berries.

In the meantime, be sure to develop a strong navy. The Palmyrans, who live on the easternmost island, have a strong navy, many transports, and a will to move west. Stopping their transports will be a fairly simple task, however, as they have to pass through a relatively narrow passage around the horn of the middle island. Send five or more war galleys to the southern corner of the map to stop up that passage. Building a dock on the southern tip of the island will further hamper their invasions.

Having been thwarted in their attempts to get to the western island, the Palmyrans will try and invade the middle island as well. This will actually work to your advantage. Place towers along your eastern shore, and station priests near them. Convert the Palmyran's transports and send them off to a safe harbor where no one can get to them. Every time you convert a transport without sinking, the passengers on board count against the Palmyran's population level, meaning you'll face less resistance in your final battle.

By the time you get to the Palmyrans, they will have towers, priests, catapults, and all kinds of archers—most of whom have been made more dangerous with alchemy. The good news is that your eastern shore is so close to Zenobia's western shore that you can use catapults and heleopolises to clear the way for your invasion.

Place heleopolises and priests along your shore to convert or kill the Palmyran ships. Then send in two catapult triremes to clear their towers and crush their priests. Be sure to destroy their docks quickly. The Palmyrans have fire galleys.

Once you've destroyed the Palmyran docks and chased them inland, begin ferrying your men from the middle island to Palmyra. Have your siege weapons to destroy their towers and archers while your priests convert their academy units and buildings. By converting their buildings, you'll be able to replenish your army with ease.

Ways to Lose

The Goths are clumsy in their attacks and do not pose much of a threat if you get to them quickly. The Alemanni, on the other hand, will build ballistas as soon as they have the chance. Kill them quickly, before they develop a real population.

The biggest threat from the Palmyrans is a successful invasion. If you don't stop their transports from landing on your shores, they'll have the upper hand.

Additional Hints

Go to the granary on the western island and begin researching towers quickly. Your villagers will need that information by the time they reach the Alemanni village.

Be alert to distress calls from your navy. Remember that the Palmyrans have fire galleys, and they may try to burn their way to your island.

Be sure to build your perimeter against the Goths even as you build towers near the Alemanni. You must execute both operations simultaneously and quickly so that you can grab control of the map. Once you control both islands, this mission becomes fairly easy to win.

Chapter Ten

Rise of Rome

This is it. Rome in its fierce infancy, fighting the Gauls, beating the Etruscans, and unifying sections of Italy. Rome was not the biggest country in the world, nor did it have the largest population. But Rome was organized and practiced. Enemy armies broke formation in battle—or had no formation at all—but the Romans ran each play by the numbers.

Mission 1: Birth of Rome

Just starting out and already in trouble—the Romans are up against no less than six angry neighbors. It's proving time. If the Romans are going to become world shakers, they'll have to prove that they thrive on challenges like this.

Okay, so much for the big build-up. The truth is, this is possibly the simplest scenario in Microsoft's Rise of Rome. You are not asked to kill your six neighbors, though at times you may wish to. You are directed instead to locate 12 flags and build towers over them. Most of the flags are around your base of operations, too, so building towers in those locations will boost your security. (If you look at the miniature area map on the bottom of your screen, the smaller illuminated spots are areas with flags.)

You begin this mission with a Bronze Age village, six villagers, a small army of short swordsmen and bowmen, 200 units of wood and food, and 150 units of stone and gold. You first goal should be to get your village running smoothly. Start by assigning your villagers to forage in the berry bushes by your granary. Use this food to train new villagers whom you will assign to chop wood and mine stone.

There is an additional stone deposit on the hill to the west of your town. Send some bowmen and a villager to build a storage pit and start mining the stone. As your stone supply grows, train villagers and send them out to start building towers on the flags.

AGE of EMPIRES

Build your towers directly on top of the flags.

In this mission, you are to build your towers right over flags, so place the ghosted-tower icons over the flags when showing your villagers where you want them to build. The final product will be a tower with a flag draping from it.

This mission is not simply a tutorial on tower building—you will face challenges. For some reason, your little corner of the map has become a crossroads for the world. There are several land bridges crossing rivers around your territory. You could build walls to block them, but it would slow you down beyond reason.

Build two docks in the deep waters just north of your new storage pit, then build a fleet of fishing boats to supply your food once the berries run out. Next, upgrade to war galleys and have your navy help protect your shores.

Your neighbors will test your resolve, so be prepared for lots of visits. The first visitors will be slingers, bowmen, and scouts. But it won't be long before the first Umbrian cavalry comes trotting in. Cavalry can do a lot of damage to a tower, so move quickly.

By having your villagers concentrate on building towers and gathering wood and stone while your fishing fleet takes care of your food, you'll be able to erect the towers around your village quite quickly.

There are three flags located in enemy territory. Two are just across the river from your land, and you will have no trouble chasing enemies from those areas with a small expeditionary force. The third flag is farther north, near the Umbrian border. While the flag is in a secluded area, getting to it will be more difficult.

The Umbrians began this scenario in the Iron Age, and they have composite bowmen, cavalry, and other nasty weapons. You may wish to

advance to the Iron Age before going to the last flag so that you can do Jihad research and speed up your villagers.

Even with the Umbrians nearby, you won't need a huge army to erect this last tower—sending any of your original bowmen, five cavalry units, and a priest to escort your villagers should suffice. There are rivers between you and the final flag, so you will have to head a little east, then backtrack to the flag. Once you get there, have your cavalry charge any enemy units while your villagers build the tower. You win the moment the tower is complete.

Ways to Lose

While you can certainly be overrun by your neighbors, this is a fairly tame scenario. Work quickly to establish your stronghold, and it will be only a matter of getting out and building your towers.

Additional Hints

Upgrade from watch towers to sentry towers as quickly as possible, and build a government center so that you can research architecture. Your enemies are after your towers, so strengthen them.

There is no law that says you can only build one tower in each location. Build additional towers around towers your enemies visit.

Use packs of bowmen as guards until you have the food and gold to build more durable units. Five bowmen make a powerful force, even in the Bronze Age. At 40 units of food and 20 units of wood, they are the cheapest defense.

Mission 2: Pyrrhus of Epirus

Rome's great expansion has made its neighbors nervous. Greek colonies have called for help from Macedonia, meaning you will be meeting a professional army in the field.

You begin this mission with two town centers—one on a small and somewhat vulnerable island, and one on the eastern side of an arch-shaped continent stretching across the map.

Your goal is to destroy the Macedonian town center while protecting your own, but that will be challenging. The Macedonians have an Iron Age civilization with catapult triremes and heavy transports. They will certainly take

the fight to you before you're able to invade them—so like it or not, you had better dig in for some defensive action.

Begin this scenario by building a huge villager work force to harvest all resources on your island. Protecting this island will not be worth the effort. The Macedonian catapult triremes will be able to hit any spot on the island and 80 percent of the island's coast is tailor-made for landing transports with armored elephants.

Instead of wasting time fortifying the island, wall-up and tower the western half of your inland base. The Macedonian base is on this same continent with only a bridge separating the two of you, so do all you can to keep your enemies from having access to your mainland, too.

Send three villagers to the northern edge of the map. There are two alcoves in the northern forest—one has an enormous gold deposit, the other has stone. These deposits are deep inside the forest, and the Macedonians are unlikely to notice a couple of lone villagers hidden behind trees. Place a villager in each alcove, then seal the way behind them with walls. Have each of them build a storage pit and begin mining as soon as you have enough wood.

There is a river to the north. Have your third villager build a wall blocking the land bridge on the west side of the river. Have him build a second wall on the east side of the river, and a third wall after that. Leave him by the walls so that he can build towers as soon as you have enough stone. (You should also build walls along the shore just south of your city—build them against the water so that the Macedonians have nowhere to land.)

The Macedonians have ballistas and armored elephants. Your western walls will be destroyed if you cannot get back to them quickly—but if you can stall the invasion and soften up the first wave of invaders, your stone was well invested.

When the Macedonians arrive, they will focus on capturing your island. They will start their invasion with catapult triremes, smashing your towers and killing anyone they can hit. Hide one or two of your villagers in the trees along the northeastern side of the island. The Macedonians may miss them.

After the triremes, heavy transport will arrive to drop off some centurions. More often than not, these centurions will attack everything around their landing, then settle together in the northeastern corner of your island. Dimwitted and near-sighted, these deadly soldiers usually don't notice if your villagers start chopping wood and hauling it to the town center. You may even be able to slip a villager over to the gold deposits on the other side of the island. That gold will be very helpful later on.

Continue gathering resources and advance all the way to the Bronze Age. Remember to upgrade your towers and walls, and upgrade your nave—if it still exists.

Once you go Bronze, build a government center and a temple. Both of these buildings are essential, so build them as quickly as possible. You need the government center so that you can research architecture and strengthen your walls and towers. The temple is even more important,

This barricade would stop most armies, but against this Macedonian band, it's not even a detour.

however, because it will enable you to build your army.

Train five priests and send them to your western wall along with three villagers. The Macedonians will send centurions, cataphracts, armored elephants, and elephant archers to break through your walls. Have your priests convert them. One of the strengths of the Macedonian civilization is its conversion-resistant units—but that does not mean that they won't see the light. Blocked by a wall, they will pound at it in an effort to get to your priest and eventually change to his way of thinking.

As soon as you've converted your assailant, hide him against the edge of the map, and have a villager repair the wall as you await your next recruit. Do not use your priests when ballistas and horse archers attack—the walls will offer them no protection. Have your converted centurions and armored elephants take care of these pests.

You can, however, use your priests to convert elephant archers. Wait until the elephant archers begin shooting at your towers, then have two priests begin chanting. The Macedonians will start to thin out after a while, and then it will be your turn to do the invading.

Having harvested two huge gold mines, you will have enough gold to make whatever kind of army you like. (Actually, since the Romans do not get heavy

Once you've cleared away the ballista towers, you can send your army into the enemy town and finish the mission on automatic pilot.

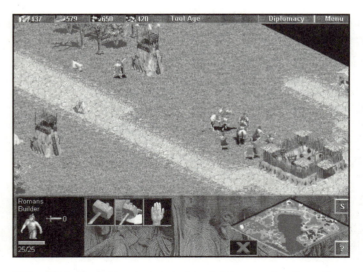

If the Macedonians manage to break into your territory, the battle will be a complete mismatch. These axemen will crumble when attacked by a cataphract and two centurions.

horse archers, chariot archers, or elephants, there are some limitations.) You will need a siege weapon, though—either heleopolises or catapults—to destroy the Macedonian ballista towers.

Heleopolises are fairly good at destroying towers but are very fragile, and you will lose quite a few to the Macedonian catapult triremes as you cross unprotected shorelines. It is far less expensive to use triremes to destroy Macedonian ships and seaside towers, and catapults to destroy landlocked towers. Just be sure that your catapults are far away when you battle enemy troops. Catapults are easy to destroy, and they often kill your soldiers when firing at enemies.

The rest of the scenario is really a clean-up operation. Use your priests to convert cataphracts and elephants on your way to the Macedonians' city, then use your catapults to destroy the towers along its walls. Once the towers are gone, you can send your armored elephants

and soldiers into the city to destroy the buildings while your trireme fleet picks off survivors at sea.

Ways to Lose

If you can hang on and protect your town centers during the early going, you will almost certainly prevail. By taking control of the northern mines, you will have access to much better resources than the Macedonians, and your priests will turn their assets into your assets.

Even so, do not underestimate the fury of their initial attacks. You are starting in the Tool Age and they have an array of upgraded Iron Age weapons. Their catapult triremes will destroy your shoreline defenses, but triremes cannot land troops. Just keep their units off your shores until you have priests.

Additional Hints

Remember to make a gap between your towers and your walls. If they are too close together, the Macedonians' armored elephants will be able to destroy them both at the same time.

Remember, using two priests at a time shortens the conversion time and confuses attackers so that they do not harm your priest.

Mission 3: Syracuse

The people of Syracuse are rebelling and have created a living, working mathematical puzzle out of their city. You must figure out how to break into their defenses and demonstrate Roman ingenuity by parading ten legions across their forum (a raised area marked with yellow flags).

This will not be easy. Archimedes, the great mathematician, designed the layout of the city specifically to foil your invasion. Furthermore, he is still in the city. You will lose face, and the mission, if he is harmed—so destroy the city, but do not harm the man who designed it.

This is the only mission in all of Rise of Rome that lets you relax and prepare for battle. You begin with a small Iron Age city on a small island with more than only enough resources to start your army.

The people of Syracuse have all of the resources, but they do not have villagers to harvest them. In other words, take your time—those resources will

Archimedes is the only priest in the city—kill him and you lose the mission.

Focusing virtual sunlight through virtual magnifying glasses with virtual mirrors, these mirror towers are the dominant force in this mission.

be waiting for you when you arrive. Further, though Syracuse has so many soldiers it looks like an organized anthill, the people of Syracuse show no desire to come after you. So take your time, harvest your resources, build a full city, and research every upgrade.

Now for the bad news. Archimedes didn't just reinvent city planning in this scenario, he also discovered laser beams. Some of the towers around Syracuse are called mirror towers. Mirror towers are the terrors of the game. They shoot a deadly red bolt of light with a better range than heavy catapults. Use fishing boats as sacrificial goats to make sure there are no mirror towers along your routes before sending triremes or transports.

As far as resources are concerned, you have access to more gold, stone, and wood than you could possibly use. There is a decently sized gold deposit on your home island. A tiny uninhabited island halfway up the northeastern edge of the map has more gold

should you need it, and a small island off the coast of Syracuse has more. And then there are the plains in front of the city, which are covered with gold, stone, palm trees, and berry bushes.

Shortly after the mission opens, Syracuse fire galleys and triremes will descend on your fleet. You will have the power to beat them off, but the holes in your fleet will be felt. Build more triremes. Resources are not an issue, and you can always Delete units you no longer need.

Once you have rebuilt your fleet, send it south along the eastern edge of the map to the small island in the south. This island is inhabited by two axemen and a tower. They're enemies, so kill them.

You will also find merchant ships, triremes, and fire galleys off the shores of that island. Sink the ships. You do not want them to interfere with your tiny invasion.

Next, send nine priests and a villager to Syracuse's island. The safest way to approach Syracuse is to travel north along the southwestern edge of the map. You will come to an unguarded beach leading to a slope. There are huge supplies of stone and gold at the top of the slope. Staying as close to the edge of the map as possible, ascend up the slope and have your villager build a town center. Train additional villagers, and mine the gold at the end of the slope.

While your villagers empty the gold mine, it's time for your priests to open their recruiting office. Hot-key your priests in groups of three.

Though Syracuse is not a particularly difficult scenario, it is lengthy. Be sure to save your game after successful encounters. You do not want to have to start again after failing with some dicey move.

Your first recruit will be the phalanx near the top of the slope. Have your priests get within chanting range, and bring him into your fold.

Your next converts will be a more valuable acquisition—a pair of armored elephants mulling about on the far side of the plains. Staying near the edge of the map, cross the island, and you will see the elephants. Send two of your hot-keyed groups of priests. Assign a group to each elephant. As soon as they convert, have the elephants attack the nearby ballista tower. These big boys will be able to destroy the tower, kill any heavy cavalry interfering with their work, and still come home alive. Heal them. You're going to use them to destroy the ballista tower on the southeastern side of the plains.

Have your priests continue to work in groups of three as they convert all of the cavalry, elephants, and phalanxes they see. Keep alert, too, there's a nasty phalanx hiding in the palm trees.

Your final obstacle will be this ledge. Both the ballista towers and the catapults will be able to hit your legions as they march into the forum.

Once you've made the Syracuse plains a safer place, it's time to work on the towers circling the plains. For this, you will need catapults. You have two catapults back on your main island. Have a transport bring them, or have your villagers build a siege workshop. (It's easier to build a siege workshop.) You can use your new wealth to upgrade to heavy catapults, giving you much better range than the ballista towers you are killing.

The mission becomes fairly routine after you bring out the heavy catapults. Simply lob stones at distant targets and have your priests convert any enemies that come to complain.

Syracuse is on a plateau overlooking the plains. Clear the towers from along the edges of the plateau, then send groups of priests to the top of the ramp to see what's inside.

Your last obstacle is a ledge overlooking the city. There are catapults and ballista towers on that ledge. What's worse: you won't be able to get your legions to the yellow flags marking your goal until you destroy the catapults and the towers.

Use martyrdom to destroy the catapults. Get your priest to the heart of the city, assign him to preach to a catapult, and Delete him as he starts to chant. The catapult will convert, and its ledge mates will kill it. Destroy both catapults this way, then send your heavy catapult to destroy the towers on the ledge.

Once the towers are gone, send in your legions. The victory is yours.

Ways to Lose

In truth, Syracuse is not so much baffling as it is lengthy. Once you see the lay of the city, you will realize that the correct paths are obvious—all you have to do is clear the way.

Additional Hints

The reason you do not want to take catapults with your priests during your initial landing is that your catapults will shoot at your potential converts, and may even kill your priests. Catapults are hard to control, so don't bring them to the action until you need them.

Build your food supplies by fishing, but Delete your fishing boats when they have outlived their value. You don't want idle boats counting against your population.

It will be much easier to complete this mission if you have martyrdom. Just remember to keep your finger on the Delete key and execute the moment your priest starts chanting.

Always keep your priests in groups of three, and always try to send at least two groups of priests for every conversion. That way, if another likely prospect should appear, you can convert him by pressing the right number key, and clicking on the new target with your pointer.

Mission 4: Metaurus

It has been observed that Hannibal was better at waging wars than winning them. That may be true, but who could ever have had the confidence to risk a final assault on Rome? There was one moment, however, when it looked like that might happen.

Hannibal crossed the Alps and won several impressive victories in Italy, then called for more troops. His brother, Hasdrubal, tried to bring them, but the Romans intercepted him, and Hasdrubal was killed.

In this mission, you control a small Bronze Age village in a seemingly precarious situation. Hasdrubal and his men have set up a city to the south, and Hannibal's camp is to the north. Like you, both Hannibal and Hasdrubal have Bronze Age cities.

Send bowmen up to Hannibal to eliminate him from the fight.

The scenario opens with several of Hadrubal's axemen attacking your village. Fortunately, you have a sufficient force of axemen and bowmen to drive off this first attack. He will be back quickly, however. The majority of his population is made up of military units. His next visit will include scouts, and it won't be long until he brings short swordsmen and even a catapult.

The easiest way to survive his next offensive is to have one of your villagers build towers on the west side of your village, between your town center and berry bushes. Then, congregate all of your men around them. Pump out villagers as quickly as you can, and assign them to forage berries and cut wood so that you can train bowmen as quickly as possible.

An army of bowmen under an umbrella of towers will have no problem neutralizing a sprinkling of axemen, scouts, and short swordsmen. As your army grows stronger, you'll want to spread out, build more towers, and begin farming. Don't let the river on this map fool you—there are no fish to be caught.

The next step in turning this situation around is placing bowmen near the land bridges leading north across the river. Several of Hannibal's villagers will cross that bridge—you want to kill them the moment they do. As soon as you can muster a force of ten bowmen, send them across the river and massacre Hannibal's people. His resource—rich territory will then be yours.

There's one catch, though. The only way to get to Hannibal quickly enough to slaughter his men is through gauntlets of four towers at the north end of each of the bridges. Send ten bowmen in your invasion—only eight will make it through. But eight bowmen will be more than enough to finish Hannibal. By the end of the first ten minutes of this scenario, you should have finished Hannibal and built a strong enough defense to keep Hasdrubal at bay.

The easiest way to take possession of your new territory is to train five villagers and send them through the towers. One or two of them will die, but the survivors can construct a government center and a town center.

Hannibal's towers will not fire at Hasdrubal's men. Don't be surprised if Hannibal finds ways to bypass your southern village and attack you up north.

Set up your northern satellite so that it is easily defended. Several bowmen from your initial assault should still be in the area. Find the location where you would like to build your new town center, group your bowmen around it, and begin building. Be sure to select a location with good access to resources. There are large gold deposits in the north. Build around them.

The action for the remainder of this scenario is fairly obvious. Develop a strong army in your southern city and wipe out Hasdrubal. His city, located in the south, is an easy one to assault. He has towers along the edges of his territory, but they are too spread out to offer adequate protection.

The best way to eliminate Hasdrubal is with a rapid Bronze Age attack—chariots are your best bet. Build two or three stables, train ten to 15 chariots, and head south. Keep your chariots bunched together so that they always gang up on their targets, and you should be able to kill Hasdrubal's fairly ragtag army.

The final step in this mission is to build a couple of stone throwers to demolish the Carthaginians' buildings. Once the buildings are gone, you win.

Ways to Lose

After the complexities of Syracuse and the fury of Pyrrhus, Metaurus is somewhat relaxing. Once you survive the initial Tool Age rush, this mission goes by very quickly. (It takes place in the Bronze Age, but the units are all Tool Age units.)

Be sure to keep your men grouped in the early stages. They can be overwhelmed if caught individually, but they can survive if they fight as a team.

Additional Hints

Remember to upgrade to sentry towers as soon as you can do it without hurting your work force.

Researching artisanship will increase your productivity and make your towers and bowmen more effective. This will be helpful. Do it as soon as you have reached the ten-villager mark.

Mission 5: The Coming of the Huns

Few give the Huns their due. We hear so much about how Alexander the Great conquered from Europe to India, and everyone knows about Rome, but the Huns managed to cut a path all the way from Mongolia to Switzerland.

Now is your chance to face them. You begin this scenario with a Stone Age village and six villagers in the north. The Huns, who have a very comfy looking Iron Age city in the south, have three Bronze Age allies—one in the east, one in the west, and a third one that appears to be nothing more than a cluster of brown towers in the center of the map. The Huns are neutral but demand tributes. Their allies are antagonistic toward you.

Fortunately, the Huns are fairly reasonable. As long as you pay them tributes of 300 units of gold whenever they ask, and make sure not to hurt their citizens, they will leave you alone. Unfortunately, in a mission in which total annihilation is the ultimate goal, you can't keep buying your enemies off forever.

The mission begins in a fairly straightforward fashion. You have a few minutes to build up, but the yellow army in the west will come up along its riverbank and attack you with increasing regularity if you do not act quickly.

Build a strong villager work force as quickly as possible. Build docks on the rivers to your east and west, and fish for food so that you can have your villagers concentrate on mining gold and chopping wood. Research leather armor and woodworking, and then train standard Tool Age bowmen. Go right to the population limit in building this army—numbers will count.

Send your bowmen south along the western river. You will find a Hittite city at the end of the river. Destroy the people, the houses, and the town center. Keep an eye open for chariot archers and attack them as they approach you. Watch out for swordsmen, too. You may think that these numbers give you an overwhelming army, but this mission will prove that untrue.

If you work very quickly, you should be able to obliterate the yellow army's town center, villagers, and houses. Don't even bother trying to attack their granaries, towers, or storage pits. The Goths, the Huns' allies from the east, will come to the yellow army's aid—but if you worked quickly, they will be too late.

Chances are you won't be able to destroy the yellow army's stables and barracks. You may get a visit from a few last stragglers looking for revenge, but the yellow army will be out of the picture.

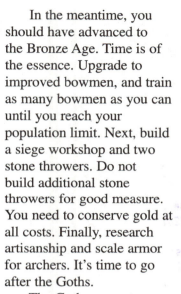

In the meantime, you should have advanced to the Bronze Age. Time is of the essence. Upgrade to improved bowmen, and train as many bowmen as you can until you reach your population limit. Next, build a siege workshop and two stone throwers. Do not build additional stone throwers for good measure. You need to conserve gold at all costs. Finally, research artisanship and scale armor for archers. It's time to go after the Goths.

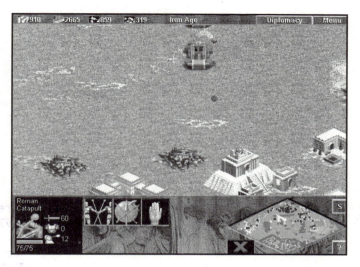

Use your catapults to destroy the Goths' towers and temple, but beware of their priests.

The Goths are not as easily defeated. They have more towers, slingers, more swordsmen, and excellent priests. They plan to build a wonder too, so get to them quickly. You'll need every last unit of stone and gold you can get your hands on in this mission, and you don't want to see precious resources vanish into a Goth wonder you'll have to work hard to destroy.

Use your stone throwers to destroy the Goths' towers, and your swarm of improved bowmen to massacre everything else. Kill their villagers and soldiers, and destroy their houses, town center, even their dock. As soon as you have destroyed the Goth's towers, send your stone throwers to find any final towers that might block your access to stone and gold deposits around the map.

Once you've eliminated the Goths, Delete all of your improved bowmen. They won't do you an ounce of good in the next part of this mission.

Next, create an entire population of villagers. Use these villagers to collect every shred of gold and stone on the map. Believe it or not, stone will prove to be more valuable than gold in this mission. Once you have scoured the map and collected all of the stone and gold, as well as significant quantities of wood and food, send your teeming population of villagers to visit the Huns.

Since you've been good about paying the Huns, they will not balk when you enter their land. You will be able to walk around their grounds, view the

AGE of EMPIRES

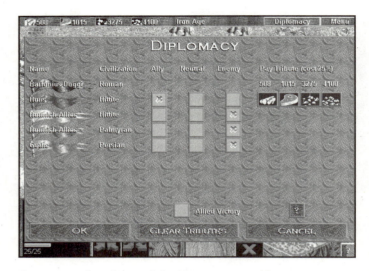

Be sure you've changed the Huns to neutral in your
diplomatic menu to avoid any costly mistakes.

magnificent wonder they will likely have completed, and do whatever you like. What you would like to do is build towers.

Before building these, however, do two things. First, save your game. There is a very real chance that the Huns will fight their way out of your trap.

Second, be sure that the Huns are still listed as allies on your diplomatic menu. One small slip, and your work is for naught.

Having taken these precautions, build towers. You should have thousands of units of stone and dozens of villagers. Since Roman towers cost only 75 units of stone, you should be able to build as many as 40 towers around their grounds.

As soon as you have built as many towers as possible, move your villagers to safety, and declare war on the Huns. Your sentry towers will be no match for their heavy catapults and ballista towers, but the numbers will be in your favor.

The battle is not over yet, however. The Huns' heavy catapults have 300 hit points, and their armored elephants have 600 hit points. With that kind of power behind them, they are going to bulldoze their way out of your sentry tower forest and find safe havens. You will need to mop up any survivors, and destroy any remaining towers.

It's time to build more heleopolises. In this case, heleopolises are not just convenient, they're also essential. No other unit has the range to hit ballista towers and the rapid firing ability needed to beat off armored elephants.

Unfortunately, you may find that heavy catapults can destroy nine heleopolises with a single shot, so you will need a second weapon for catapults-chariots. What you need is a unit that can get to the catapult and stop it from

firing. Fast-moving chariots can accomplish that task. Cavalry can do that, too, but chances are you'll need all of your gold to build heleopolises.

Once you have destroyed every Hun building, you win.

Ways to Lose

This mission is long and difficult. Beating the Huns' allies is not so hard, but taking it to the Huns is next to impossible. Spread your towers too far apart on their fort, and they will survive your ambush. Accidentally mistake a Hun for a Goth, and you won't get close enough to make an ambush.

Additional Hints

The Huns and the Goths have very similar colors. Be careful not to kill a Hun when you attack the Goths. Why? The Huns will declare war on you. Change the Huns to allies in your diplomatic menu—now you only have to worry about accidentally hurting a Hun villager who happens to be near a target your catapult is hitting.

Be sure to research architecture, jihad, and wheels. Architecture will make your towers stronger. Researching Jihad and wheels will make your villagers faster.

Chapter Eleven

STRATEGIES FOR WORLD DOMINATION

The people who worked on the original Microsoft's Age of Empires obviously knew they had a great game and that it was every bit as exciting a multiplayer title as it was a single-player game. They anticipated good sales of the game since the campaigns were so challenging and addictive, but they never dreamed it would become a multiplayer phenomenon. In many ways, Age of Empires has had an even bigger impact in multiplayer circles than it did as the shelf game for single play.

While most of the tricks and skills people use to beat the campaigns can be applied to multiplayer matches, others are painfully obvious to skilled human opponents. (Anyone thinking they've mastered Age of Empires by beating the campaigns should challenge a few players on Microsoft's Internet Gaming Zone—in terms of skillfulness, expect the unexpected.) Top multiplayer Agers debate such topics as the benefits of ballistas over catapults, whether the Babylonian priest and tower advantage cancels out the Assyrian archer rush, and which nations combine to make the best teams. Meanwhile, most single-player gamers simply want to know how to get to the next campaign.

Several skilled multiplayer gamers allowed interviews so that I could add their strategies to this book. An interesting note about their comments: They seldom agree with each other on any one point (other than the fact that the Choson is a civilization that gives them a lot of trouble). One of these experts favors a defensive strategy, while the others think it's foolish. One likes Egypt and relies on priests—the others think priest offensives are fruitless. Despite the differences, there's one common denominator in this group—hugely impressive winning records.

You might have the misfortune of running into one of these guys if you play on the Zone. If you do, knowing their strategies could help.

John Romero

As the co-founder of id Software, John Romero played a major role in the creation of Castle Wolfenstein 3D, the game that popularized first-person perspective shooters. His next title, Doom, was arguably the most popular computer game in history and certainly the game that established shareware as a viable way of marketing software.

Having left id Software to start up his own company, ION Storm, Romero is currently working on an elaborate first-person perspective game to be titled Daikatana.

Romero's success is no accident. A dyed-in-the-wool, dedicated gamer, Romero is nearly as talented at playing games as he is at making them. He is also a student of computer game history.

"Age of Empires is one of my all-time favorites," says Romero, who has a copy of the game on a shelf over his desk. According to several Ensemble employees, Romero is a dangerous opponent. He and a team of ION Storm employees routinely challenge Ensemble players to Random Match battles, and the ION Storm team generally wins.

PC Press: Do you play Age of Empires often?

Romero: A group of us here at ION Storm are pretty good at Age of Empires, and we heard that the guys at Raven Software (creators of Hexen) were getting into the game as well. I emailed them and cajoled them into playing us. A massive beating ensued.

They vowed to get better and smack us down the next week.

The next week came, and so did their next beating. Fast-forward past many weeks of Raven beatings—we stopped playing after nine straight wins. The prize for winning was that they had to change the name of their game, Hexen II, back to my original name of Hecatomb. (Hecatomb is the follow-up game to Heretic and Hexen—when Romero left id, the marketing folks renamed the game to capitalize on its predecessor's success. The game was published as Hexen II, but Romero proudly displays a mocked-up Hecatomb box over his desk.

PC Press: What civilization do you generally choose?

Romero: I play different civilizations depending on the style of the map I'm playing on. For water-based maps, like Small Island or Large Island maps, I

really like taking the Phoenicians because they have lots of great water units—plus, they have both types of elephants and, man, they are tough! (Since Romero had not played Rise of Rome at the time of this interview, he had not yet seen armored elephants.)

For land-based maps, I like to play the Yamato. They really blast through the ages and can early-attack with cavalry in no time at all. Plus, it's nice to have all the boats and still be able to train centurions.

PC Press: What nations do you like to partner with in team battles?

Romero: For water maps, I like to partner with Yamato because I can handle the water-based warfare really well while my Yamato partner dumps off heavy cavalry and takes over their islands. If we're playing on a land-based map, I usually take the Sumerians, and my partner is Yamato because I can wall-up and generate tons of food and go to Iron while my partner early-attacks and slows down their Age advancement. Then, when I get to Iron, I come out with the most upgraded units in all the categories. Total destruction!

PC Press: Which nations give you the most trouble?

Romero: All of the early attackers like the Yamato, Assyrian, and Shang are troublesome because they come after you early and destroy your villagers, slowing down your resource gathering and Age advancement. If I'm playing against an early-attacker, I wall-up, build towers, and Age advance as fast as possible.

PC Press: Do you go straight to the Iron Age or do you do an early rush?

Romero: I like a balance of both. I do a little bit of early attacking, which makes my opponent think that's my entire strategy, when, in reality, most of my work is geared toward age advancement.

PC Press: Do you play an offensive or defensive style?

Romero: I do both. In the beginning, I wall-up and gather resources quickly, then do some early attacking. I'm mostly on the offensive later in the game, when I have the upgraded units.

PC Press: What is your strategy for building your nation quickly?

Romero: Gathering resources as fast as possible is the quickest way through the ages, so putting out as many fishing boats [as possible] is priority one, hunting animals is number two, and picking berries is number three.

While this is going on, I keep half my villagers chopping wood and a few busting down rocks. When I hit Bronze, about a third of my units become bearers of death. Then in Iron, I start increasing the death squad to 50 percent and up, until it gets to be about 100 percent.

PC Press: How do you beat off early rushes?

Romero: Walling-up and building towers at key points is a good way to discourage an early attacker. Throwing some chariot archers near the walls is also a good idea.

PC Press: What are your favorite Iron Age weapons?

Romero: I love playing water-based maps. Triremes and juggernauts are my favorite water weapons. On land, I just love heavy horse archers and upgraded catapults.

PC Press: What special tricks do you have for deploying those units?

Romero: I keep the juggernauts in a row behind my triremes because juggernauts are wimpy and get taken out easily. The triremes beat on the opposition, while the back row juggernauts destroy their buildings.

When I attack with heavy horse archers and catapults, I do the same thing by having a solid row of heavy horse archers in front and catapults in back, bashing down all buildings in sight. You know, sometimes I like to use the catapults on the little dudes.

PC Press: Describe your strategy through the stages of a game.

Romero: The very beginning is extremely time-critical. You have to have a constant stream of villagers being generated at every second and keep 80 percent of your units on food gathering while the rest are chopping wood. As soon as I have 20 villagers, I go to the Tool Age and start farming and building a few stables. I go Bronze as soon as possible and start pumping out cavalry units, then send them to my enemy and take out his villagers first and his houses second.

I use whatever tricks I know along the way. I like researching wall building and sending a villager into the enemy camp to build a wall around his town center.

In Bronze, I am still in major resource-gathering mode because I like to finish a game in Iron. If my opponent likes to finish in Bronze, I will upgrade

everything and finish the game. If I get to go to Iron, I will pump out centurions, cataphracts, and heavy horse archers and rumble all over his town.

Normally, I consider building a wonder a cheap and cheesy way out—but if your teammate is not doing well and it looks like you might lose the game (and you have enough resources), build one in a corner of the map as far away from ships as possible. Open areas behind heavily wooded forests are great locations since the forests provide natural barriers.

Normally, you would surround your wonder with stone walls to keep marauding enemy units at bay—but stone is scarce and is better used to keep the enemy from getting anywhere within sighting distance of your wonder. The trick is to build a double or triple wall of Town Centers around your wonder. Not only do they only cost wood (which is plentiful), but they also take an awesome 600 hit points—and if enemy catapults get too close, you can use them to generate villagers to come and pound them down, right on the front lines.

The other cheesy way of winning, in my opinion, is by gathering all the artifacts or capturing all the ruins. But, ya' know, when your teammate is falling behind and it doesn't look like he might make it much longer, an all-out rush to gather the artifacts might be in order.

The sneakiest way of winning the game with artifacts is to gather them all up in one location (if possible), put them on a light transport, and float them into a corner of the map where no one will find them. If you can't get all the artifacts in one spot, cruise the boat around and capture them one at a time.

PC Press: Got any other dirty tricks?

Romero: As soon as you research walls, you should attempt to build walls all around your perimeter. Of course, it would take a long time for your villager to go around to all of them and build them—but what happens is that you just built a barrier, however weak, against your enemies. If they attack it, you will know that they are attempting an invasion.

It's like having towers all around your land. And if you're playing against the computer, their villagers are really stupid and will just bunch up against the invisible walls.

It's also cool to build walls around your enemy's town center.

Duncan McKissick

Duncan McKissick has been a 3D Artist at Ensemble Studios for about two and a half years.

Before joining Ensemble, he worked for Origin Systems, maker of the Ultima and Wing Commander games.

On the Zone, McKissick goes by the name Reverend. "I use the name 'Reverend' because I am an ordained minister," says McKissick. "You'll find me using Yamato horse archers, Carthaginian elephants, or Minoan composites and heleopolises to sway you to resign."

PC Press: Which civilizations do you prefer?

McKissick: Either the Minoans or the Yamato—the Yamato because they have good cavalry and villagers, and the Minoans because their composite bowmen have a +1 line of sight allowing you to see farther with them. You can hunt down villagers really easy with Minoan composite bowmen.

PC Press: So you like to go after villagers and houses first?

McKissick: Exactly. That's usually the first thing I go for. I'll almost always go right past the other units and go straight for the villagers. That's probably my number one thing—I want to slow down your production. Number two, if there are any enemy units around, you want to try and get rid of them so that you can take out houses. Take out his houses and he can't build more units or more villagers.

PC Press: Of the new civilizations in Rise of Rome, which is your favorite?

McKissick: I usually like to play with Carthage. Their fire galleys do +25 damage. Also, hoplites are one of my favorite units. Carthaginian hoplites have +25 hit points. Oh, and I like playing on water maps. They have faster transports so you can get your guys over more quickly.

PC Press: What do you think of fire galleys?

McKissick: Fire galleys take extra damage from catapult triremes. It's tricky— you usually don't want to have just fire galleys naked like that because their line of sight is almost nothing. They are definitely a close-range hitter, so you usually want to keep triremes or catapults around.

PC Press: Which civilization gives you the biggest fits?

McKissick: I would probably say Egyptians. Egypt has a relatively solid navy, and they counter your elephants and hoplites with excellent priests.

PC Press: How do you counter against Egypt's priests?

McKissick: I would probably counter with priests, to be honest.

PC Press: There's nothing unusual about Carthaginian priests.

McKissick: No, but they have martyrdom, and that's definitely one of the new things that we've been using over here at Ensemble. Martyrdom is extremely valuable to get you out of a tough situation quickly. I'll trade 125 gold for an elephant any time if it will get me out of a situation.

PC Press: Describe your strategy for the typical death match?

McKissick: Nowadays, walling off is critical. You can never predict when the enemy is going to attack, especially in death matches. If he finds you early enough, he could rush you in the Stone Age. He could rush you in the Tool or any Age, especially Bronze. So, get to the Tool Age as quickly as you can and wall-off immediately so that you've got a little bit of time to think about what you're going to do next.

When I hit Bronze, I build two of everything...two markets, two government centers. Having two of everything means I can research more quickly. I also build at least six stables. I build some towers, but I'm not much of a tower guy. I spend the stone on walls rather than towers.

PC Press: Do you protect your walls with archers or slingers?

McKissick: With catapults and ballistas, most likely. It's always good to have a combination of both. If I were to pick one, I'd probably say ballistas because en masse they do a hell of a lot of damage—especially heleopolises. They do a ton of damage and they have the range from hell. The tricky thing is that catapults will take four or five ballistas out with one shot.

PC Press: Is there any unit that you don't like to see your opponents using?

McKissick: I'd probably say priests. I love to use them, and I hate when they're being used against me. It's a love/hate relationship with priests.

The new unit that I have a lot of trouble with is scythe chariots. Scythe chariots are so fast, hit so hard, and are rather inexpensive. You can pump a lot

of them out and just swarm somebody with them really easily.

The best way that I found to deal with scythe chariots is to send armored elephants after them.

Chea O'Neill

A 2D/3D artist at Ensemble, Chea O'Neill is considered one of the company's best players. On the Zone, O'Neill plays under the name Truck.

PC Press: Which civilization do you usually use when you play?

O'Neill: I tend to lean towards the Yamato. Lately, I've dabbled with the Assyrians—but I think my favorite is still the Yamato. They have good, cheap cavalry, fast villagers, and a lot of the government center research [options] that are important if you have horse archers in the Iron Age.

PC Press: So, you favor a horse attack?

O'Neill: Depending on the circumstance. Cavalry are quick, but they don't have a good line of sight. Typically, I like to send a scout with my cavalry. Scouts have a greater line of sight. If I'm going into somebody's town and their villagers run away, chances are my scout will see the ones that the cavalry wouldn't otherwise see.

PC Press: Do you prefer the Yamato to the new nations in Rise of Rome?

O'Neill: Yes. The Yamato do not have fire galleys, scythe chariots, camel riders, or martyrdom. It doesn't sound like they get any of the new units. The Yamato are very capable even without the new stuff.

PC Press: What civilization gives you the most trouble?

O'Neill: So far, the one that's given me the most trouble is probably Rome. With logistics research, the Romans can build two legions and it only counts as one in their population. When somebody comes into your town with 50 legions backed with heleopolises, it's a pretty hard force to go up against.

PC Press: What do you do to try and counter that?

O'Neill: The Yamato don't get the big catapults, but even a stone thrower stands a better chance at taking out a few heleopolises than a foot solider trying to run up and hit it. As far as the legions go, hoplites and phalanxes seem to do

fairly well against them. Horse archers do pretty well against the foot units when you send them in groups.

Horse archers are so fast, you can do what's called a "dance" with the legions. You shoot at them, turn and run a little distance while they're still coming, take another few shots, and then run. You can lead them around until they're dead.

The heleopolises are a little harder [than foot soldiers and catapults] because they seldom miss and it doesn't take but two shots from a heleopolis to drop a horse archer. In my opinion, you want to take out the siege engines first because they will do a lot more damage than the foot soldiers.

PC Press: Do priests give you much trouble?

O'Neill: By the time I'm in the Iron Age with the Yamato, I have a lot of horse archers. Heavy horse archers are typically my favorite unit in the Iron Age.

They are one of the fastest units in the game and one of the hardest units to convert. The first thing that priests don't want to walk into is a pack of chariots or chariot archers. The second would be horse archers.

I also try to build beyond my population limit.

PC Press: How do you do that?

O'Neill: Let's say the game has the population level set at 50, and you have 49 units on the board. If you have 20 or 30 barracks, you can go to each of them and start training one unit, which would give you a good 19 to 29 units over the population limit.

A lot of people will do that. They watch their population limit very closely. When they know that they're extremely close to the limit, they hit every military building and create something just so they have more units.

PC Press: Do you prefer fighting on one front or a multifront battle?

O'Neill: One front is easier to manage, but it seems like you really can't get through a game these days without playing on at least two, if not three, fronts. Three fronts is fine. It's tougher to manage, but if your economy allows, it's really not that difficult.

One thing that a lot of people don't pay enough attention to is their economy. Typically, I try to maintain a good economy at all costs. If your economy ever falters, it can essentially cost you the game because you will not have the resources to produce military units to protect yourself.

PC Press: When do you explore the map?

O'Neill: Typically, I have one of my very first villagers that I start with scour the map. First, he looks around my town center and then a little farther out. That way, as I create villagers and as they're resourcing, this guy's already found where my next food is coming from. When that first berry patch runs out, he knows where to go for gold, trees, and shore fishing. As soon as I've established my first run of resources, I'll send him all over the map and pray he doesn't get mauled by a lion.

If I find an enemy, I'll typically just keep my villager back in a corner until I hit Tool Age. When I hit Tool Age, especially as the Yamato, I build three or four stables behind that person's town. By the time I hit Bronze, I've got all kinds of cavalry coming into their town, and there's not a whole lot they can do because they don't have a military front on the back side of their town. They're not expecting the attack to come from the back side, so that's typically where the houses and economy are.

PC Press: How do you fight off early rushes?

O'Neill: It's a little easier to fight off a rush if you have scouted around because you know which direction to run and you know where land barriers are. If you get to the Tool Age and you suspect a rush... if you're a person who checks your opponent's achievements, you can generally tell if somebody's going to rush based on what type of units they're building.

By keeping an eye on Achievements, you can typically tell if somebody's going to rush or not. If you know somebody's going to rush, the best defense is to wall-off. You don't lose any units and it will take them forever to get through your walls with Tool Age units—and while they're doing that, you can continue resourcing, advance to Bronze, and take them out.

Keep in mind that since they did a Tool Age rush, they had to use a lot of resources. That means they are behind you in resourcing and technology. If their Tool Age rush is ineffective, you can basically wipe those people out when you get to the Bronze Age. It's been a long time since I've been rushed.

I'm not a big tower person. I really don't build towers because I think walls are plenty of defense. If I see an incredible number of units coming and I know they could break through my wall any minute, I'll go on ahead and build some military units—typically archers—to defend with.

It's been a long, long time since I've been through a Tool Age rush, but I think the Tool Age rush will be back. My prediction is that it probably will consist of a couple of scouts, four or five archers, and probably four to six slingers.

PC Press: Do you prefer playing offensively or defensively?

O'Neill: Offensively, absolutely, and for several reasons. Number one, if somebody plays defensively, they wall themselves into an area and are confined to that area's resources. If you know that person is walled in, you basically have free reign of the rest of the gold on the map. No matter what the defender has, his resources will never outweigh the resources the offensive person can throw at him because he's walled himself in.

Dave Pottinger

Though he does not readily accept the title, most of his co-workers say that Dave Pottinger is Ensemble's best Age of Empires player. Pottinger, who led the engine development and designed the artificial intelligence for Age of Empires, is currently working on a next-generation engine for future Ensemble Studios games. On the Zone, he goes by the name Bigdog.

PC Press: Do you prefer playing random map or death match?

Pottinger: I pretty much don't like doing death matches. I prefer playing random map with the default starting values of 200 wood, 200 food, 150 stone and no gold. All of my comments are going to be based off of that because I definitely don't like to play death match. They just turn into tactical games of who can click their mouse faster, and there's not any sort of real strategy.

In a standard random map game, when it takes 15 minutes to get to the Bronze Age, we're all quizzing ourselves about which unit we're going to build next. If you make a mistake and it sets you behind by ten seconds to a minute, it can cost the game. In a death match, it's really just a question of who can crank out the most stuff.

PC Press: What is your favorite civilization in the original Age of Empires?

Pottinger: It would depend on the map type. If it's a water map, I definitely like the Minoans because of the cheap boats. If not the Minoans, then somebody

like the Phoenicians because they get the undocumented wood bonus and the faster firing catapult triremes.

PC Press: Undocumented wood bonus?

Pottinger: Yes. We had an oversight in our database in the original game, and we didn't notice that they [the Phoenicians] got a wood carrying bonus. We documented it in the "read me" for the patches, but it was not in the original game documentation.

The Phoenicians also have cheap elephants which are really good for landing on islands.

PC Press: How about land-based games?

Pottinger: Playing the Shang is always fun because they get up so quickly through the ages.

The Palmyrans are kind of the opposite of the Shang. I mean, the Shang work really well in getting you up quickly when you have a low food situation—but if you start a regular game with high resources or a death match game, these things don't have much impact, and the Shang don't get any bonuses for combat.

Palmyran villagers work faster, so they provide a better advantage in games in which you don't have to worry about how much they cost. Palmyra is a very, very slow civilization that is susceptible to getting rushed early, but once in the Iron Age, they're almost pretty unstoppable.

PC Press: How long do your games usually last?

Pottinger: Anywhere from one to two hours. The best game is an eight-player game with two four-player teams. Playing with teams is nice because it makes it harder for you to get wiped out early. If somebody comes into your town early, you can evacuate to somebody else's town or they can come help defend you.

PC Press: Of the four new civilizations in Rise of Rome, which is your favorite?

Pottinger: Of the new civilizations, Rome is a favorite of mine because it builds up quickly thanks to cheap buildings. I think Roman buildings cost only

85 percent of what other civilizations' buildings cost. Rome is cool because it has forced me to rethink all of my strategies about the build-up.

The cheap buildings kind of forced me to rethink all of my decisions about when to build buildings. If I can sit down and play the Shang, I know pretty much what the first ten minutes of my game is going to be like. I know exactly what I'm going to build and in what order—but facing a civilization with less expensive buildings made me rethink things.

PC Press: What would you normally build as the Shang?

Pottinger: The first thing to do is to cue up all of your villagers [in the town center] that you can. The next thing to do is to build one house.

I have my second villager start walking in concentric rings around the area while my third guy is chopping a nearby tree. As soon as I find berries, I put down a granary and put about two-thirds of my guys on the berries—five villagers, assuming nobody gets killed by a lion.

You still need to have two people getting wood so that you can get the storage pit close enough to your forest. Hopefully, you have found a forest by then. If not, you're going to be a few seconds behind.

If you found a forest quickly and your initial trees were nearby, you can put the storage pit down before you build your eighth guy. That helps you gather 30 wood quickly to build a second house, so you don't have to wait to build more guys.

PC Press: How long before you start worrying about stone?

Pottinger: If I'm playing the Shang, I don't worry about stone unless somebody else is playing a fast civilization like the Assyrians, Minoans, or Shang. Actually, in the expansion pack, the Assyrian and Yamato civilizations are not as fast [as they were in the original game] because their villagers have been tweaked back a little bit.

I don't start gathering stone until I reach the Tool Age, then I research the stone upgrade.

Ideally, I won't build barracks until I have started researching the Tool Age. If things go correctly, I can put the barracks down while I'm advancing to the Tool Age, and I'll have 800 food and 300 wood to plop down on my stable and market by the time I advance.

Then I can make the Tool-to-Bronze jump in as much time as it takes me to build two of those buildings. The trick there is that you want to basically plop your buildings down with all of your civilians building them.

If you do that right, you'll be in the Tool Age for approximately 30 seconds before you start researching Bronze. Then, while you're researching Bronze, you can research the gold mining bonus and the woodworking bonus at the market.

PC Press: How many villagers do you train?

Pottinger: I generally never build any villagers past the initial ones that I build in the Stone Age. I usually build between 20 and 25 villagers. You need even less when you play the Palmyrans—usually all I train is between 13 and 17. Now, if they get killed off, I'll replace them—but generally I try not to build any villagers past the Stone Age.

PC Press: You're trying to keep your population low?

Pottinger: Yes.

PC Press: What do you think of logistics?

Pottinger: If you're Roman, you definitely want logistics. Instead of having 25 villagers and 25 legions, you can have 50 legions pouring into somebody's town, which is pretty unstoppable.

Robert Howg

A game tester at Microsoft, Robert Howg is one of the better Agers in the company. Playing on Kali under the unusual name Sipsip (the word his two-year-old son used to ask for a drink of water), Howg has compiled an amazing record of 179 wins and 28 losses.

PC Press: Which civilizations do you prefer?

Howg: I would have to say either Assyrian or Yamato. I would go more with the Assyrians for coastal maps in which I can do a lot of fishing. On island maps I go with the Yamato—on landlocked maps I go with the Assyrians.

PC Press: The infamous Assyrian archer rush?

Howg: Not an archer rush, a chariot archer rush. I love playing 90 percent of my games in Bronze. I like chariot archers because they're fast and they don't take gold.

That means you can concentrate on two resources instead of three. You get your wood and your food. You have to factor in peasants for gathering gold with the Yamato.

The Assyrians have to do the wheel upgrade to make chariots, but it's a double upgrade. You get your chariot and you also get faster villagers.

PC Press: But chariots are vulnerable to cavalry attacks.

Howg: There's a trick to use when your chariots go against cavalry. Unless the other guy is really paying attention, cavalry tend to head for one particular chariot. Once you see which chariot they're heading for, peel it off from the back of the pack. The cavalry will follow it around while your archers continue shooting them. Chariots are a little bit faster than cavalry, so you can always keep a little ahead of the pack.

If the cavalry switches to another chariot, you peel that chariot off. Basically, you keep moving the one chariot they're going after. That leaves you to use your other guys to take them out.

PC Press: Do you favor any of the new civilizations in Rise of Rome?

Howg: Even though they're slated as an economic civilization, I like the Palmyrans. I see them as a tribe with a lot of hidden potential. Everybody's going to look at this tribe, and they're going to say, "No way. It's not worth it to pay the extra 25 food." But they work 20 percent faster and that means you need 20 percent fewer villagers.

And once you get started, you only have to make 16 villagers before you go to Bronze, as opposed to making 20 villagers with other civilizations. That means your Bronze time is going to be cut down potentially because they're working faster.

I'm working on it with a friend, and we've got the Palmyrans down to about a 12-minute Bronze time with the potential to go even lower. We're coming a little bit too heavy on the wood side of the equation. When we go Bronze, we'll have like 120 extra wood. That means we could peel a couple of guys off of wood and put them on food to go Bronze in less than 12 minutes.

PC Press: What do you think of Rome?

Howg: Rome has the potential for early attacks, I think, with their cheap towers. They have a good defense. Your ground troops attack faster. With logistics, you can pump out a lot of ground troops.

Rome is a pretty civilization. They're like a show-piece civilization, but they're not the strongest civilization. I'll take the Choson any day.

PC Press: The Romans have scythe chariots.

Howg: The best use I've found for scythe chariots is to break up a catapult attack, but they have other uses, too. If scythe chariots attack your barracks buildings, they'll damage your new units as soon as they pop out [since their attack damages everything within the area they are attacking].

Once you get scythe chariots in the other guy's town and make contact with the buildings, don't worry about killing villagers or houses. Go directly after their military buildings. Get them to surround siege workshops, and they'll chew through ballistas as soon as they come out. The ballista pops up and gets off maybe one shot.

The Choson have archers—the remedy for scythe chariot attacks. They just pincushion them.

PC Press: Describe your basic battle plans for, say, a Mediterranean battle against Rome.

Howg: I'll probably go with about 20 villagers. I'll go as hard as I can on food, taking only as much wood as I need until I'm getting ready to go Bronze. Once I have the food I need to go Bronze, I'm probably going to put 90 percent or 18 of the guys on chopping wood; two guys will go out and build a few docks.

I know it sounds like I'm shorting myself on food, but you're generally going to have a couple hundred extra food by the time you reach Bronze.

I'll probably put up three or four docks, and I'll put out fishing boats. As soon as I put up my docks, I'll probably throw down about five archery ranges. By that time, I should be Bronze and having my wheel upgrade done.

Meanwhile, I'm assuming that since you're Roman, you will be towering up and putting up some walls.

PC Press: What if your opponent sends scout ships after your docks?

Howg: If you're doing that, I'll probably manage to get 300 or 400 food together. I'm going to build some chariot archers to defend my docks. If you manage to kick me off the water, I'll just throw up 12 farms.

I'll be exploring this whole time, and I probably will have found where you are. You will probably be walled off on the Mediterranean. I'll probably just keep you busy. Let you think I'm coming for your walls.

In the meantime, I will build another dock away from where you've been attacking my docks. I will make a transport, put five villagers on the transport and come over onto your side of the map.

I'll probably land my villagers and throw up four or five ranges. By this time, it will probably be 20 minutes into the game.

I'm assuming this is all going pretty fast because generally I like to hit Bronze in about 12 to 13 minutes. I'm not going to bother walling in because it's all about putting the other guy on the defensive and making the other guy react to you.

PC Press: What do you consider the most powerful unit?

Howg: If I had to take my pick as far as the strongest unit, it would be heavy horse archers. You have the most potential to do damage with them, and that gives the Yamato an advantage because their heavy horses are cheaper.

Heavy horse archers do surprisingly well against ballistas. If you have ten horse archers and you run into five or six ballista or three or four heleopolises, just make sure you have your guys divided into two groups, with five or six in each. You target one [ballista], target the next, target the next, target the next, target the next.

PC Press: Should you hot key them?

Howg: Hot keying the heavy horses into groups is very important. Also, before you go in to attack, make sure you have your army laid out the way you want it. Hot key them in the order you want to use them. Number one will be your first troops to hit the walls, number two and three might be your archers that come up and give support on the sides, number four might be your priest come to do some conversions. Number five is going to be your siege weapons that come after you open the gap.

PC Press: Got any dirty tricks?

Howg: There is a dirty trick strategy involving the Yamato. It's a combination of scout and tower rush. That makes it a Tool Age attack.

You're going to want to get to the Tool Age as quickly as possible. That means you'll probably want to make 14 to 16 villagers. As soon as you start to go Tool, put all but six guys on stone so you're mining stone like crazy. You want to hit Tool in about seven or eight minutes, and once you hit Tool and have about 300 food, you've put a lot of guys on stone.

Now, make a scout and find the guy your playing against with the scout. As soon as you find the guy, have your scout start attacking one of his villagers. Meanwhile, send six or eight villagers along with two or three other scouts to build a tower next to his storage pit. Next, send your villagers to build a tower near his town center. Then have your villagers build a tower near a couple of his houses. Do this right, and you can kick him out of his base.

Another dirty trick, if you find somebody who's mining gold, is to tell a villager to build a wall there. You'll throw down the wall with only one hit point—but if the other guy is not paying attention, all of the villagers will just go up the wall and stop. Until he actually looks and sees what you did, all of his villagers will just stop there and bunch it up. By the time he finally kills your wall, he's maybe lost 30 seconds or a minute worth of production.

Bryan Trussel

This guy is the kind of person who most people would euphemistically label a brat.

A team leader at Microsoft, Bryan Trussel has amassed an impressive record of more than 40 wins with only two losses in multiplayer death matches. Playing on the Zone under the name GanGus, Trussel's modus operandi is taunting victims right before launching his final invasion by sending them the message, "I am GanGus. FEAR ME." As many of his victims attest, like him or hate him, Trussel has the skills to backup his big talk.

PC Press: What is your favorite style of game?

Trussel: I like to play death matches with a low population setting. Most people don't go above 200. A lot of people go 200. I prefer to keep the limit at 100. At a population level of 50 on an island map, I don't think anybody can beat me.

PC Press: What civilization do you pick?

Trussel: I always choose Egypt. Egypt has a full navy, which is nice, and long-range priests. When you play Egypt, you're playing a priest-type game. The way to counter that is with strong chariots, but Egypt has both strong priests and strong chariots.

Egypt has tough chariots to counter other civilizations' priests, full naval capabilities, and a pretty good spattering of other stuff. Egypt has war elephants and pretty good walls.

PC Press: Which civilization is the toughest to defeat?

Trussel: The Choson is the hardest civilization to go up against. Egypt against Choson is almost a neck-and-neck game. The Choson are very hard to attack because they have long-range towers. You can't launch an attack with your priests because they'll get wiped out. You can't use elephants because their catapults will kill any elephants that their priests don't convert. All that leaves [in the Egyptian arsenal] is stone throwers, and stone throwers can't reach the towers because they're very weak. That almost leaves you hoping you can get through with your navy.

PC Press: And if you're playing on land?

Trussel: And if you're playing on land, you're hosed. You just have to do an all out march—send out your catapults, elephants, and priests all at the same time. You try to march your elephants through to draw some fire, then advance your priests and hopefully convert some of the enemy guys. If you can get to the towers, you hope you'll feed them enough chaos so that you can break through the towers by the time they clean it all up.

The Choson are the toughest, but I think the Greeks are almost as tough for a lot of the same reason that the Choson are tough.

PC Press: If the Choson and the Greeks are so tough, why go with the Egyptians?

Trussel: This is why I like to play with a small population limit. That's when the priests become very effective. If I get ten priests, and the population limit is 50, I can convert one fifth of your guys every 15 or 20 seconds. That's enough to wipe you out.

You make ten priests and put walls around all sides of them with a couple of towers in there and a villager for fun. And as the other guy attacks, you just sit there and convert them.

If you send in 200 Choson guys and I convert ten of them, you don't care—the other 90 you've got can kill my priests by the time my priests rejuvenate. So, large populations are tough.

The Choson have these little guys that aren't worth your time to convert. Converting them doesn't buy you that much because they can build more. With the other races, if you can convert a catapult or an elephant, it's a very worthwhile trade for your priest.

There's no way for them to get to your priests. People just send in waves and waves and you just go "thank you, thank you, thank you, thank you, thank you, thank you."

The other thing is that you have to watch out if they send catapults against your priests...then they're in trouble. What I do on that is I'll space my priests out. Remember the key thing is then that you hot key each priest with Control-1 and Control-2, so each priest has his own hot number. Then even if you're on offense or defense and the other guy charges you with 20 elephants (they always try do that), you just go: 1. click on an elephant, 2. click on an elephant, 3. click on an elephant.

It's just hilarious. Then you just sit back and watch as they just change to your color, your color... your color, and then your first priest is rejuvenated and you just go through your priests again. It's almost like having this hot key to turn their guys into yours.

PC Press: What is your overall strategy?

Trussel: I play death matches, so I usually go for a quick kill.

When I start my game off, depending on the population setting, I build four to eight cities all next to each other. That's the very first thing I do. I've tried other things and this is by far the best because the idea is to get as many villagers out there as quickly as you can so that then you can go out and build more and more and more. You get that curve ramping up really quick.

I'm very heavy on the offense initially. I usually try to control just over half the map, then I start building my offense out there. I build everything in groups of six. I build six stables next to each other, because the first thing I build is six elephant stables and then I build usually temples.

All I build, when I play Egyptian, is priests, elephants, and villagers. If they [my opponent] have priests, I'll build chariots—but really priests and elephants are all I use.

So I build the stables and the priests, then I'll build a tower up around them. I'll do that across my front, across the whole map or across two-thirds of it. Then I leave my back end pretty much open.

PC Press: Do you ever get worried about a Stone or Tool Age Rush?

Trussel: Oh, they wouldn't have time. They've either got to build those clubmen or send them across the map. It's the same problem the British had— you have to haul all your armies all across the ocean before they get a chance to fight.

They can run across and build up their barracks right next to my city. If I see that happening, I just build a bunch of priests in my city and some towers. As they train units I convert them.

I love it when people rush me and try to build towers around my city because I'll just build a couple of things to draw fire, then build up a ton of priests. Priests are great in chaos. If your opponents don't see a priest coming and kill it, they'll direct their fire at the wrong place and let you convert everything they built.

If somebody comes in and builds stables and towers around me, I say, "Great! That's free stuff for me. I'll win them in the long run." Remember I'm building all those villagers in my cities as fast as I can, so I can build anything I need quickly.

PC Press: Are towers an important element in your strategy?

Trussel: I have to have towers everywhere. They give you a big range of sight.

Any time somebody comes to attack you, they'll come and attack your tower, which gives you time to build a few defenses. The big plus is being able to adapt really quickly to the game.

PC Press: Do you build your towers in clusters?

Trussel: Nope. The only thing towers offer me is an early warning sign. Once I see where the attack is coming from, I've got so many villagers that I'll run in and build more towers in time if I need them. I'd rather save the resources, see where they attack, and then build up before they can get in.

PC Press: You begin death matches with 20,000 units of wood and food, 10,000 units of stone, and 5,000 units of gold. Do you find that you need to harvest more resources or is that enough to keep you going through the whole game?

Trussel: Actually, the mistake that most people make is that they don't go after more wood and food initially. I hardly ever run out of wood unless it turns into a big naval battle.

If we get into a stand off in which we're just going back and forth and nobody launches a full-fledged attack, I sit back with my villagers building my food supplies. When it looks like the big rush, I build elephants. Once he goes away, I go back to farming. So, if your opponent's not doing that, you'll win in resources in the long run.

I always assume that I'm entering a battle of attrition, and that if I can get 51 percent of the map or of the resources, all I do is wait. I just build up my resources, strengthen my defenses, and sit and wait for them to attack.

Since we're playing death match, I ignore trees and food initially. I send all of my villagers to mine gold patches and I gradually move my way back.

I prefer to play a defensive game because you lose more resources attacking than defending. So the idea is to get those high resources, make the other guy waste a lot of time [trying to reclaim his land], and by the time he breaks through, there's nothing there for him but a bunch of wasted land.

Another thing is people get this emotional attachment to their base like "Oh, gosh, I better not let him kill my village." The only thing you've really got there is houses, and they're easy enough to build somewhere else.

PC Press: When you take the offensive, do you go after villagers and houses?

Trussel: No, they're too easy to replace. When you're playing a death match against somebody who's good, they're going to have city centers everywhere. And that's the other thing...I never build storage bits. Always city centers.

I go after conversions. You convert a tower and you've not only taken their offensive weapon but you've got an offensive weapon now. The villagers are easy to wipe out after you own the towers and the barracks.

PC Press: You've been known to cajole opponents.

Trussel: I once got a guy down to his last man—a villager—and I walled him in. I built a wall around him and sent in an army of villagers to beat the crap out of him.

I learned about checking achievements from somebody I was heckling. I sent him a message saying, "I can give you some gold, I've got plenty." He responded, "I know." I asked him how he knew, and he told me that he had checked my economy achievements.

One last thing that get people's goats is to convert their transports before they land. Convert a loaded heavy transport and move it to safety, and you take ten units away from your opponent's population because there is no way to kill the units on that boat.

Making Your Own Worlds

Once you've played through all of the missions in Rise of Rome, you may want to try your hand at creating some scenarios of your own. You'll be amazed at how easy it is to make an attractive and challenging level with the tools in the Scenario Builder.

Start by clicking Scenario Builder in the main menu, then click Create Scenario. You'll see a large, featureless (except for grass) map and menus along the top and bottom of your screen.

If you're in an ambitious mood, you can start building your map—or if you'd rather tweak a ready-made map, click Random Map on the bottom of the screen, then click Generate Map. (Since map tweaking is one of the steps in creating a map from scratch, we will cover it later in this discussion.)

The first step in creating a scenario is to decide what kind of mission you want to make. If you want epic naval battles, for instance, set your scenario in the ocean instead of the desert. By the same token, you probably won't have exciting chariot battles if your map is set to island terrain.

"I usually start with a clean green map and start drawing in where I think the water should be, and I usually use those as strategic spots as placing grounds. I'll decide that I want a battle to take place in a certain spot, so this is where I want to throw some people," says Chris Rippy, the Ensemble mastermind behind many of the cruelest levels in the Age of Empires games.

By way of example, let's assume you want to make an inland mission. Click Terrain along the top of your screen. Menus for setting your brush type and size will appear on the bottom of your screen along with a list of terrains. To form cliffs and hills, click the elevations option in the Brush Type menu and experiment with the different elevations. (Don't worry about creating a realistic-looking landscape. If you don't like what you make, you can always start again.)

Elevation 1 indents the ground. Use this to create slopes and small valleys. Elevation 2 creates flat ground. Use this to erase holes or hills you don't want. Elevation 3 creates single-terraced hills. Sacred buildings such as ruins and temples look great on Elevation 3 hills.

Elevation 4 creates double-terraced hills, Elevation 5 creates triple-terraced hills, and you can probably guess what Elevations 6 and 7 create. To create these hills, choose a location on your blank map, select the elevation of the hills you wish to lay down, move the hills in the right location on the map and left click your mouse to place them.

Placing cliffs is even easier. Click Cliff in the Brush Type menu. To place cliffs, click the left button on your map. If you don't like how they look, you can erase them with the right button.

(If you want to restart your scenario, click the Map button at the top of the screen, click the Blank Map button on the bottom of the screen, and erase your map by clicking the Generate Map button.)

Now that you've got the cliffs and hills in place, you may want to add streams, lakes, and maybe even an ocean. Click the Map button in the Brush Type menu at the bottom of your screen and you'll bring up a new menu titled Terrain.

You may want to place deserts around your cliffs and then a river running through your desert—the options in this menu will let you place terrain tiles throughout your map. You may, for instance, try clicking on desert terrain and small brush. Bring your pointer to the map and place desert tiles one at a time by left clicking your mouse, or lay a row of desert tiles by holding the left button down and dragging your mouse.

Try experimenting with the different terrains. You may want to build a forest-covered island in the middle of your lake, or place a stream running along the top of your cliff. Hey, no one is checking your map for accuracy, so you can put that pine-forest island in the stream in the middle of your desert, on the top of your mountain.

Now that you have the basic map, it's time to decide how many and which nations will be competing. Click the player button at the top of the screen.

There's nothing tricky about setting up the game. Simply click each of the 13 menus along the bottom of the screen and select the options that fit. It's very straightforward. If you want your nations to concentrate on fighting from the start, give them lots of food and resources and start them in the Bronze or Iron

Age. If you want a freewheeling battle, create several players. If you want a straightforward fight, create two nations.

Okay, so now you've got a Garden of Eden with no Cains and Abels to fight in it. Where should you put your nations and how will you set your battlefields?

"I usually put down player one and then the enemy so I know where they are going to be, then I start dropping in all the resources where I want battles to take place and stuff," says Rippy.

Rippy makes an interesting point. If there is one place where your men are likely to fight your opponents' men, it's near gold mines or quarries.

Look at your map and decide where you want to place your civilizations. It's usually a good idea to put a lot of space between your nations to act as a buffer, but you can place them right beside each other should you wish. You can even create a nomadic nation with nothing more than a villager and enough wood to build a town center.

You should begin by building your Player 1 civilization. Choose men and buildings from the scrolling menu along the left side of your screen, and place them wherever you wish. (Remember, if you have decided to create a mission that begins in the Stone Age, you will create an anachronism by placing centurions and juggernauts in the middle of your village. Not that anachronisms aren't great fun, it's just that a single centurion can skewer a tremendous number of clubmen, and that may take some of the mystery out of your mission.

The next step is to place resources around the map. If you want a scenario in which your civilizations spend time developing lots of technology, place lots of gold and stone around the map. If you would like to see a battle of attrition in which clubmen bash it out like college frat-boys in an apocalyptic pillow fight, limit the resources to wood and very little food. (Interestingly, Stone Age civilizations have no use for stone.)

To place stone, gold, trees, gazelles, elephants, lions, wild horses, alligators, and berry bushes around your map, stay in the Units directory, but select "Gaia" from the menu at the bottom of the screen. They're all there—the fish, the animals, the trees, the pathways, all of the ingredients that made the missions in Rise of Rome so attractive and wonderful.

Having these ingredients does not guarantee that your recipe will be a success. "Balance usually comes from watching people play," says Rippy.

"I've gotten it right on the first try a couple of times, but that's pretty rare. I usually have to go back and make a couple of changes."

Of course, some scenarios are fun precisely because they are out of balance.

Appendix B

CHEAT CODES

Suicide? Omnipotence? Nuke power? Flying cows? Yep, even Microsoft's Rise of Rome has weird cheat codes.

Making Rise of Rome Do What It Shouldn't

Before discussing the cheat codes in Rise of Rome, let's look at another fallen empire—Atari.

Warner Communications purchased Atari in 1976, and eventually installed a president named Ray Kassar, whose previous experience was managing Burlington Industries. Kassar tried to reign in the wildness that had nearly bankrupted Atari on multiple occasions, but his efforts often had stringent results and Atari became a repressive place.

Nervous that a competitor might try to hire his game designers, Kassar would not let his employees put credits on their games. Seeing themselves as artists, several game designers said that Kassar's policy was simply unfair. One of the offended designers was Missouri-born Warren Robinett.

As one of the first ten programmers hired to create games for the Atari Video Computer System (later known as the 2600 or VCS), Robinett saw Atari making millions of dollars from the VCS while he and the other programmers made far less than robust salaries. Most of the other original programmers left Atari and started their own companies, but Robinett stayed on.

In 1978, as he worked on a game titled Adventure, Robinett came up with a way to get his name into his game, even if no one would ever see it. He created a secret room with his name in scrolling rainbow colors.

Of course, no one would find that room. To enter it, you had to use a ladder to climb a wall, find the single active gray pixel in a wall full of gray pixels, take that pixel all the way across the game, and use it to open a single doorway.

Robinett never told his co-workers about his little prank. When he left Atari, in 1979, he believed that no one would ever know his secret. Then the

Egyptian
Black Rider

8
0
2
7

6/60

*Dark riders are tougher
than heavy horse archers
and cost no more than
villagers—literally.*

company got a telephone call from a kid in Salt Lake City, and Easter Eggs were born. (There is some debate over the first Easter egg. According to Keith Feinstein, founder of Videotopia—a traveling museum exhibit chronicling the history of video games—Space Invaders has an Easter egg, too. According to Feinstein, if you repeatedly pound all of the buttons on an arcade Space Invaders at the same time, a little banner appears.)

Easter eggs have become an accepted and encouraged part of the computer game industry. All of the fatalities in Mortal Kombat are nothing more than well-publicized Easter eggs. Galoob, 3DO, and Interact have manufactured products to help players access these cheat codes. There are books and magazines that publish cheat codes and Easter eggs, and there are dozens of sites on the Internet with these nuggets of information.

This brings us to Age of Empires and Microsoft's Rise of Rome, two games that would not be complete without a couple of Easter eggs. Having worked hard to invent these fun pranks, the jokers at Ensemble Studios are reticent about giving out their Rise of Rome codes without a fight, but the following is a fairly complete list of Easter eggs from Age of Empires. (Every code has been tested and works with Rise of Rome, too.)

To access these codes, click Enter to bring up the message window, then type the codes as they appear below. You'll get some fairly crazy results.

Lazy Good for Somethings

Tired of hardworking obedient villagers? Type MEDUSA in the message window and your villagers will turn into lazy sheep that go where you tell them to go, but refuse to chop wood, pick rock, or mine gold.

Why would you turn your villagers into such sloths? Simple, kill a medusa and it turns into a dark rider—something similar to a heavy horse archer with +1 attack points. If you're Shang, that gives you units better than heavy horse riders for 35 units of food!

And it doesn't stop there. Kill the dark riders and their strange metamorphosis continues as these once—useless villagers change into catapults.

Quiet and deadly, Ensemble Studio's laser gun-toting astronaut toasts all who get in his way.

Caffeine High

It doesn't make them move any faster, but if you're hoping to get a little more work out of your villagers, try typing STEROIDS in your message window. Your villagers will become veritable supermen—able to erect a town center or any other building by touching its foundation. Put a granary beside a berry bush, and your villager will turn into a blur as he strips berries and stores them away. They'll chop trees in the blink of an eye, kill elephants with a single spear, and mine stone and gold with insane efficiency.

It's not a perfect solution, however. Steroid-fueled villagers may work more quickly, but they'll still be half-brained drones who get lost easily and cannot defend themselves against axemen.

It's worth conjuring the Nuke Guy just to see the explosions he makes.

Darth Invader

Want to shoot something other than arrows, stones, villagers, and spears? Type PHOTON MAN in the message window and a little astronaut will join your army. This is no sweet, benevolent ET. Point him at the bad guys and he'll wipe them out with his rapid-fire, long-range laser gun.

Faster than a horse archer, more powerful than a heavy catapult, and more durable than an armored elephant, Winsett's Z is so cool you hate to call it cheating.

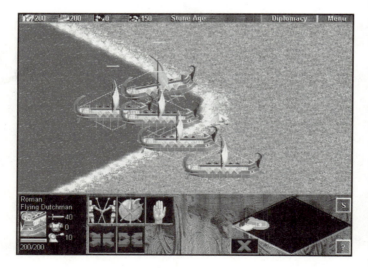

If only they could have done this with the Exxon Valdese!

Rocketman

There are two silent spacemen types in the Age of Empires universe. There's Photon Man, the guy with the laser gun, and the Nuke Guy, a missile-packing astronaut who can take out ships and elephants with a single shot.

To get the Nuke Guy, type E=MC2 TROOPER— but be warned, this guy is the catapult of the cheat code army. He's got a big and powerful weapon, but he won't fire if enemy units are crowding him.

Knight Rider of the Appian Way

If you thought horse archers were fast, just wait until you see Winsett's Z, a zippy little black Camaro that comes with a high-powered rocket launcher as standard equipment. Fast, sleek, and powerful, this weapon of the nineties makes the scythe chariot look obsolete.

To add Winsett's Z to your arsenal, you should type BIGDADDY.

True All-Terrain Vehicles

By definition, juggernauts are supposed to be unstoppable and indestructible. Ensemble Studios got it half right. Type FLYING DUTCHMAN in the message window and your juggernauts will no longer be bound by lack of water. They'll sail right up to and over the shore, across the plains, and into your enemies' territory.

How do flying juggernauts compare to heavy catapults? They don't shoot as far or do as much damage, but they are more than twice as fast and one-third more durable.

When Nature Calls

If you're tired of seeing cruel villagers subjugating poor defenseless animals, you can join the virtual animal liberation front by typing GAIA in the message window. You'll lose control of your villagers, but gain control of the animals on the map.

The gazelles do little more than hop around, the birds barely change direction at your command, and the villagers you once controlled will eat your new subjects for dinner.

Snatched From the Jaws of Defeat

If you think winning with a wonder is cheap gaming, just wait until somebody pulls this prank on you. Type HOME RUN in the message window, and the computer instantly credits you for winning the match or the scenario!

You Won't Take Me Alive

You're playing some Microsoft team leader, and he sends you the message, "I am GanGus. FEAR ME." You know what's next: an all-out assault, and you're not going to win. Type HARI KARI in the message window and everybody in your civilization dies. Sure you lose, but old GanGus will have done all of his boasting for nothing—unless he was bluffing. In which case, you're really toast!

Smart Bomb

If there's no way out, and you absolutely can't cope with the thought of losing, here's a really despicable code you use. Typing DIEDIEDIE kills all of your opponents. You might also want to type, "I am a really, really bad sport who should be ostracized from future games," but that doesn't activate any special codes.

The Honorable Exit

While one of the pleasures of Rise of Rome is getting to finish off your enemies, there is nothing wrong with admitting defeat. If your civilization has been crippled and it's just a matter of waiting for your opponent to finish the job, you can forfeit the game by typing RESIGN in the message window. It's not as sporting as allowing your enemy to savor his victory, and it's not as cinematically gruesome as killing your civilization off with HARI KARI.

Eliminate the Competition

You're in an eight-man game. Seven of you are mortals, and one of you is Robert Howg (see Chapter 11). You could all gang up on him, but do you really trust those other guys? Type KILL8, assuming Howg was player number eight on the Settings screen, and your problem is solved.

Typing KILL and an opponent's civilization number instantly annihilates that opponent.

I Can See Clearly Now

Ever felt like you'd give your soul to know what your opponents are doing? Type NO FOG in the message window and the fog of war will lift from the map. You won't see areas you've not explored, but you will be able to see if enemies have moved into areas you've explored without having to place a unit in their line of sight.

The Columbus Command

There are three ways to reveal the entire map. The first is the honest and old-fashioned way: have your units explore every inch of it. The second works only

if you have allies. Research writing in your government center and you get to see the areas your allies have explored.

The third way involves a cheat code. Type REVEAL MAP in the message window, and you'll be able to see everywhere on the map, but the fog of war will prevent you from seeing if your enemies are there. (Type NO FOG and the fog will go, too.)

Remember: just being able to see something doesn't mean you can build here. Just because you've cheated doesn't mean that your villagers have. You will not be able to place buildings in areas not yet explored until you send a unit there.

Free Stuff!

Looking for a handout? Using codes to add to your resources isn't as cheap as killing your opponents, but it's pretty cheeky.

Typing QUARRY gives you 1000 units of stone, PEPPERONI PIZZA gives you 1000 units of food, COINAGE gives you 1000 units of gold, and WOODSTOCK gives you 1000 of wood. These codes seem almost forgivable for players in a handicapped situation.

The Broccoli Men

You may already have horse archers and elephant archers, but here's a new one to add to your collection: tree archers. By typing DARK RAIN, you will disguise your bowmen as trees. When they move or attack, they will turn back into humans—but when dormant, your bowmen will reassume their arbor disguise.

This, believe it or not, is one of the few tricks that works better against human

Popping in and out of disguise, these archers look like a cross between a maple tree and a clump of broccoli.

One cheat code makes your priests veritable supermen, able to approach and convert such previously unattainable prospects as ballista towers and scythe chariots.

Borrowing a page from Monty Python and the Holy Grail, the catapults in Rise of Rome hurl more than stones.

opponents than the computer. The computer seems to see right through the costume, but an unalert human is likely to overlook a small grove of trees in the middle of a barren desert.

They Won't Take No for an Answer

Martyrdom is a very good weapon, but why kill yourself when it's so much easier to be an immortal? Type HOYOHOYO, and your priests' hit points go from a maximum of 50 to a chilling 600 points. With 600 hit points, you can send your priests to convert ballista towers and they will survive.

Human Cannon Fodder

Type JACK BE NIMBLE and your catapults begin hurling villagers and cows instead of stones. The human projectiles fly like skydivers when fired at distant targets and tumble in the air when

fired at nearby marks. The cows are less acrobatic in their final moments.

The good news here is that flinging villagers does not count against your populations, and it does not reduce the amount of damage you inflict.

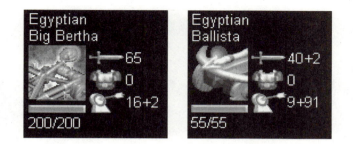

A less dramatic but more reasonable cheat: upgrading your siege weapons.

More Fun with Catapults

The car, the futuristic warriors, and the enemy-killing codes may all be completely below the belt, but other codes are merely mild.

If you would like to increase your ballistas' attack range, type ICBM and it will increase 1000 percent. While there is no code to increase your catapults' range that much, you can increase their range and attack strength slightly while raising their hit points to 200 by typing BIG BERTHA.

Appendix C

THE RISE OF ROME TEAM

Ensemble Studios is the perfect name for the company that designed Microsoft's Rise of Rome. The dictionary definition of ensemble—"a group comprising an organic whole"—fits the development perfectly. Speaking with Tony Goodman, whose Ensemble Studios titles include founder, CEO, president, lead art director, and executive producer, you quickly realize that Rise of Rome was the product of many talented people working together in an amazingly cohesive environment.

Though he downplays his involvement, Goodman brought a certain practicality to the project. He is a businessman with an eye for projects stamped for success. His approach to making games is intelligently customer-driven. Goodman knew he had a winner in Age of Empires because he had all of the right elements.

"We had done everything we could do to position Age of Empires to be the program that could take over the world," says Goodman. "We got Bruce Shelley, co-designer of Civilization. We picked the most epic topic—the Greek Empire. We put together a team of fantastic artists and technical people."

The plan worked. Within four months of its release, Age of Empires hit the million mark in units shipped. It was an international success. It sold very well in the United States, but did even better elsewhere. Sixty percent of the game's sales were overseas. When asked if he expected the game to sell as well as it did, Goodman admits surprise. "Yes, we were very surprised. This was the year of the strategy game. I remember Johnny Wilson [editor of Computer Gaming World] doing an article about 50 strategy games coming out this year. I mean, every company was doing one, and which ones would survive and which one will actually win were big questions."

"StarCraft was the earliest favorite, but it shipped last. Everybody knew that StarCraft would be a big winner because it was sort of like a sequel. Then Dark Reign was the big thing, but Total Annihilation came up on it. Age of

Empires always got a, 'Keep your eyes on Age of Empires' write-up. People knew that Bruce Shelley was doing it, and that stood for something—but when it released, we didn't know how the other products were going to do."

Much of the team that created the original Age of Empires returned to work on Rise of Rome. One particularly noticeable exception, however, is Rick Goodman, Tony's brother. The lead designer of Age of Empires, Rick has gone off on his own to form his own company. Sandy Petersen, formerly of id Software, has stepped in to fill his space.

"Sandy Petersen was the senior non-owner at id," says Goodman. "He worked at id for years. It was a great opportunity for him to work at id, but if you look at the kinds of games he's designed, he's really a complex game designer, and he wasn't fulfilling his life's quest."

"Bruce Shelley, who knew him from MicroProse, called me and mentioned that he had a friend who might be interested in our game design position. We talked to him, and it was just the perfect match. He's happy because he gets to do the complex types of games that he likes to do."

According to Bruce Shelley, Petersen brought an everyday gamer's tastes and sensibilities to the Rise of Rome project. "Sandy's got an incredible imagination. He's a very good writer and researcher. I consider him like every man in terms of his tastes about what is fun to play, so he was the perfect balance for Tim Deen [lead programmer on Rise of Rome], who is a very hardcore gamer and a very detail-oriented player."

This goes back to the Ensemble team being an organic whole. Despite all of his wide-market savvy and success, Petersen is not the company's most experienced gamer. That accolade, according to Goodman, would belong to Tim Deen.

"Tim Deen understands games better than anybody in our company. He can do anything in the company. He can be a designer—he can be a producer. He loves programming. He knows games and real-time strategy games better than anybody in the world."

"I always thought Tim was an astounding genius. He can tell instantly whether a game idea will or will not work. If anybody has an idea, they run it by him and he can tell you if it will be fun. He buys two games a week and plays them all the way through. He doesn't pick up a game unless he is going to finish it."

Petersen and Deen are not the only Ensemble forces that counterbalance each other. Even with this duo wrestling together to create a game that will thrill casual gamers while keeping the hardcore audience happy, Ensemble needed skilled programmers to bring Rise of Rome to life. Those skills came in the form of a team of programmers, each with unique skills and talents.

One person whose skills have been invaluable was Dave Pottinger, the man who designed the Age of Empires game engine and artificial intelligence. According to Goodman, Pottinger's meticulous nature melds perfectly with the ultra-fast programmers on the Ensemble team. "I met Dave over the Internet and we decided to get together at a Computer Game Developers Conference, and it was like an instant match. It was perfect. He was exactly what we needed."

"We had Angelo Laudon and Tim Deen on board. Those two are incredibly fast programmers. Dave Pottinger's skill is thinking the model all the way through from the infrastructure and building the perfect engine. He's incredibly structured, and the other guys are incredibly fast."

Goodman says that the programming team was perfected when Matt Pritchard joined. "The next guy to come in was Matt Pritchard, one of a few people in the country like John Carmack (the game engine designer of id Software). Just a few people have the incredible low-level optimization skills to do what he's done."

One person who seems to prefer going unnoticed is sound director and scenario designer Chris Rippy. Gracious and genuinely friendly, Rippy is the varmint who came up with most of the puzzles and tricks that have permanently marred the lives of so many single-player gamers. He is also the sound director. Every time you hear a villager scream or a fishing boat sink, that's Chris Rippy's work.

In typical Ensemble fashion, however, Chris is not the only Rippy who had a hand in Age of Empires and Rise of Rome. David and Steven Rippy, Chris's brothers, did the music for the games. As Goodman put it, "Now here's a family of people with ears."

Finding detail-oriented programmers and time-efficient workers is challenging, but getting them to work together in a perfectly orchestrated mass takes a more rarefied talent. It takes leadership, a quality the Ensemble team gets from one of its newest members. That leadership came in the form of production leader, Harter Ryan.

"Harter Ryan was a key acquisition. He's the leader around the company now," says Goodman. "He's the person who rallies the troops, the person who can lead the troops through hell. He sends out orders and everybody wants to do it. He's not hesitant about giving marching orders, and he has a way of doing it that gets everybody on board."

Loading and Starting

First things first. You're anxious to start playing, but installation and setup are necessary first steps. And you've got to get these right.

Loading Rise of Rome

It's time to discuss the basics of playing Microsoft's Rise of Rome.

First, in order to play Rise of Rome, you must have Microsoft's Age of Empires already installed on your computer (which means you must have an IBM-compatible personal computer with Microsoft Windows 95 or Windows 98). To load Rise of Rome, place the CD into your CD player—that's the little sliding tray that first-time users sometimes mistake for a drink holder. (No, I did not make that up. Ask a repairman at your local computer store.)

Both Age of Empires and Rise of Rome are Windows 95-compatible, meaning that if you have Windows 95 or Windows 98, your computer will recognize your CD when you place it in the drive. Help windows will automatically appear to walk you through the loading process.

The first screen will ask if you want to install Rise of Rome, exit the installation program, or connect to the

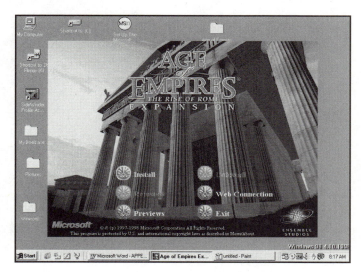

Click the top icon on the left to load Rise of Rome on your computer.

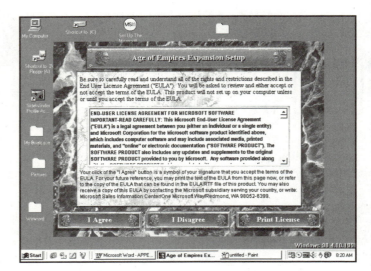

This screen informs you of the implicit legal agreement that comes with installing a game on your computer.

This screen lets you decide which Rise of Rome files to load into your hard drive.

World Wide Web. The answer to this little multiple-choice ditty is A. Install. Click the little round seal beside that selection.

Before beginning the loading process, the installation program will display a window describing the legal ramifications of loading software on to your computer. It's all very standard—just click Yes and respect Microsoft's copyright.

The next screen lets you decide how much of Rise of Rome you want to install on your computer. The Minimum Setup option places only those files needed to run the game into your hard drive. The Typical option stores the same files as the Minimum option, but also includes on-line help files in the installation.

The final option, Full Setup, places the cinematic files on your hard drive. The only reason for installing these files is so that they come up quickly when encountered in the game (you only see these cinematic sequences as you start the game and when you begin or end an entire campaign). You don't need to load these files into your computer to see them, so Typical Setup is likely the best choice.

You will next be shown a screen with a large oval meter which indicates your computer's progress as it loads Rise of Rome into the hard drive.

Next, you are asked if you would like to register Rise of Rome electronically. If you have a modem, on-line registration is a very easy option. If you would rather get to playing, click the Continue option and your computer will complete the installation process.

Once you have registered or selected to continue, you'll return to the help screen displayed at the start of the process. Note that the screen now has three new options—Play Rise of Rome, Reinstall Rise of Rome, and Uninstall Rise of Rome. Click Play to move on.

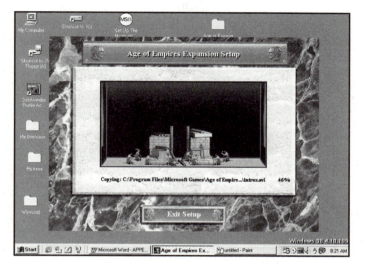

This meter displays the progress of the loading process.

This screen lets you quickly register your copy of Rise of Rome via modem.

Starting the Game

Rise of Rome opens with an animation of an ancient battle. Glorious and cinematic as it is, you may get tired of watching it after you've seen it several times. You can skip it by clicking the left button on your mouse or by tapping the space bar on your keyboard.

After the animations, you'll see a screen with buttons that let you access single and multiplayer games, on-line help, and the scenario builder. Each of these options are discussed elsewhere in the book (see the Table of Contents for specific information).

The Original Campaigns

The following is a complete mission-by-mission account of the campaigns presented in the original edition of *Microsoft Age of Empires: Inside Moves*. The scenarios have been variously rewritten or re-edited for presentation here.

The Egyptian Scenarios

The Egyptian missions of Microsoft's Age of Empires may be considered a unique tutorial designed to acclimate players to the game. It's nearly impossible to lose the first few missions, but the scenarios become more challenging quickly.

Mission 1: Hunting

The goal is to increase the population of a Stone Age village from one person to seven.

You begin this mission with one villager, 50 units of wood, 30 units of food, and a town center. Assign your villager to hunt gazelles. As he increases his food supply to 50 units, create another villager and assign him to join the hunt. Continue training new villagers and sending them to hunt every time you accumulate 50 units of food.

Once you train your fourth villager, assign him to build a house. When the house is complete, send him to join the hunt.

Continue training villagers. You complete the scenario when your seventh villager appears.

Ways to Lose

The only plausible way to fail this mission is to kill your first villager by having him meander aimlessly around the island until he is caught and killed by either of the two tremendously slow-moving alligators residing along the shoreline.

Additional Hints

Chase the gazelles toward your town center as you hunt them. It will cut down the time your villager spends traveling to deposit the meat from his kill.

Do not worry about gathering wood—you are given enough wood at the beginning of this mission to survive.

Mission 2: Foraging

The purpose of this mission is to acquaint you with gathering berries from bushes. You are also required to build a granary, a storage pit, and a dock to complete it.

You begin this mission with three villagers and a town center. There are two palm trees and two bushes within sight of your town center. Start this mission by assigning all three of your villagers to pick berries—that way they will quickly pick enough food for a fourth villager. As soon as you have 50 units of food, you can train a new villager and assign him to cut down wood. (You can also assign one of your original villagers to cut down wood so that you have quick progress on both wood and food. You'll need a lot of wood to finish this mission.)

You will need to build a house before you can create a fifth villager. Once your woodcutters finish chopping down the first palm tree, assign one of them to build a house. By the time he finishes, you will have more than enough food to create more villagers and begin looking for more trees and food.

Though it's no Yosemite National Forest, there is a nice grove of trees just east of your village. As you get more villagers, begin sending some of them to this grove for wood. Once they've gathered 120 units, you can build a storage pit by the forest.

With a team of three or four woodcutters shuttling wood to a nearby storage pit, you'll quickly accumulate more than enough wood to successfully finish this mission.

The next job is locating a big cache of berries and building a granary beside it. Send two foragers across the sandbar, located southeast of your village, where they will find enough berries to feed all of Stone Age Cairo. Build a granary beside the berries.

The last task is to build a dock in any large body of water on the map. Once you build the dock, the mission is over.

Ways to Lose

There are three alligators on this map. Avoid them or kill them—but do not let them kill your villagers.

Additional Hints

You can make this scenario go faster by pressing the plus key on your keyboard and making the game move at twice the speed.

Mission 3: Discoveries

Your job is to find five hidden sacred symbols before the Libyans find them. Before you can look for the symbols, you need to establish a village.

You begin this mission with one villager, 15 units of wood, and 90 units of food—more than enough food to create your next villager. Start training a second villager as you send your first one to chop down the nearest tree.

When your second villager appears, send him to forage berries from the bushes southeast of your town center. As soon as your villager drops his first load at the town center, begin creating a third villager. When that villager appears, assign him to forage from the same bush as the first villager.

You should have three or four villagers before the first Libyans show up at your front door. These first Libyans are hunters who won't cause any problems—they are looking for sacred sites.

You goal is to create villagers, gather food, and build a couple of houses as quickly as possible. Assign one of your berry pickers to build a house, create more villagers, and keep the raw materials pouring in. You need villagers—fast! Once you have two houses, you can stop chopping wood and concentrate on food.

When Libyan scouts ride in to your town, group your villagers together and attack them. Five villagers will have little trouble defeating a scout.

Once you have between eight and ten men, you should search for the sacred symbols. The first site is just below the stand of trees to the south of your village. Send a group of villagers to kill the lion guarding the site, then have a villager walk over the site to mark it. A blue flag will appear.

The second sacred site is in the southeast corner of the map. Send four villagers to this site. If you send a single man, he may fall pray to the Libyans. Leave a marker on this site by walking over it and move on to the next site.

Site number three is north of your village, just past the herd of gazelles. The fourth site is in the middle of the map, just beyond the stony ledge of that cliff. There is a Libyan village by this site—and they may spot and attack your villagers.

Should a Libyan scout attack you as you pass the town center, do not stay to fight. There's no advantage in fighting at this point. As he attacks one villager, send the others toward the grove of trees to the east. The last site is right beyond the trees.

Be sure to send more than one villager on this last leg, there is a lion guarding the last site.

Ways to Lose

Spend too much time trying to decide what to do next, and the Libyans will find all of the sacred symbols before you. Do not waste time building too large an army or fighting the Libyans.

Additional Hints

Do not bother trying to defend the southwest site even if it is just below your village. You will need too many men too quickly, and it will distract or stop your all-important race to forage for food and create more men.

Mission 4: Dawn of a New Age

Your goal in this scenario is to advance your civilization from a Stone Age tribe of hunter-gatherers to a Tool Age town of fisher-hunter-gatherers.

You begin this mission with three villagers and no supplies. Send your villagers to chop enough wood to build a dock, three houses, and fishing boats. You will need 100 units of wood to build a dock, and an additional 50 units of wood for each fishing boat you construct.

Once you have 100 units of wood, begin building a dock in the water with one edge touching the shore. As you gather more wood, build at least three houses and four fishing boats.

You need to construct two Stone Age buildings and gather 500 units of food before you can advance to the Tool Age. The dock counts as one building, and you can build a storage pit near your wood supply as your second.

Once you have built the dock and one house, you can start launching fishing boats. Look around the water for fish or whales. When you find some, left click your boat to select it, then right click a tile in which you saw the fish or whales to send your boat fishing in that area. The boat will automatically shuttle between the dock and the tile until it has caught all of the fish in that area.

You can advance to the Tool Age as soon as you have 500 units of food. Left click your town center, then click the Tool Age icon along the bottom of the screen to evolve to the Tool Age.

Ways to Lose

Send lone villagers after elephants—and he'll get stomped.

Additional Hints

There are no other nations in this level, so don't bother building a trading ship—you'd just waste wood and time.

Once you launch your fishing boats, your landlocked woodcutters become unimportant. Do not create more villagers—it will needlessly prolong the mission.

Mission 5: Skirmish

The Upper Egyptians have sent three archers and four axemen to raid your territory. You must kill the invaders.

You begin this scenario with three archers and four axemen, the exact same army the Upper Egyptians have sent against you.

Begin the mission by separating your men into two groups—axemen and archers. You may wish to hot key the archers as group one and the axemen as group two by

selecting the archers and pressing Ctrl-1 on your keyboard, then selecting the axemen and pressing the Ctrl-2. Whenever you press the 1 or 2 key from this point on, you will automatically select your archers or axemen. Keep your axemen in front of your archers to protect them, and use your archers to soften up the enemy at long range before your axemen confront them.

Once you have grouped and arranged your army, march them toward the north edge of the map. They will come to a small grove of trees just east of the lake. Send your axemen around the top of the grove and have your archers move around the lower edge of the trees.

There is an Upper Egyptian axeman guarding a stone ledge just below the trees. Have your archers get close to the edge and shoot him. If you position your archers so that they face northwest of the axeman instead of parallel to him, you will pin him against the ledge and he will not be able to escape.

Next, have your archers rejoin your axemen at the top of the trees, then send your entire army up the slope to the right of the trees.

There is an Upper Egyptian axeman in a crevice just beyond the top of the slope. Have your archers march to the edge of the crevice and shoot him. He will walk out of range and attempt to climb out of the crevice and attack your archers. Have your axemen kill him.

Two Upper Egyptian archers will follow him. Have your archers take out one archer and one of your axemen kill the other.

You will find the last Upper Egyptian archer by the cliff to the south. Have all three of your archers shoot him.

The final Upper Egyptian raider is an axeman hiding in the easternmost part of the crevice. Have all four of your axemen hack him apart.

Ways to Lose

Do not rush into this battle. Remember, your archers take out their axemen, and your combined forces demolish their archers. Lose your axemen and your archers won't stand a chance.

Additional Hints

Do not let your archers follow that first Upper Egyptian axeman if he walks away. He will lead them toward the two enemy archers guarding the cliffs to the east.

Try to herd your axemen so that they are always in your archers' line of sight.

Have your archers attack enemy soldiers when they are in geographical traps such as on ledges and in crevices from which they cannot fight back.

Mission 6: Farming

There are two distinct objectives to this mission: finding the fabled ruins and building farms.

You begin this level with a Tool Age village, three villagers, three clubmen, and 100 units of wood, food, gold, and stone. You also have barracks and a granary with three nearby foraging shrubs.

Assign all of your villagers to forage those bushes. As your foragers gather food, create one villager to help forage, and three soldiers to guard your village, then upgrade your soldiers from clubmen to axemen.

You will be attacked from the north—a hunter, followed by a lone clubman, followed by four axemen, followed by a fifth axeman, followed by another clubman. The axemen are the only real threat—but if you keep your foragers gathering food while your axemen fight the invaders—you will be able to create additional soldiers should you need them.

Once this initial battle is over, the Nubians will not attack for a while. Use this time to store up food and build your village. Build your work force to six villagers— two chopping wood and four gathering food. Once you have 150 units of wood, assign one of your villagers to build a market.

By the time the market is finished, your villagers will have picked all of the berries from the bushes near the granary. Have them clear the trees away from your granary and build a ring of three farms around it. You will want to build a second granary and have up to six farms up and working before too long.

Build a storage pit north of your village around the area where you fought the Nubians. Once it is erected, your woodsmen will harvest wood more quickly. At this point you should rebuild your army and take the offensive.

Research the toolworking to increase your axemen's attack strength, then send your axemen to destroy the houses that the Nubians have constructed on your side of the river. Once the houses are destroyed, place some axemen and some bowmen by the land bridge to guard against further Nubian encroachments.

By this time the Nubians will have also built a dock just north of the land bridge. Build your own dock and a fleet of four scout ships to destroy their scout ships and their dock.

With their dock destroyed and your territory well protected, prepare to invade the Nubians. If you have worked quickly, they will not have much of an army. Their defenses will consist of bowmen and a guard tower.

Assign your axemen to their archery range, stables, and barracks while your bowmen engage their bowmen and villagers. Once their population is destroyed, destroy their town center. (If you built a navy, your scout ships should be able to do the job.)

After you have finished massacring the Nubians, send a single axeman or scout along the southeast edge of the map. The ruins will change color, once he passes them, from red to blue signifying that you have captured it.

The last objective in this mission is to accumulate 800 units of food. Once you have neutralized the Nubians and found the ruins, simply wait until your farms produce enough food.

Ways to Lose

That first Nubian incursion poses a very serious threat. If you have thrown all of your resources into creating villagers and harvesting food, they may overpower your soldiers and destroy your village.

Additional Hints

If it looks as if your soldiers are going to lose that inaugural fight with the Nubians, have one of your villagers abandon the village and hide in the southern corner of the map. Have him return and resume picking berries when the Nubians are finished destroying your houses.

You can defeat an entire enemy fleet with one ship if you have the ship fight from along the shore. Post a villager beside the ship and have him do repairs on it as it takes damage. Enemy ships usually ignore peasant repairmen—so they will not shoot him.

Make sure to watch for new villagers as you destroy the Nubian town center. Kill them as they appear.

You do not have to destroy every Nubian building and kill every Nubian to win this mission. Once they are too crippled to stop your progress, concentrate on finding the ruins and producing food.

Mission 7: Trade

Pharaoh requires that you give him a tribute of 1000 units of gold and 1000 units of stone to help him build a monument. You have a good supply of stone near your village, but you'll have to trade with your neighbors for the gold.

You begin this mission with a Tool Age village, three villagers, a dock, a granary, and a storage pit. Your resources include 200 units of food, 200 units of wood, and 200 units of stone.

Start by training new villagers while assigning your existing villagers to forage for berries in the nearby bushes. When your fourth villager appears, have him chop wood from the forest by the storage pit. As you create new villagers, assign them to chop wood and forage. When you have enough wood, build a fishing boat and two trading boats.

To get through this mission quickly, you may want to train as many as 20 villagers. In the beginning, you will need to build a few farms, but as you gain control of the waters, you can send fishing ships to take care of your food. At that point, you should assign 16 of your villagers to chop wood while the other four mine stone.

All three of the civilizations in this scenario have ports, but only the Canaanites are friendly. That does not mean, however, that the Libyans and Babylonians cannot be made to cooperate.

Build stables and a market, then build farms and gather enough food to enter the Bronze Age. Research wheels in your market and train chariots. Upgrade from scout ships to war galleys in your dock, then send a fleet to destroy the two Babylonian catapults on the small island at the bottom of the screen. Next, send ten chariots to kill the Libyans and destroy all of their buildings, except their docks.

You now control the waters and have no enemies left alive.

Upgrade from trading boats to merchant ships and begin sending ships to trade wood for gold at all three docks. The Canaanites will give you the best terms, so be sure to send the biggest fleet of merchants to their dock. Send them to these ports to trade lumber for gold.

Along with 1000 units of gold, you need 1000 units of stone to complete this mission. There is a large deposit of stone in a desert west of your village. Build a storage pit beside the stone deposits and collect your quota.

Ways to Lose

The Libyans have a ballista and the Babylonians have two catapults. Be careful as you destroy these targets—they can get the upper hand if you're careless. Once you've destroyed their weapons, you've pretty much won the match.

Additional Hints

Have your first villagers forage for berries so that you can create more villagers to chop wood. The key material in this mission is wood. You need wood to build boats and to trade for gold. Don't waste time and materials building lots of farms—they won't help.

Mission 8: Crusade

The objective of this scenario is to convert the Libyan's ballista.

You begin this mission with 100 units of wood and food, a Bronze Age village, four villagers, and a priest. The village has bushes for foraging, a temple, barracks, a storage pit with nearby forests and stone deposits, and a granary. There's a small gold deposit (300 units) a little southeast of the village, just beyond the fog of war.

Begin by training two villagers and assigning three of your villagers to gather food. Send the fourth villager to mine gold. When your two new ones arrive, send them to mine gold, too. Use the gold to purchase the astrology (conversion effectiveness) upgrade, to train a second priest, and to train composite bowmen.

As your foragers store more food, train eight axemen and four bowmen. Once you've upgraded your priest and created axemen and bowmen, send them to the southern edge of your city.

Your village is built along the northeast edge of a lake.

If you are playing on the easier difficulty levels, the Libyan's bowmen will be spread out along the southern shore of the lake. Send your bowmen south, a few inches away from the eastern shore of the lake. When you get within range of the first bowman, have all four of your bowmen fire at him. Two more Libyan bowmen may come—you can kill them or have your priests convert them.

Next, sacrifice your axemen by sending them after the Libyan bowmen. Have your priests convert the ballista as it shoots your axemen, then bring it back to your town.

If you are playing on the harder levels, the entire Libyan army, complete with a ballista and several archers, will be in a clearing in the center of the map just south of that lake. On the harder levels, you should send your bowmen across the lake and have them attack from the west, then send your priests and axemen to come in from the east. Have your priests convert the ballista, then have your axemen escort it to your village.

Ways to Lose

If your priests die, you will be unable to convert the ballista. Protect them or you will have to start again. Also, make sure that your units do not attack the ballista. If it is destroyed, you lose. Finally, the Libyans will attack the ballista the moment it is converted. Make sure that your composite bowmen kill the Libyans before they kill the ballista.

Additional Hints

Don't bother upgrading your priest with double-hit points—use the gold for composite bowmen.

While priests can convert enemies from far away, they need to get close to their target when they heal. Bring your ballista to your priest—so that they are both far from the battle—if you need to heal the ballista.

This is a particularly fast mission. It should take between 20 and 30 minutes to complete. Do not waste time building too big an army—it's unnecessary and it can even work against you.

Mission 9: River Outpost

Your goal in this mission is to build a town center and two watch towers on the large island in the middle of the screen.

You begin this mission with a Bronze Age village, five villagers, 400 units of wood and food. There is a substantial deposit of gold in the northern corner of your village right beside a storage pit. You also have a granary, three berry bushes, and an elephant for food.

Assign one of your villagers to build a dock and one to chop wood while the other three pick berries. Begin training more villagers. You should train between 10 and 15 villagers with at least eight villagers cutting wood.

Upgrade to fishing ships and build two fishing ships to supply food once the berries are gone.

Upgrade your naval vessels to war galleys and build three war galleys. Have them go to the island in the middle of the map and destroy the watch towers. Once the towers are gone, use your galleys to kill the lions and alligators on the island.

Have one of your villagers build a government center, then build a light transport and send five of your villagers to the island. Have them build a town center near the stone deposits, then have them mine stone. Once you have 300 units of stone, divide your villagers into two groups and have them build towers.

Ways to Lose

Sending your villagers to the island before the towers and animals are gone will set you back, but nothing in this mission is likely to cause you to fail.

Additional Hints

At this point in the game, you should be looking for efficient ways to run your campaign. The waters around the island have several fishing holes and a couple of whales. Don't waste your time and materials building farms. Instead, create a couple of fishing boats and your food needs will be solved for the entire mission.

Remember, you cannot build a town center until you build a government center.

Sending your transport to bring a second load of villagers to the island will speed the construction process.

Mission 10: Naval Battle

The Libyans have stolen the Pharaoh's tribute. You must defeat the Libyan fleet, take the battle to their homeland, and recover the stolen booty.

You begin this mission with a Bronze Age village, three villagers, a market, a granary with nearby foraging bushes, a stable, a storage pit, a dock, and 200 units of wood, food, gold, and stone. Your first objective should be to gain control of the sea. Assign all three of your villagers to cut wood in the beginning, and purchase the war galley upgrade in your dock as you train more villagers.

Train more villagers. Send two to forage berries and have the rest chop wood. You will need the wood immediately as two Libyan scout ships will attack your dock.

Build a war galley as soon as possible. Send a villager to start repairing the galley as he defends the dock. As soon as you have enough wood, build two more scout ships to protect your shore, then build two fishing boats and upgrade to fishing ships. Send your fishing fleet after the schools of fish to the west of the dock—a Libyan sentry tower guards the waters to the north.

Have your galleys destroy the tower to clear the way for your fishing boats. Once you've finished with the tower, take control of the sea by destroying the Libyan dock, located on an island in the north corner of the map.

Group your galleys together, then send them to the dock. Libyan archers will attack your ship as you destroy the dock. Kill the archers as soon as they appear.

While your galleys clear the waters, create more villagers and begin mining gold from the deposits near your village. If you keep your gold, food, and wood harvesting teams throughout the naval battle, you'll have more than enough supplies to last you for the rest of the scenario.

Once the dock is destroyed, use your galleys to pick off the people and buildings on the Libyans' island. The galleys should be able to destroy all of the military buildings, the bowmen, the towers, most of the houses, and most of the villagers.

Next, build a light transport and train three scouts in your stables. Have the scouts board the transport and send them to the Libyans' island to reclaim the tribute.

By placing your galleys near their landing, you can set up protective cover should the last Libyans try to stop you. Have your scouts ride to the tribute and reclaim it, then bring the tribute and your scouts back to the transport. Load them and return to your base.

Ways to Lose

Do not let the Libyans overwhelm your dock in the beginning of the scenario. Also, monitor your galleys as you attack the Libyan dock. Their bowmen and towers will damage your ships, so make sure you have enough ships to sustain an attack, and be sure to send damaged ships back for repairs.

Additional Hints

Make sure you have a villager/repairman to fix your first galley. Two and possibly even three scout ships will attack it the moment it appears.

There are schools of whales in the waters off your shore. Don't waste your time on farms, make a fishing fleet.

This is a very easy level. Don't make it harder by over-strategizing.

Mission 11: A Wonder of the World

Pharaoh wants to build a wonder to celebrate the victory against the Libyans. You must collect 1000 units of wood, stone, and gold and build it.

You begin this mission with a Bronze Age village, four villagers, and 100 units of wood, food, gold, and stone.

Shortly after the scenario opens, Canaanite scout ships attack your dock. They will be followed by a transport loaded with swordsmen and archers. Begin the scenario by assigning all of your villagers to gathering wood as your train more villagers. You need to build at least three war galleys, which means that you must upgrade your navy as quickly as possible, then build at least three ships to fight off the Hittites' scout ships and stop their transport.

Once you've fought off the Canaanite, build fishing boats and upgrade to fishing ships. There are lots of fish in the waters off your dock, so fishing will be your best supply of food once you take control of the waters. The Canaanites will continue to harass you, so you'll have to send ships to their shores to destroy their dock and cripple their economy.

As you begin to accumulate wood and food, build up your navy and send a fleet of at least four ships to attack the Canaanite's dock and kill any villagers that come into range.

The dock is below a cliff along the southwest edge of the screen. A sentry tower overlooks the dock, so be careful not to get too close as you attack or the tower will attack your ships. The Canaanites also have priests, so be sure to kill them as soon as you hear them chanting.

Once you confine the Canaanites to their island, you can establish bustling trade routes. Both the Minoans and the Hittites have docks along the southeast edge of the map. Lead your trading boats to these docks and start your routes.

There is a huge deposit of stone on an island in the east corner of the map. Build a transport ship and send at least five men to mine the stone piles.

Only an Iron Age civilization can build wonders, so you are going to have to advance your people before you can start building the pharaoh's monument.

While your men mine stone and wood, construct two Bronze Age buildings. Continue collecting resources. When you have 1000 units of wood, gold, and stone, group all of your villagers together, get them in a wide open area, and begin building your wonder.

Ways to Lose

You must stop the Canaanites from harassing you. This mission will never end if they continue to send transports with swordsmen and catapults.

The only way to get gold if you accidentally destroy all of the other nations' docks, is to take it from the Canaanites island—and they don't seem to want to share. Don't get overly aggressive and accidentally attack the Hittites' and Minoans' dock.

Additional Hints

Wood is the key to everything in this mission. You need wood to build fishing boats for food. You need wood to take the battle to the Hittites. As soon as you have a decent fleet of galleys and fishing boats, go to your market and upgrade your woodcutters.

The Canaanites' dock has the most favorable trade rates. Kill them off without destroying their dock and the scenario will end more quickly.

You will be able to accomplish everything you need to with ships and villagers.

If you want to hurry through the end of the mission, use the Delete key to destroy your ships once you begin building the wonder. That will enable you to train more villagers to work at the construction site.

Mission 12: Siege of Canaan

To complete this scenario, you must develop a strong army and destroy the Canaanites' government center. You begin this scenario with a Stone Age village, three villagers, three archers, three clubmen, and 200 units of wood, food, gold, and stone. Your village consists of a few houses, a town center, and a barracks. There are berry bushes near your town center and trees just outside your village for wood.

Your situation is tenuous at the start of this scenario. The Canaanites have a larger and stronger army than yours just across a shallow river bank. They also have several bowmen and a sentry tower just north of your town center. Give away your position, and they will rush your village and kill your men.

Begin by sending your villagers to forage, training new villagers, and sending them to forage as well. You want to build a 15-villager work force to strip those berry bushes as quickly as possible.

Once the berries start to disappear, send several villagers east along the southern edge of the map. They will come to a large grove of trees. Have them build a storage pit and start chopping wood. As soon as the pit is built and you have 500 units of food, advance to the Tool Age.

Once you enter the Tool Age, build a market and two granaries near the southern edge of the map. When the market is complete, you will be able to build farms around the granaries.

You should also build a dock in the bay near the top of your grove of trees. There is a school of shore fish there, and you can build a scout ship. Use the scout ship to kill the Canaanite villagers who are foraging berries across the river. Then build a light transport and send a villager to build a granary and forage the berries.

With several farms and the berries from across the river, your food supply will be sufficient to upgrade your barracks units from clubmen to axemen. You can also research toolworking and leather armor in your storage pit. Finally, have a villager build a couple of stables, then upgrade to the Bronze Age.

Once you enter the Bronze Age, research wheels in your market and have a villager build a government center. From here on out, you will want to build town centers instead of storage pits.

Once your market has researched wheels, train five chariots, and launch an attack on the sentry tower overlooking your village. Canaanite bowmen and clubmen will come, but your axemen and bowmen will defeat them. Have your chariots guard the land bridge across the river as you explore your land.

Next build a temple and a siege workshop. Train a priest and have him heal wounded units.

You should research craftsmanship during this period to improve your bowmen's range. You might want to research nobility as well.

There are gold and stone mines on the plateau on which you destroyed the tower. Have a villager build a town center between them, then have him begin mining gold as you train additional villagers in that town center. Once you have enough food and gold, advance to the Iron Age. (There is a much larger gold mine to the north, send a villager to find it and build a town center beside it.)

Next build your army and prepare to invade. You will need to destroy the two Canaanite towers guarding the far end of the land bridge. Send a catapult to your end of the bridge, and have either composite bowmen or chariot archers to protect your catapult.

Once the towers are down, simply work your way up the terraced hill in the north corner of the map the same way you went across the bridge—using your archers to clear the way for your catapults, and your catapults to destroy any towers. The Canaanites' government center is in a fortress at the top of the hill.

Ways to Lose

Though they never upgrade their army, the Canaanites begin this mission with much stronger forces than you. If you stumble too far north in the beginning, they will find you and wipe you out. Do not go near their ledge or try to cut down trees from the grove to the west of your village.

Additional Hints

Don't worry about destroying the Canaanites' houses and granaries. You win as soon as you destroy their government center.

The Greek Scenarios

Heroes have existed as long as mankind, but the term and its definition are inseparably tied to Greece. Greece's gallery of great heroes is filled with familiar names such as Ajax, Hercules, Achilles, and Atlas. American school children learn about the Trojan War, and modern athletes run marathons and compete in the Olympics—all borrowed from Greece.

Greece was not always so glorious, though. The great nation that modernized the world was born of smaller nations that often struggled and fought with each other. In Age of Empires, you become a general in Greece's troubled days as a tribal land and its glorious days as an empire.

Mission 1: Land Grab

To complete this scenario, you must destroy the Dorians' farms while building five of your own. The Ionians and the Tyrinians will intervene on the part of the Dorians, making your job considerably more difficult.

You begin this scenario as a nomadic tribe consisting of six clubmen, four villagers, and 400 units of wood and food, and 100 units of stone. Your first task is to find a good place to settle and build your town center there.

As it turns out, there is a great spot to the east with lots of wood, berry bushes, and a lake with fish. Unfortunately the Tyrinians own it, so they become your first victims. Swarm their clubmen with your entire population. Once they are dead, have your villagers construct their town center beside the berry bushes and close to the trees.

Now that you have a home, get ready to defend it. Dorian clubmen will begin pouring in, and it won't take long until they upgrade themselves into axemen.

Though you start this scenario with the same amounts of wood and food, a lot of your wood goes into making your town center. Build two houses and send all of your villagers to collect wood as you train more villagers. Send one of your new villagers to build a dock on the lake in the southern corner of your land and rely on fishing for food.

Now that you have food and an ever-growing work force, build two barracks and two more houses. Work to enter the Tool Age as quickly as possible—your clubmen are no match for Dorian axemen.

Build a granary by one of the knots of berry bushes as soon as you can. Though there is more than enough fish to get you to the Tool Age, you will want to research walls as soon as you enter the Tool Age. Walling the Dorians out will give you an opportunity to build up your army and take offense.

Once you've secured control of your area, build two more granaries and place farms around them. This will give you good food production and fulfill one of the scenario objectives: to build five farms.

The Dorians' village is toward the western corner of the map. They have constructed watch towers in their village. While you should take eight or nine axemen to destroy the Dorians' houses and buildings, your army should consist mainly of bowmen. Even though towers have a larger attack radius than bowmen, your bowmen will be able to stand just outside that range and attack many of the farms that the Dorian towers are defending.

You complete the scenario when you destroy the Dorians' farms.

Ways to Lose

Heading north toward the Dorians' town center is sure death. They are already dug in, and they have a much larger population than you do.

Additional Hints

You are going to lose men destroying the farms closest to the Dorian watch towers. Deal with it!

Play aggressively. Build lots of villagers, advance to the Tool Age quickly, and march into the Dorian village as soon as you have at least 15 bowmen and 10 axemen.

If you see Dorians, Ionians, and Minoans attacking the same building, don't try to stop them. There are no allies in this scenario. Given the chance, the other nations will attack each other—you can kill the wounded survivors.

Mission 2: Citadel

In this scenario you are to capture the ruins outside of the Thebian city and build two Bronze Age sentry towers beside them.

You begin this mission with a Tool Age village consisting of a town center, a market, barracks, a granary, a storage pit, and some houses. You have three villagers, three clubmen, 400 units of wood, stone, and food, and 200 units of gold. Your village is in the southern corner of the map. The ruins are located along the northeast edge of the map, across a large body of water. Start this mission by sending your villagers to forage from the bushes in the western end of your village and building your forces.

Upgrade your army from clubmen to axemen while your villagers collect food. Position your axemen near the top of your village to intercept any Thebian soldiers that come to invade.

The Thebians are entering your land by crossing a land bridge from an island north of your territory. Send a villager to build a wall across that narrow neck of land. Build a dock near the wall and build two or three scout ships to defend that area. Then build fishing boats. There are several schools of fish in that area.

Since this scenario begins in the Tool Age, you can build an archery pit as soon as you have wood. Training archers to defend your wall is a good idea.

The Thebians will send scout ships and transports to harass you. Their dock is near the eastern corner of the map, at the end of a fairly narrow waterway that has watch towers along its northern shore. Once you have advanced to the Bronze Age and upgraded your ships to war galleys and artisanship, you'll be able to destroy the towers and the dock with a fleet of four galleys.

The Thebians have constructed several key buildings along the edge of their cliffs overlooking the water. You should use your ships to destroy these buildings as well.

Once you enter the Bronze Age, there's not much skill needed to finish off this battle. Your war galleys can clear the way to the ruins, near the west corner of the map. You can use your galleys to clear the Thebians away from the gold deposits that are on the peninsula north of your land, then send villagers to build barracks and a storage pit to hold the gold and barracks to train broad swordsmen for protection.

You should probably build a siege workshop and make a stone thrower to clear away the inland Thebian towers that your ships could not reach. There are two towers beside the ruins. Obviously they must be destroyed before you can claim the ruins and build your sentry towers.

Once you have your stone thrower and five or ten broad swordsmen, slash across the land bridge to the west and cut your way through the Thebians' land. This will knock the Thebians out of the rest of the scenario, and it will get you within catapult-range of the towers guarding the ruins.

Once the towers are down, send villagers to the ruins in a light transport and have them build two towers beside it. If you have not upgraded to sentry towers, you must do so now.

The scenario ends when your towers are upgraded.

Ways to Lose

In order to accomplish your mission, you must construct two towers sentry beside the ruins. You start the scenario with 400 units of stone—building the towers will require 300 of those units, researching towers costs 50 units of stone, and upgrading to sentry towers will cost an additional 50 units. In other words, build a wall or a tower in this mission and you will need to find more stone—and there is very little on this map.

If you are short of stone at the end of this unforgiving scenario, you'll have to start all over again.

Additional Hints

Don't build towers until you get to the ruins and you've disabled the Thebians to the point where they cannot destroy your towers.

Watch out for archers as you clear the buildings along the coast with your ships. A single archer can do a lot of damage to a galley, especially if it is too busy shooting a building to fight back.

Mission 3: Ionian Expansion

Your objectives in this scenario are to expand Athens' influence by building a government center in a flagged area on a heavily fortified Ionian-held island, or to find three sets of ruins.

You begin this mission with a Tool Age village, four axemen, five villagers, and 400 units of wood, food, gold, and stone. There is a small forest near your village, and you have a granary and plants to forage. You also have a storage pit, a market, and a dock on your shore. Once you gain control of the waters, fishing will be your best food source.

Build your work force to 15 villagers with 11 villagers chopping wood and four foraging berries. Your first task is to take control of the water, and to do that you will need to advance to the Bronze Age and create a fleet of five war galleys. Use your galleys to fight off any ships the Ionians send to invade you, then take the war to them.

The Ionians' are on an island along the northeast edge of the map. Have your galleys destroy any ships along their coast, then have them destroy one of the towers guarding their dock. Next, destroy their dock and everything and everybody that comes in range.

With your ships guarding your beachhead, you should be able to establish a powerful city on the Ionian island. If you have not already done so, build a government center on your island, and send four bowmen and a villager to the area you control on the Ionians' island.

Have your villager build a town center, a siege workshop, two barracks, and four archery rangers. You should have no trouble overrunning the island with axemen, bowmen, and two catapults. The Ionians will try to hit you with siege weapons, but their most effective weapon will be cavalry, which you can overwhelm with a swarm of bowmen.

Make killing military units, villagers, and houses a priority, and the Ionians will simply trail off. Once you control the island, have your catapults destroy the towers on the northwestern end, and build a government center.

Ways to Lose

This is a solid mission requiring good basic skills. It has no unique elements that threaten your success—you simply need to take control of the water, then invade.

Additional Hints

Attack houses and other buildings until they catch on fire, then stop. Then kill the Ionian villagers who come to repair the damage.

Don't worry about advancing to the Iron Age in this scenario. If you move quickly, you'll be able to finish the job with bowmen and stone throwers.

Make sure to upgrade your ships' attack range with woodworking and artisanship.

Mission 4: Trojan War

The King wants you to kill Hector, the hero of Troy, and capture a Trojan artifact.

You begin this mission with a large Bronze Age village that includes stables, barracks, and an archery range. You have ten villagers, several archers, axemen, farms, a heavy cavalryman hero, and 300 units of wood, food, gold, and stone.

The Trojans will invade you with a small force of axemen, catapults, and bowmen—just enough of a force to cut across your land if you do not prepare. (You can actually wipe out the entire invasion with your hero.)

Assign your villagers to chop wood and forage as you fight off the invasion and build your work force. You will need to assemble ten additional villagers so that you can assemble enough wood and gold to build a strong invasion force.

Build two additional docks along the beach on the western edge of your island, and make a large fleet of sea galleys. You will be able to seize control of the waters, but expect a tough a fight trying to destroy the Trojans' dock. They will greet you with catapults.

The Trojans' island is located along the southeastern edge of the map extending from the southern corner to the halfway point of the northeast edge. Their dock is straight across the map from your dock. While your fleet takes control of the waters, you should gather gold so that you can advance your civilization.

There is a small island off your shore, in the southern corner of the map that's crawling with gold and lions. Send a transport with four archers, and then a second transport with five villagers to the island. Have the archers kill the lions and leave, then have your villagers erect a storage pit and mine the gold. If the gold on that island is not enough, there's a second island just north of your base island that has 1500 units of gold and 600 units of stone. (This mission does not allow you to advance to the Iron Age, and you will not need to mount a major invasion—but if you want lots of wood, gold, stone, and food, this is a mission that provides it.)

There is a small island off the northern coast of Troy. This island is separated from Troy by a channel. Transport two stone throwers to the southern shore of that island and destroy the tower guarding Troy's north shore. A third tower, in the top corner of the island, will be just out of reach. Send your galleys to destroy it. You will likely lose one or two ships, but taking out that tower will set you up to finish the scenario.

With that tower destroyed, you can land your stone throwers on the Trojans' beach and have it destroy some of their other towers. Hector and several cavalry units will come to attack your stone throwers. Have your galleys kill them.

Once Hector is dead and the towers and cavalry are destroyed, you need simply send some cavalry into the walled area just below that beach. The artifact is behind those walls. The scenario ends the moment you reach it.

Ways to Lose

As usual, you are most vulnerable at the very beginning of this scenario. The Trojans will continue sending invasion parties until you knock out their dock and destroy all their transports. You need to block them as quickly as possible. (The double docks on your beach will prevent any landing in that area.)

Cutting off the Trojans' gold is also important. They will squander their gold on catapults if they have it. Trojan catapults will make your invasion far more difficult. Your ships will not have enough space to maneuver in the channel between the islands, and your stone throwers will not be safe as they attack the towers and walls around the artifact.

Additional Hints

Do not bother building farms or upgrading your farming capability. The foraging bushes and farms in your village will provide sufficient food until after you've destroyed the Trojans' dock. After that, get your food by fishing.

Other than storage pits, the only buildings you need to construct are a temple and a siege workshop.

Do not bother attacking the towers along the western edge of Troy—they are of no consequence.

Mission 5: I'll Be Back

After fighting a battle alongside the Minoans, you discover that they are not such great guys when they convert or kill everyone in your army. Your objective in this scenario is to help a few people escape, find a new army, destroy the Minoans' temple, and steal their precious artifact.

You begin with several cavalrymen and archers, but within seconds you will see the Minoans turn the fury of their army on you, and your last remaining cavalry must flee to safety. Your only chance is to select as many cavalry units as possible and have them run east to the beginning of the zigzagging trail that leads away from the Minoan stronghold.

Once your men get to the bottom, a team of archers will meet them. There's no time to fight these archers—flee to the shores to the east. With some luck, you should have four or five men left.

Get to the river quickly, enough and you'll see several Minoan ships sinking two Greek galleys. You will also find a transport. Load your men on that transport as quickly as possible and head south and west to an island in the middle of the map. There are several trails that lead across the island, but sandbars that make good unloading areas mark the two most direct trails. Once you have unloaded, hide your transport in a far corner of the map.

The first of these trails is a little narrower and more heavily guarded, but you can get to it quickly. It's in the center of the island. Have the transport take your men to the first trail if there are galleys chasing it.

Follow the trail south as quickly as possible. It will lead you past archers, towers, and a couple of ballistas. Run past them.

There's a very thin shoreline that leads west around the southern edge of the island. Parts of this shore may look blocked, but you can and must navigate that shore. Follow the shoreline west as quickly as possible. Three quarters of the way across the island, you will find a friendly transport. Load your men on the transport and head toward the southeastern or southwestern edge of the map.

Have the transport drop you on the east or west edge of the island in the corner of the map. One incredible army awaits you there. Revenge is at hand.

Your new army includes two catapults, six composite bowmen, four ballistas, four heavy cavalrymen (which are tougher than the men you started out with), four priests, six horse archers, six long swordsmen, four elephant archers, three heavy transports, two galleys, and the light transport which brought you to the island.

As commander of a new military machine, you should begin your revenge by taking your cavalrymen to the priests and having them healed.

You'll have to return the same way that you came. If you use your priests carefully on your return, you will be able to convert some of the ballistas on the island in the middle of the map. You do not need these ballistas, but the challenge of converting them is fun.

If the Minoan fleet has not destroyed your transports, use them to cross back to the first island. If they have, you will need to use your priests to convert transports and galleys from the center island so that you can take new army to fight the Minoans. To do this, use your elephants as bait to lure enemy galleys toward your men. While they shoot at your elephants, have your priests convert them. Repeat this process several times and you will have converted enough of a navy to do the job.

Next, use your freshly converted galleys to chase Minoan transport boats toward your priests. Your original transport only held five passengers. Dropping off five soldiers near the Minoans would be the same as giving them the death sentence.

Having cleared the seas between your forces and the Minoans, it's time to begin your landing. The Minoans still have four archers and a tower on the beach, your first ten invaders should combine power and fast shooting. Send two or three ballistas to clear out the archers, a catapult to destroy the tower and elephants for protection and you will clear the beach quickly. Send cavalrymen and archers for reinforcements while your first party clears the beach.

After you destroy the first tower, have your ballistas form a protective barrier blocking the mountain pass, and send your catapult to destroy the two towers on the lower levels of the mountain. There are six towers along that pass—use your catapult to destroy all of them.

As you destroy the towers, the Minoans will send waves of soldiers to stop you. Use your ballistas to chew through them before they make it down the mountain. The Minoans will also send priests down the path to convert your men. Have your catapult mash them. Once you have cleared your way to the trail, use you catapults to clear the train and your archers and cavalry to protect your catapults. Make killing priests your top priority, and you should have little trouble reaching the Minoan temple and taking their artifact.

Ways to Lose

The entire first half of this mission is one long opportunity to lose. Do not try to fight, just get as many men as possible on the transport and across the island.

Make sure not to lose all of your priests going after ballistas on your way back. Also, be sure to kill enemy priests quickly. If they manage to kill or convert your catapults, fighting your way back up the hill to the Minoan temple will be considerably more difficult.

Additional Hints

Have your catapult creep across the island in very small increments as you clear the ballistas, archers, and towers from the center island. Your catapults have a wider field of vision than ballistas.

Have your priests heal each other as soon as one gets wounded. Priests have only 25 hit points—they usually die if you wait to heal them.

Only include one catapult in your party as you make your way up the mountain for the final fight. In their zeal to assault the enemy, catapults tend to kill everything in sight, including your men. Keep the other catapults in a transport offshore for safekeeping.

Mission 6: Siege of Athens

The Spartans have declared war on Athens. (At least the red Spartans have—the yellow Spartans and the gold Spartans are still on Athens' trade route.) Sparta has sent an enormous army with cavalry, phalanxes, and more.

The Spartans will come with a large army and lay siege on your city, but you can prevail. Assign the farmers outside your city walls to seal the walls in front of your towers. There will be just enough stone to do this, so don't try to be fancy and make double walls, just something to cut off the Spartans' access.

Once the walls are sealed, you can try to protect the villagers outside the walls by hiding them in the trees at the top of the screen. They will be killed if they are discovered, but this gives them a chance of survival.

Next, place all of your archers along your walls, and place your war galleys at the corners of your walls. The Spartans may still crack through your walls—but even if they do, your towers and archers will have thinned and hurt them so much that they will pose no threat once they enter.

Once you have withstood the siege, the next steps will be rebuilding your economy and reclaiming the land outside your walls. To rebuild your economy, send villagers outside to the stand of trees along the top of the map, have them build a town center and begin cutting wood. Expand your fishing fleet, and send merchant ships to the friendly yellow Spartan dock in the bottom corner of the map to trade wood for gold.

Reclaiming your land should be equally simple. Having thrown themselves into the siege, the red Spartans will have few units left on your island, but the Aeginians have several heavy cavalry units waiting to attack you as you venture out from behind your walls.

You have the home-field advantage, however, as you can rebuild your forces as you fight. Train an army of 12 or more heavy cavalry and three priests, and you will easily overpower the Aeginians. The artifacts are on your island, in the west corner of the map. Defeat the Aeginians and no one will challenge you as you claim your prize.

Ways to Lose

Seal your towers and place your units near your walls to attack any Spartans who get through, and you've pretty much won. The only other danger is alerting the Aeginians to your city and having to endure a second siege.

Additional Hints

In some ways this mission is actually easier to beat on the harder levels. The Spartans will throw so much of their might into attacking your walls that you'll have less of an army to confront at the end of the mission.

If you are worried about food, you can send two of your villagers to hide in the northern corner of your land while the Spartans attack your walls. Kill enough Spartans outside your walls and they will leave without finishing off your farms.

Be sure to place archers along the inside of your wall to shoot the enemy.

Mission 7: Xenophon's March

In this scenario, you must help build an army, capture an artifact, and deliver it to your government center.

You begin this mission with 120 units of wood, four villagers, a priest, two heleopolises, and eight phalanxes. Use the wood to construct a storage pit, and harvest

all of the wood in your launch area. Then build a town center, houses, and farms so that you can build your food supply. By the time you leave your starting point, you should have over 1000 units of wood and food.

Moving ahead in small increments, lead your men north out of the valley. Have your phalanxes lead the way, moving nearly to the edge of the unfogged area created by your heleopolises line of sight, then move your heleopolises behind them. Move your priest and villagers last, and keep them a short distance behind the line. You will encounter lions as you move ahead. Kill them.

The Persians have a small town with barracks, stables, houses, and a town center just past the mouth of the valley. Use your heleopolises to destroy the entire town. Several broad swordsmen will attack your army as you destroy their buildings. Make sure your phalanxes are stationed in front of your heleopolises to protect them. Once the battle is finished, have your priest heal any of your men that were wounded.

There is a river behind the town you just demolished. Build a dock and a transport to get across it. There are enemies along the river, so build a trireme to any towers and archers. Now take your army south.

Bring your entire party to the clearing on the east bank of the south end of the river. Build a storage pit for your villagers to mine the gold in the clearing. Next, build a siege workshop and an academy and enlarge your army. Once you've added some heleopolises, several phalanxes, and a catapult to your ranks, head forward along a twisting path.

Blast through any walls you encounter, and kill all enemies who try to stop you as you head east. You will meet several enemy soldiers and a couple of buildings in the east corner of the map. Have your heleopolises level them all, then mine the gold behind the town center.

You will come to a city along the side of the lake. With ziggurats and more firepower than the other places you've destroyed, this sleepy hollow is prepared to defend itself and a temple with priests who may convince some of your men to switch sides.

Clear out the temple and the ziggurats, then blast a hole in the wall and place your catapult inside the wall for safekeeping. There is an artifact walled in the center of this area. Once you've destroyed the people guarding the artifact, punch and collect your prize. This will initiate a 2000-year clock—you have 2000 years to build a dock and a transport on the lake and get the artifact to your government center.

Have your catapult and heleopolises destroy the ziggurats guarding the lake, then have your villagers build a dock. Build your transport, and ship your cargo.

Ways to Lose

Waste your wood on anything but a storage pit at the very beginning of this scenario, and you're history. Just make sure that you keep a few healthy villagers nearby.

Additional Hints

Leave a villager and a storage pit in the clearing where you killed the two lions. He can continue to cut trees for you through much of the mission.

Leave a villager by your first town center to tend farms. Have him build two farms so that he can go to the second farm when the first one dries up. That way you will not have to check back to see what he's doing.

Don't bother trying to convert enemy archers—they are too likely to kill your priest. Converting war elephants and swordsmen is much safer.

Keep your catapult in the very back of your line with your priest and your villagers and only bring it out when you have to destroy walls and towers.

Mission 8: Wonder

In this scenario, your neighbors to the east and west are constructing wonders. Your job is to destroy both wonders or the civilizations building them.

You begin the final Greek mission with five heavy cavalrymen, five phalanxes, five composite bowmen, and five villagers. There are foraging bushes in your village, and you have 1000 units of food, 500 units of stone, 500 units of wood, and 500 units of gold.

You need to build up your workforce and your army as quickly as possible. Train 10 to 15 new villagers to chop wood, forage berries, and tend farms when the berries run out. You also need to build walls and towers at the north end of your city for protection—meaning you will need to mine stone.

While most of your villagers chop wood and forage berries, send three villagers to build three siege workshops and another three to mine stone. Create more villagers to cut wood, build a network of towers along the north entrance to your village, then build three towers along the western entrance and build a wall between the clumps of trees in the south.

The Persians have a large and powerful city guarded by ziggurats and filled with composite bowmen and legions. They also have a couple of catapults which must be destroyed before they get to your city. Since you will not have gold until you conquer Lydia, train scouts to attack the Persians' catapults.

The nation to the east, the Lydians, will complete their wonder shortly after the scenario begins. You must throw together an army with at least three catapults and all of your heavy cavalry to and break through their walls and destroy their wonder while fortifying your city to withstand the Persians. Make sure to include villagers in your army. The Lydians have two gold mines, and you will need that gold and more to succeed.

To make matters worse, you may not even reach the Lydians' wonder before the Phoenicians complete their wonder.

Do not stop building your army or your city while you attack Lydia. Construct a temple, train more scouts, build houses so that you don't get a "need more houses" message during the heat of battle, and build two more catapults.

Do not charge straight toward the Lydian's wonder with your invasion force. Head slightly north, then east so that you end up just north of Lydia when you reach the end of the map. Now move slowly southward with your catapults leading the way until you see the first guard towers along the Lydians' northern wall.

Have your catapults kill the archers inside the Lydians' walls, then destroy the towers. Once the towers are gone, inch forward killing archers and towers as they go. On the easier levels, the archers will simply wait to be slaughtered. On the harder levels, they will try to fight back.

Blast a hole in the wall and have your catapults inch forward, killing archers as they go. They will be able to fire on the Lydians' wonder before entering the wall. Have them destroy it, then send two of your catapults and all of your army, except your villager, back to your city to prepare to invade Phoenicia.

Have your remaining catapult inch through the city and kill the remaining archers and towers, then have your villager build a storage pit. As your catapult leaves, have your villager build a town center on the eastern side of the city by the larger gold mine. Then train a few new villagers and clean that mine out.

The next step is to invade Phoenicia. You should have at least three to five catapults, at least four heleopolises, and 25 foot or horse soldiers for this siege.

Approach the Phoenicians the same way you approached the Lydians from north of their city. Use your siege weapons to destroy the Phoenicians' towers. Though your catapults will do that job more quickly, you may want to use your heleopolises as Phoenician swordsmen and scouts will pour out in an effort to attack your catapults if you breach the walls. On the other hand, their greater range makes your catapults less likely to fall to the Phoenician priests who will try to convert them, and you can have your heleopolises pick off the priests and soldiers that come through the walls as your catapults destroy the towers.

Once you have punched out all of the towers, assemble your soldiers and heleopolises along the north wall and have your catapults destroy it completely.

As soon as the wall is down, have your heavy cavalry charge straight for the wonder. Only a few will make it, but they will distract the Phoenicians as your catapults and heleopolises move in. Though the Phoenicians will turn and attack your siege weapons, they will fire several shots before being destroyed, and your cavalry will be able to finish the wonder if your catapults and heleopolises are destroyed.

Ways to Lose

You must rush in every phase of this scenario. Take too long getting an army east and the Lydian wonder will cost you the game. Take too long rebuilding and going west and

the Phoenicians may be able to hold you off. Ignore the Persians and they may wipe out your base.

Additional Hints

Forget about Persia once you have a strong fighting force outside of Phoenicia. You won't win this scenario by having a town to return to. The only way to win is to destroy both wonders, and you must be prepared to sacrifice every one of your people to do it.

Continue manufacturing catapults, heavy cavalry, and heleopolises throughout the mission. The only time you should stop is after your invasion force has entered Phoenicia's walls.

Have a villager build a tower within ballista-range of the Phoenicians wonder when your men and catapults go in for the kill. If the Phoenicians manage to destroy your army, the tower may be able to finish the job before time runs out.

Avoid going to battle with the Persians if at all possible. This mission is not about revenge—it's not even about survival. You simply want to stop two nations from immortalizing themselves with wonders.

The Babylonian Scenarios

Don't waste time trying various options in the Babylonian missions—once your enemies get the upper hand, you'll see the proverbial handwriting on the wall. (Of course, seeing your empire crumble every now and then is a real character builder.)

Remember the lessons learned in the Egyptian missions. In Age of Empires, the Babylonian Empire is more of a defensive power. Babylonian priests rejuvenate faster, their towers have more hit points, and they mine stone more quickly. Of all of the resources in the game, stone stands out as the only resource with no real offensive value.

Historically, the Babylonians built huge towers known as ziggurats. Though real ziggurats were mostly used as places of worship, the ones in Age of Empires have a practical side to them—shooting nasty arrows at oncoming armies. It doesn't cost any more stone to build a fully upgraded ziggurat than it costs to build Egyptian or Greek towers, so if you find yourself guarding territory with a little extra stone in your bank, by all means build a ziggurat.

Mission 1: Holy Man

Your calling is to establish a city along the Tigris River by converting the people who already live there. Your only assets are a priest and 200 units of wood. (Incidentally, this is my favorite mission in Age of Empires.)

As the scenario opens, you find your priest standing beside a river in the southern corner of the map. A lion is hiding in the blacked out area just ahead of you, so stay close to the river as you head north. Turn right when you come to the land bridge leading east across the water. The Akkadians on the east are far less formidable than the Elamites who live in the west.

Convert the first villager that you see once you've crossed the river, then start looking for a suitable spot to build a town center. You'll find a grove of trees and some foraging bushes east of the land bridge, have your villager build your town center near the bushes, then have him start foraging. Convert as many of the Akkadians as possible (later you'll have to kill any Akkadians that remain unconverted).

This is a very short scenario if you play it aggressively and do not allow the Akkadians and the Elamites to tap into their resources.

Between training villagers and converting Akkadians, you should be able to assemble a 15-villager workforce quickly. Build your city as quickly as possible. Mine the stone and gold along the eastern edge of the map, then send villagers south to get the wood and stone down there.

The first Elamites will roll into your territory quickly, so advance to the Tool Age and Bronze Age as quickly as possible and train axemen, and then cavalry. You can avoid a protractive battle if you launch a decisive invasion within 20 minutes of starting this mission. The Elamites may have already entered the Bronze Age, but they are unlikely to have much of a standing army at that point. You will undoubtedly encounter some resistance and a couple of towers, but you will be able to massacre their villagers and stop their progression, and then finish off their army.

Ways to Lose

The surest way to fail this mission is to lose your priest. He's a fragile guy, doesn't move fast, and doesn't carry any weapons. If he stumbles across a lion, he dies. If he comes upon a group of soldiers, he may convert one, but the others will kill him.

Additional Hints

Finish the Akkadians quickly, you don't want to be sandwiched between two hostile armies.

Take a villager with you when you invade the Elamites. You may need him to erect barracks so that you have quick access to more soldiers if the battle goes against you. Your villager can also build towers.

Keep your priest away from the heavy fighting. Remember, it doesn't take much damage to kill a priest.

Mission 2: Tigris Valley

The objective in this scenario is to recapture the famous Code of Hammurabi (represented by two artifacts) from the Akkadians and Elamites who stole them.

You begin this mission with a small Stone Age village consisting of three villagers, four houses, a town center, and a dock. You also have 500 units of wood, food, gold, and stone.

Begin by growing your workforce to 15 villagers, with 12 chopping wood and three mining stone from the deposit in the northernmost point of the map. There is a dock in your village. Create a six-boat fishing fleet, but also make sure to launch five scout ships as soon as you advance to the Tool Age—you're going to need them.

If you work quickly, you should have two or three scout ships up by the time the first Akkadian scout ship arrives. The Akkadians will advance to the Bronze Age shortly after that, so try to sink that scout ship before it turns into a war galley.

The first Akkadian transports will arrive shortly after you sink their ship. Having enemy soldiers walking around your Tool Age village is fairly destructive, so try to trap and destroy the transports with your scout ships, build a market and an archery range, and advance to the Bronze Age.

Both the Akkadians and the Elamites have Bronze Age harbors, and they are going to continue to harass you until you close their docks down permanently. Upgrade your ships to galleys, build a fleet of between five and 10 ships, and head over to the Elamites dock. (Remember, the Babylonians have a lame navy that does not advance beyond the Bronze Age. If you end up advancing to the Iron Age before sending your fleet to destroy the enemy docks, research engineering, alchemy, ballistics, woodworking, artisanship, and craftsmanship to give your ships every advantage.)

The Elamites have a dock on the southwestern edge of the map. Have your ships surround the dock and sink it, but watch out for catapults.

The Akkadian dock is located on the northwestern shore of a large island near the southeast corner of the map. Be warned, you will be met by catapults and towers as you arrive. This dock is worth the trouble, however. Destroy it and the Akkadians will remain stranded for the rest of the mission.

You can now focus your efforts on invading the Elamites and reclaiming your artifacts. The first artifact is on a small island just south of your base. The island is crawling with clubmen.

Load one or two cavalry units on a light transport and send it to the island. Have your war galleys thin out their ranks, then send a cavalry unit to recover the artifact and bring it to your transport. Once you get the artifact, return it to your base.

There is a large deposit of gold on that island. Send three villagers back to the island to build a storage pit and mine the gold, and you'll have enough materials to advance to the Iron Age.

The second artifact is on the Elamite's main island. This island has several towers and the Elamites have cavalry everywhere. Be sure to purchase every available upgrade to extend the range and power of your ships. The more buildings and units you can clear from the island, the easier it will be to get the artifact.

When you launch your invasion, make sure to aim at the northwest corner of this island. The Elamites have built a wall around their island, but there are two gaps along the northeastern shore. Destroy the towers and secure the north shore of the island with your ships, then wear your enemies down.

Horse archers are probably the best choice for this invasion. They are fast and you can combine their arrows with those of your ships to wear the Elamite cavalry down. When you have control of the island, retrieve the final artifact.

Ways to Lose

If you don't upgrade to the Tool Age and start cranking out scout ships as quickly as possible, the Elamites and Akkadians will destroy your city during their repeated invasions.

Additional Hints

One ship, even a scout ship, can destroy an entire battalion of catapults. When you see catapults coming for your ships, move all but one or two of your ships to safety. Have your remaining ships do the catapult shuffle—shoot and move, and shoot, and move until the catapult crumbles.

Use your gold wisely—you won't get much of it. Don't waste it on technologies you'll never exploit.

Place a villager on the small wooded island just north of the Elamites' island before attacking their towers. Your ships are bound to take damage while attacking their towers. With a villager on that island, your ships will not have far to go for repairs.

Mission 3: Lost

The Hittites have sacked Babylon. Now you and a handful of men must defeat them.

You begin it with a ragtag army—six composite bowmen and a priest—that is trapped on a tiny island with very little resources and no way to harvest them. Your first trick is to find your way off of the island.

Move your army to the north end of your island. There is a priest and some bowman on an island just north of yours. Have your bowmen focus all of their firepower on the priest.

There is a heavy transport in a little bay on that northern island. It will come to you with a load of archers. Have your priest convert the transport. If it unloads the archers,

have your bowmen cut them down. If you convert it first, dump the archers on some small island, then load your men into the transport.

The Hittites have built a city on an island in the eastern corner of the map. Unload your archers on the island just west of the Hittites' island, then send your priest to the Hittites' island to convert a few villagers. Once you get a convert, load your priest and his new follower on your transport and return to your island.

From this point on, this scenario becomes a bit more standard. Use your 500 units of wood to build a town center near the trees on your island, then develop a 15-villager workforce to harvest stone, gold and wood. Have your composite bowmen destroy the towers on the western point of the Hittite island so that your villagers can collect the gold on your island.

Build several docks. You need to destroy the Hittites' dock so that you can have free reign of the ocean, then you can fish for food. The best way to do this is to have your bowman and war galleys attack the Hittites' ships while your catapults bombard their dock from the eastern tip of your island. You should be able to convert some of the Hittites' galleys with your priest during the battle, but don't take too many chances.

Now that you have control of the waters, have your ships patrol the Hittites' coast and demolish any houses, archery rangers, barracks, stables, or academies that are within range. You will probably have the opportunity to slaughter a few enemy soldiers while you're at it.

Establish a beachhead and send catapults, priests, and archers to the island to finish the Hittites and end the scenario.

Ways to Lose

The easiest way to lose this mission is to lose your priest before you convert a villager. The next most vulnerable spot in this mission is the time your men spend on your transport. Let that boat get cornered by enemy ships, sunk by catapults, or shot down by towers while it's carrying your priest and the mission ends in failure.

Additional Hints

Don't bother building a government center or a market—your entire village is already upgraded. Government centers and markets are only important if you want to make upgrades.

Mission 4: I Shall Return

The Elamites are launching a massive invasion into your city. Don't bother trying to defend your land, you've lost this battle before the scenario begins. The best you can do is hope to escape with a good supply of villagers and rebuild your forces.

This mission begins on a frustrating note. The opening screen shows your dock and a transport, the only units in your entire nation not getting creamed by Elamite ballistas and soldiers. Quickly shift the view to your city, select every person on the screen, and have them flee east to your transport. Load them aboard, then head north. There are only two islands on this map, so unload your men as soon as you find land. Send your transport to a far corner of the map, then build your town center near the gold and stone mines against the far edge of the map.

The first thing you need to do is secure your island, and this means killing the lions in the corners. Stay in the clearing in the middle of the island until you have the manpower to kill them. Build a town center beside the stone and gold mines, then begin cutting wood and building your workforce.

The Elamites have not finished with you yet, and they have a fishing boat snooping around, mapping the ocean. Your best bet is to stay far inland, forage berries from the plateau on the eastern end of your island, build granaries, and circle them with farms. With any luck, the Elamites will not notice you until you are ready to take the fight to them.

Harvest all of the natural resources around your town center before branching out. You will be able to use all of the stone to build towers around your territory and upgrade them. Use the gold in the nearby mind to advance to the Iron Age. Once you've advanced and have a navy, go to the western end of you island and claim the gold in that mine.

Once you've advanced to the Iron Age, build a government center and research ballistics, engineering, and alchemy, then build three or four docks, upgrade to triremes, and prepare to take control of the waters. Once you've researched these technologies, your triremes will be much more powerful than the Elamites. Hunt for their ships and transports and sink them.

Now that their ships are gone, have your triremes circle the Elamites' island killing anybody they encounter and destroying buildings and towers.

You can now launch a fishing fleet to stock your food supply. Use that food to research catapult triremes and juggernauts, then make one last pass around the island killing any enemies you see.

The final step in your revenge is clearing the island. There should only be a few buildings by this time. There may be some cavalry and scouts, but most of the people left on the island will be villagers. Send a villager and some cavalry to the island. Have the cavalry kill everybody they see as your villager builds a siege workshop. Build ballistas and use them to destroy the Elamites' final buildings and people.

Ways to Lose

The easiest way to lose this scenario is to dawdle as the Elamites destroy your first town. Run to safety, build up quickly, and you should have few problems.

Additional Hints

Make sure to research alchemy, ballistics, engineering, and all other technologies that have to do with your boats.

Mission 5: The Great Hunt

The Elamites have stolen a valuable statue (handily represented by an artifact), and the king wants you and nine axemen to get it back. Your job is to lead this weak-but-homogenous party through the winding hills in search of a powerful stronghold that could cut down your axemen before they get within striking distance.

Group your axemen and lead them south along the trail. Move cautiously a little at a time—there are lions waiting. As soon as you see them, attack them one at a time, and know that you're going to lose some men.

Continue south and you'll find another lion and two elephants. Lead your men through this area as fast as you can, and run away from the elephants.

Don't worry if you continue to lose. This scenario is a relay race—as long as one of your men makes it to the next marker, you'll go on stronger than before. A group of six bowmen is waiting to join you just beyond the animals.

You will be met by ten enemy bowmen just a little further south. Do not get in a tit-for-tat firefight with these archers. Kill the ones that block your path, and run from the ones that you can avoid. Once you get past the trees, you'll run into two friendly scouts that will join your party.

The next set of obstacles will be four more archers followed by eight towers. Your axemen and archers will not survive this. Get your scouts past this gauntlet and know that you've done well.

Make it past the towers and you'll be met by six friendly cavalrymen whom you must lead north past towers, elephant archers, ballistas, and catapults. Have your cavalry swarm the ballistas, but don't stop to fight the elephant archers, you want them to follow you.

Thread your men through two sets of two towers followed by a pair of stone throwers. Run past the towers and attack one of the stone throwers at close range. Make sure that your men do not harm the second one.

Make it past all of this and you get your first prize—a pair of imprisoned priests. Draw close enough to the priests to bring them to your side, then have them convert the stone thrower. Now break the wall and release your new priests.

There are two stone throwers on an island just to the east—they shot at your cavalrymen as they rode through the gauntlet. Have your priests chant to one of them from the cliff, then move them safety as they rejuvenate their faith. Be sure to move

them back and forth as you perform this conversion so that they do not get hurt. You will need these priests throughout this scenario.

Once you convert one of the stone throwers, they will destroy each other unless you act quickly. Move your converted stone thrower right up to the enemy stone thrower. Siege weapons cannot attack adjacent enemies, so both weapons will be safe until your priests can finish the conversions. Once they are converted, use the stone throwers to destroy any towers within their range.

Next, use your cavalry to attract the elephant archers north, past the towers, then use your priests to convert them.

There is a light transport waiting for your party in the river just east of the cliffs. Once you convert the catapults, send a cavalry unit along the river to claim the transport, then use it pick up your catapults.

There's a thin shore that runs along the cliffs on the far side of the river. Have your transport drop a priest there. Do not take any units with your priest—he'll need the space to move around. His job will be to move south along that shore and convert any enemies on the far side of the cliff.

The Elamites have catapults, stone throwers, and ballistas on the other side of the cliff. These units may kill each other off if your priest converts them, but even that is better than having them shoot at your men later in the mission.

Now come the toughest legs of this mission. You have to cross over the lake to the next row of cliffs, where a row of towers blocks your path. Beyond the towers is a row of six ballistas and a catapult, and beyond that four more catapults. Destroy the towers with your stone throwers, and prepare for a fight.

Expect casualties, but keep your priest healthy and proselytizing, you may walk away with some excellent rewards.

The six ballistas and catapult will attack as you get to the top of the cliff. Use one of your priests to convert a ballista and the other to convert the catapult as your elephants and cavalry destroy the rest.

Just beyond the dogleg bend in the cliff, you'll be met by five catapults. Try to convert at least one of these catapults as your cavalry destroys the others. Remember, you cannot afford to lose your priest.

Next you'll encounter a line of bowmen and five priests. The priests constitute the greater danger, take them from long range with your siege weapons as your elephant archers and cavalry attack the bowmen.

The next leg of your mission involves shuttling across some marshes to pick up those catapults you converted, then mounting an attack on a mountain teeming with priests and ballistas. Go down the slope to the waterside where you will find a transport boat waiting. Have it pick up the stone throwers you converted along the side of the cliff. It's time for another little skirmish.

There is a land bridge leading from your shore to a small island. On that island you will find stone throwers, cavalrymen, and archers. Try to lure them in small groups with one of your elephant archers, convert as many of them as you can and kill the rest.

There are ballistas and catapults on many of the islands in this marsh. You will have to clear a path for your transport to get to the island in the northern corner of the map where the Elamites have the statue your artifact. To get to it safely, you are going to have to blast or convert the ballistas and catapults in the western side of the marsh.

You should have a decent enough army to invade the Elamites' island. The final stumbling block is a lone ballista guarding the only part of the island on which you can land. Destroy it with your catapults.

The cliffs around the Elamites' island form a spiral with the statue of Marduk at the top and hordes of catapults, ballistas, and soldiers blocking the way. You enter this spiral on the west side by going up a slope that touches the edge of the map. Your forces will have to land on a sandbar, and, yes, it is a trap, and the moment you entered it you set off a time clock. You now have 20 minutes to fight up that mountain and capture your prize.

Fight your way up and clear a path for a stone thrower—it's time to clear the tower that stands in your way. Place your elephants beside your stone thrower—they'll do a decent job of protecting it. Work your way forward.

The end of this mission is a straightforward fight with you trying to clear cliffs using your archers, ballistas, and catapults.

Ways to Lose

You automatically lose if your parties of axemen, bowmen, scouts, or cavalry do not make it to the next marker. You will also lose if the Elamites manage to kill one or both of your priests early on. The only way to beat this scenario is to keep your priests healthy so that they can heal your vital units and convert enemies along the way.

Additional Hints

Make sure to have your priests heal each other while they heal your army.

When your cavalrymen run into the ballistas on the mountain trail, have them swarm the second ballista. Because they're so close together in such a tight space, both units will stop firing when your men crowd them.

Keep your transport right beside your priest when you send him to convert the catapults on the far side of the cliff. The shoreline is narrow and he won't have room to dodge their attacks, so have him jump into the transport instead.

When you pick up your stone throwers, make sure to keep your transport as close to the cliffs as possible. These waters are filled with enemy ballistas and catapults.

Mission 6: The Caravan

Your objective in this scenario is to deliver a statue of Marduk to a Babylonian temple.

Your destination is a temple located on the northwest edge of the map. You must lead five composite bowmen and an artifact to that temple from a southern corner of the map.

Group your men so that they will all shoot at the same target. The only way to survive this scenario is to take advantage of your bowmen's superior line of sight, group your men together, and have them focus on one enemy at a time.

Your men start out in a grove. When they emerge from the grove, they will be at a fork that sends them east or west. Head east until you come to a river.

Backtrack in a southeastern direction along the river until you come to a group of lions. Kill the lions, then cross the river on the land bridge.

Head east past the Elamite flag, then head north and up the slope to the top of the cliffs. Expect to be spotted—your enemies are near. There are several Elamite hoplites below the ledge. From this vantage point you can shoot them without retaliation—they may walk out of range, but you'll have softened them up should you run into them again.

You will also see Elamite composite bowmen from the ledge. Kill them.

Once you've killed the hoplites, there is no reason to skirt around their part of the woods. Have your party walk down the eastern slope of the hill, then follow along the bottom of the cliffs back toward the river. Follow the river north and west until you pass a small grove of trees, then head straight for the temple. Deliver the statue of Marduk and you win.

Ways to Lose

Simply put, you can't lose this mission so long as you have control of the artifact. Keep your men around the artifact. The only time you don't want men around the artifact is if and when you decide to sacrifice them and have the artifact make a run for it.

Additional Hints

Avoid elephants all the way through this mission—both domesticated and wild varieties.

Stay in the center of the map as much as possible—you won't stand a chance against the armies stationed along the edges.

Mission 7: Lord of the Euphrates

Your objective in this scenario is to destroy Assyrian and Chaldean cities.

You begin this mission with six villagers, 200 units of wood, food, gold, and stone, a Bronze Age town composed of barracks, a granary, a storage pit, and houses. Assign one of your villagers to build a second barracks as your other villagers forage for berries.

The Chaldeans have more men than you and are preparing an invasion. Train six axemen and prepare to defend yourself.

Now that you've bought some time, create a 15-villager workforce to cut wood and mine stone. The resources around your village will dry up quickly, harvest them, fortify, and get ready to look for more.

You'll see your first Chaldean within the first three minutes of your mission. He'll be a lone hunter—don't worry about him. He'll be followed by axemen a few minutes later.

In this mission, given your resources, you need to train axemen quickly, but you also have enough resources to build a build a temple and train a priest. Having a priest will help your men last longer and he may be able to find a few recruits for your army.

While you work on your army, monitor the coastline just north of your village—an enterprising Chaldean builder will attempt to erect a tower along your coast. Send men to destroy his work as soon as the stakes appear.

Use this time to build a dock and galleys. If you take control of the bay that sits between you and the Chaldeans, you'll be able to stop their incursions and prevent them from fortifying their land with coastal towers. You'll also be able to stop the Assyrians from sending transports with chariots and catapults.

You need only five ships to take control of the ocean in this mission. Once you have a sufficient fleet, scour the coast along the west edge of the map and destroy the Assyrians' dock and ships. Don't leave the scene too quickly, though, as they will try to build a second dock almost immediately.

Once you have 10 to 15 axemen and two or three priests, you will be ready to march into the Chaldeans' territory. Use your priests judiciously in this invasion. Remember that even though Babylonian priests rejuvenate more quickly than other priests, they still have downtime in which they are helpless. If you squander his faith converting villagers and axemen, he may not be ready when the next Chaldean cavalryman rides into range.

Take a villager with you on this invasion to build a tower in the center of the Chaldeans' city. The tower will serve like a lightning rod—enemy soldiers will often attack it before attacking weaker targets. With a villager there to repair it, your tower will attract and kill or convert a great many Chaldeans.

Your Chaldean siege should end quickly if you mounted it early enough. By annihilating the Chaldeans you take control of the entire continent—you inherit two large forests and a couple of stone and gold deposits scattered around the map. Use these materials to prepare for your invasion of Assyria.

Before invading the Assyrians, you will need to take control of the waters. Upgrade your ships and missile weapons with ballistics, alchemy, engineering,

woodworking, artisanship, and craftsmanship, then send in a mass navy. Once you have control of the waters, send your ships to clear the Assyrian coastline. Then, send in your invasion.

The Assyrians have superior bowmen, so concentrate on cavalry and making the fight take place in close quarters. Have your cavalry rush and destroy bowmen, chariot archers, siege weapons, houses, and villagers. Don't worry about storage pits, granaries, government centers, and markets until it is time to mop up.

Send villagers as part of your invasion force so that they can build towers, a siege workshop, and stables. This will provide instant reinforcements for your army.

Ways to Lose

Though you begin this mission with Bronze Age technology and a nice location, your lack of men and facilities will open the door for serious problems. The Chaldeans are simply too close to ignore, and they are eating up resources you will need in your fight against the mighty Assyrians. If you wait too long to attack the Chaldeans, you may not be able to defeat them.

Additional Hints

There is a gold deposit east of your village—create villagers and mine it early or the Chaldeans will commandeer it for themselves.

Control the ocean between your village and the Assyrians and you not only insure that they will not interfere in your battle with the Chaldeans, you open up a good source of food. There are lots of fishing areas in the waters to the south.

Be sure to hunt down and destroy Assyrian transports or they may continue to send catapults and soldiers to harass you even after you demolish their dock.

Once you have control of the seas, make a fishing fleet. Upgrade your fishing fleet so that your boats can obtain food more quickly. You'll soon have enough food to wage a huge invasion.

Mission 8: Nineveh

The Assyrians are building a wonder—your job is to destroy it.

You start this mission on a small island in the southern corner of the map with a great Bronze Age city complete with a siege workshop, a government center, an academy, a granary, a temple. You even receive a Tool Age navy with scout ships and transports. You even have 2500 units of wood, 2000 units of food, 2000 units of gold, and 400 units of stone. What you do not have is villagers or a town center.

The Assyrians are about to send triremes and galleys to destroy the guard tower on your eastern shore. Create two or three catapults and four priests as quickly as possible. Since the Assyrians have Iron Age-ships and you do not, you will profit greatly by

converting their ships. If you cannot convert them, blow into foam as quickly as possible. Take too long and the Assyrians' catapult triremes will probably kill your priests while sinking your ships and destroying your towers.

While your catapults and priests take care of the Assyrian navy, train a new priest and send him to convert and retrieve a villager from the unfriendly Babylonian city on an island northwest of yours.

The bottom edge of the island, however, has a narrow shore running along a large and dense forest. Have your transport boat run along the southwest edge of the map and unload your priest on the bottom corner of the island. Do not let your priest travel too close to the city.

There is a villager on this island who frequently walks along the shore by the woods. Wait until he is near your priest, then convert him.

Do not try to get more converts. The moment you turn this villager, load him and your priest on a transport and return to your island, where you should have him begin building a town center. Have your priest heal the villager if he is wounded.

Once the town center is built, assign your villager to build a second one so that you can advance to the Iron Age as you begin training a workforce. Your island may not be big, but it has small gold and stone mines as well as lots of wood. Assemble 15 villagers and harvest your island's resources as you build your army and navy and destroy your northwest neighbor's harbor and ships.

The Assyrian navy will continue to harass you while you erect your town center and build your villager work force. Try to convert Assyrian triremes and catapult triremes, but have your ships and catapults sink Assyrian galleys.

In order to cut through Nineveh, you'll need a lot of soldiers, which means you are going to need a lot of food. Upgrade your farms as much as possible. You should also use your Iron Age government center to research ballistics, alchemy, and engineering. It takes a lot of gold to make these upgrades, so use your gold judiciously.

While you are making upgrades, remember to give your priests some firepower as well. Give them fanaticism and afterlife so that they convert more effectively and have longer ranges. Upgrade them with polytheism so they walk faster, monotheism so they can convert towers, and mysticism so they don't die so easily. Your entire mission hinges on the success of your priests, navy, and catapults with protective support from other units.

Send a catapult trireme, and two regular triremes as an armed escort, to the uninhabited island in the eastern corner of the map. Destroy the towers guarding the island, then transport a villager to the island. Have him build a town center, then train five villagers to harvest the island's resources. You should either assign a ship to protect the island or have your villagers build towers or walls around it.

Once you've advanced to the Iron Age and purchased the juggernaut upgrade, make three juggernauts and begin clearing the towers from the edges of the Assyrians'

island (the island along the northeast edge of the map). Do not worry about the Babylonians to the west. Once you destroy their dock, they will stay put on their island. As long as your men stay clear of their ziggurats, the Babylonians cannot hurt them.

Watch out for priests when you send your juggernauts to destroy the Assyrian towers. Their island has more priests than the Vatican, and you may find yourself having to attack your own ships if you do not blast enemy priests as soon as you see them. Keep an eye out for catapults and heavy catapults as well.

If you've upgraded your priests with afterlife, they'll have a very wild field of range. Have a priest stand on the little outcrop at the north end of the eastern island. You should be able to see a thin strip of the Assyrians' island from that vantage point. When elephants or other soldiers walk within range, have your priest convert them. They'll be killed as soon as they're converted, but it's better than losing your men.

Once you've destroyed the towers on the outside of the island, begin your invasion. Send triremes and catapult triremes to the southern shore of the Assyrian island to provide cover for your transports. Put together a landing team with at least four catapults, three priests, two villagers, and several cavalrymen.

Look for the road running between two walls on the southern end of the island. Drop your men in front of that road.

Your first job is to destroy the towers guarding the road. They are out of your ships' range, so you'll have to do it with your catapults. Arrange your soldiers in a protective formation around your catapults and begin shelling the towers. Enemy elephants and horses will come to attack your catapults. Be sure to convert at least one elephant—it will be very handy later.

If you look closely, you'll see Assyrian ballistas along the walls between the towers you are attacking. Have your catapults destroy the ballistas as well. Assyrian priests will come to try and convert your catapults. If your priests have monotheism, they can convert those priests. Either way, take care of enemy priests quickly, as they pose the biggest danger to your invasion.

Once you make it past the tower, you'll come to a crossroad with more towers and several large buildings. While your fighting forces dig in for a battle at this site, have your villagers build a siege workshop, a temple, and stables so that you have a steady supply of reinforcements without having to send ships to other islands.

Have your catapults attack the towers and building in this part of the town. The Assyrians will continue creating heavy catapults and archers until you destroy their buildings. Also, be prepared to interrupt your regular siege activities to destroy any priests that come out. You don't want your invasion cut short because of a converted catapult. Finally, save your progress after every successful skirmish. One thing you do not want is to begin this mission all over again.

If you have not received it earlier, you should receive a message that the Assyrians have completed their wonder around the time you enter their town. To get to the

wonder quickly, you must shatter the Assyrians' line of resistance with catapults and cavalry attacks. (Be sure not to use cavalry if you see enemy priests nearby.)

Have your catapults attack Assyrian priests and archers. Use your priests to convert Assyrian elephants and hoplites. Above all else, try to take out the towers guarding the wonder.

If you do not have enough time to destroy the towers, have your elephants attack them, then have your catapults attack the wonder while the towers are distracted. Remember, the Assyrians win if their wonder survives for 20 minutes, so time is of the essence. You may have your priests convert the towers while they're shooting your elephants.

Ways to Lose

There are so many ways to lose this mission that it's hard to believe you can possibly win. Failing to convert a villager is a sure way to lose. You simply cannot beat this mission with a Bronze Age army. You can also lose by playing too methodically. Don't waste your time attacking the yellow-colored Babylonian army to the north. It's nearly as tough as the Assyrian army, and the wonder will have aged several millennia by the time you finish.

Do not underestimate your enemies on this level. Send in too few men and you'll lose everything you've invested. You need several priests, several catapults, and a host of soldiers to act as a barrier for them.

Additional Hints

Keep a repairman by your ships during the early navy battles. The enemy's triremes and catapult ships will inflict heavy casualties on your scout ships and galleys. If you don't have somebody standing by to make repairs, you'll lose them.

Use your gold wisely. You need lots of gold to make juggernauts, catapults and priests, and you need several of each of these to pull off this mission.

There is a lot of gold on a tree-covered island on the northwest edge of the map. The best way to clear space for a storage pit will be to bombard the forests with a juggernaut.

Upgrade your farms. You won't get much food from fishing in this mission, and you don't want to have to keep looking back at your farms.

The Yamato Scenarios

The Yamato missions take place in ancient Japan. This is not the fairly recent Japan of samurais and shoguns—this is the practically prehistoric Japan of which little is written or known.

As a body, the Yamato missions are the most difficult in the game. Starting with Mission 1: The Assassins, you are expected to take the lessons learned in previous campaigns and adapt them to more demanding situations—so prepare to pull some bigger rabbits out of your hat.

Mission 1: The Assassins

You are to lead a small group of assassins to the Izumo Clan's capital and kill their leader.

In this scenario, you lead a team consisting of a composite bowman, three broad swordsmen, and one cavalry unit as they work their way through enemy territory. You have no resources and no way to obtain resources.

You begin in the northern corner of the map that's bisected by a river. Work your way south along the river's edge. Have your rider, who is both your fastest and most durable unit, go first. March him nearly to the edge of the fog, then move your swordsmen beside him. Finish by moving your archer.

There are several lions roaming around this half of the map. When they enter your field of vision, have your archer kill them. It should take three to four arrows to kill each lion.

There is a land bridge running across the river near the center of the map. A tower guards the other end of that land bridge, so you will have to lead you men across it quickly. As soon as they get across, have your men stay on the riverbank and head north. You will be able to follow this path all the way to the Izumo temple, located near the top of the map. The short swordsman busily pacing back and forth in front of the temple is the Izumo leader.

There is a ledge overlooking the Izumo temple. Have your bowman shoot at the Izumo leader from the top of the ledge. As he comes to attack your bowman, have the other members of your party attack him.

Ways to Lose

Watch out for lions in the east and stay away from the Izumo palace complex in the west. Do not challenge towers and avoid confrontations and you should be fine.

Additional Hints

There are four friendly priests rooted in certain spots around the map. They cannot move, and they are nearly useless at converting enemies, but they can heal your men if they are seriously wounded. Think of them as health stations. The easiest priest to reach is in the east corner of the map.

If you do not see all three of your swordsmen as the mission opens, sweep the area while pressing the left button on your mouse. One of your men may be hiding behind a tree.

Be sure to keep your swordsmen and cavalryman well within your archer's field of vision as you move across the map. Move your men to the edge of his vision and they may fall prey to lions.

Mission 2: Island Hopping

The Izumo have stolen five treasures (artifacts) from the Yamato, and scattered them throughout their islands. Your mission is to scour the Izumos' islands and recover the stolen treasure. Make sure you keep your swordsmen and cavalryman well within your archer's field of vision as you move across the map. Move your men to the edge of his vision and they may fall prey to lions.

You begin this mission with three composite bowmen, two galleys, two phalanxes, a catapult, a ballista, a light transport, and a heavy transport. The Izumo greatly outnumber your men, but your ballista and catapult represent much greater firepower.

You should approach this mission with two immediate objectives, both involving taking control of the larger of the two islands off your southwest shore. One is tiny and inhabited by a composite bowman and two enemy priests. Do not attempt to land on that island or you'll lose your men. A little farther south, there is a larger island, inhabited by lions and elephants. One of the missing treasures is there. If you can land on that island early (before an Izumo galley appears) and take control of the treasure at the outset of the mission, you'll avert catastrophe.

If you fail, the Izumo galley will come in close contact with the only treasure not controlled by the Izumo, thus gaining control of all the artifacts and setting off a 2000-year clock.

Next load your catapult and an archer on your light transport. It's time to begin island hopping. Return to the island where you got the treasure and kill the elephant and lion on its southeastern shore. Now use your catapult to kill the archer and priests on the smaller island—you're doing this to ensure that they do not convert or kill your ships—there are no treasures on their island.

Now head south to the large island near the corner of the map. (To avoid running into Izumo galleys, make sure you sail to the next island along the recently cleared eastern shore.) The only inhabitants on this island are three innocent Izumo villagers busily cutting wood. Crush them—that wood is being converted into the Izumo galleys intended for attacking your island.

The Izumo will not be napping while you capture the treasure—they will be sending galleys to annihilate your men at your home base. Move your heavy transport along the southern cliffs of your island and group your ballista, archers, and galleys, and your men will be able to fight off the first Izumo galleys on their own.

This situation cannot go on forever, however. Once the priests and archers are gone, load your men on the heavy transport and move it along with your galleys to the

north part of the woodcutters' island. Next, unload your ballista and archers on the small island and move your galleys into their firing range as you send your transport to the southern edge of the island. The final Izumo galleys are bound to find your men—this configuration will enable your men to fight them off while suffering only minimal casualties.

Land your catapult on the island in the southern corner of the map. Ignore the houses along the island. Send your catapult to the west shore of the island and destroy the Izumo dock. This will guarantee the safety of your catapult and your ballista. From this point on, you can deploy them on smaller islands to soften or destroy enemy armies and prepare the way for your archers and phalanxes.

Use your catapult wisely to land and pick off enemy defenses as you move from island to island. Once they are dead, go in and collect each treasure. This strategy works well until the last treasure. The sixth treasure is on an isolated island near the northern corner of the map. Collecting this treasure is a bit tougher because the island is so small that there is no way to sneak up on the three composite bowmen guarding the treasure. To win this island, you'll need to launch a two-pronged attack.

Load all of your men and weapons on the heavy transport, then send everything you have to that final island. Begin your assault by sending your remaining galleys to attack the archers. While they sink your galleys, make your landing. Your phalanxes and weapons should make short work out of the archers. Once the island is clear, collect your prize and celebrate. You've accomplished another mission.

Ways to Lose

There are three major threats in this mission, and you should eliminate all of them in the opening minutes of the scenario. The 2000-year clock poses a problem because 20 minutes is not enough time to hunt for six treasures and reel them in. The way to avoid this problem, as stated earlier, is to gain control of the closest treasure before that Izumo ship passes by.

The next threat comes from Izumo priests. Given the chance, they will convert your transports and catapult. Don't throw archers or your ballista at them—you need your catapult's range to take them out without being converted.

The last and most serious danger is the Izumo navy. You can only go island hopping if you have ships, and given the chance, they will overwhelm your galleys and transports. Kill the Izumo woodcutters quickly, then take the battle to their dock before they have the chance to sink your fleet. This mission becomes much easier the moment you control the waters around these islands.

Additional Hints

Leave your catapult to help defend your shores against the first Izumo attacks as you collect the first treasure. Your navy will need the assistance.

Make sure to move treasures deep within your island when returning them. If they're too close to shore, they may convert over to the Izumo.

Since the Izumo do not have a town center, they'll be unable to create more villagers once you kill their three woodcutters. With no villagers, they cannot build a new dock. Destroy their dock and kill their villagers, and you'll control the waters in this mission.

Even though only one of the archers guarding the third treasure poses any threat to collecting that treasure, they will fire at your ships throughout the mission. It's worth the effort to clear them out of the way, especially as you go to collect the fourth treasure.

You will never have to deal with the six phalanxes and three archers guarding the eastern cliffs of the island with the fifth treasure. Just kill the clubmen and slip on and off of the island quickly.

If you want additional points to achieve a high score on this mission, wipe out the Izumo. Land your catapult and ballista on the island in the center of the screen and have them destroy the Izumo army on the island to the west. Destroy their houses and their storage pit, and you will achieve a winning score.

Mission 3: Capture

Your job in this mission is to capture an Izumo artifact. This is not going to be easy— the artifact is safely hidden within the thick walls of a fortress that has been buttressed with several fully upgraded guard towers. To make matters worse, the fortress is on an island with only one entrance—a land bridge in the center of an Izumo stronghold.

To win this battle you'll need to advance to the Iron Age, and to do this, you will need gold. Unfortunately, all of the largest gold deposits are guarded by Izumo towers. They are located at 11:00, 1:00, 3:00, and 7:00 on the map. To get that gold, you'll have to make your move quickly and fight for it before the Izumo harvest it.

There is one 300-unit deposit of gold along the northwest edge of the map, at 10 o'clock, not far from your village. Mine that deposit as you fortify your village against Izumo invasions. Initially have villagers begin cutting wood and picking berries. Build four more villagers. Assign two to pick berries and two to go north with four axemen to build a tower and a storage pit beside the gold deposit (where they will mine it).

Build a dock and upgrade your ships from scouts to galleys, then build three fleets. Send one fleet to the southern corner of the map to kill the Izumo villagers as they harvest gold and stone from the rich deposits near their village. Keep another fleet in

your port to defend your village. Send the third fleet to help defend your men as they harvest the small gold deposit along in the northwest, then send the fleet farther north to kill the Izumo as they approach the gold supplies located at 11:00.

Do not send your villagers after those supplies, however, since they are guarded by a tower, as are the deposits at 7:00. At this point in the mission, you will have to accept the notion that stopping the Izumo from reaching gold deposits is almost as good as mining the deposits yourself. As long as the Izumo cannot mine the gold, you have the potential of owning it.

The Izumo will not take your expansion lightly. The yellow Izumo will march north toward your village, sending axemen, cavalry, and archers. The brown Izumo will send chariots and ships along the top of the map to attack your men as they mine gold.

Use your fleets as your primary defense against these invasions. Make sure to beef up your fleets so that you have four or five ships at all three strategic locations.

Build a tower by your dock in your village and a second tower by the shore at your mining outpost. With only 400 units of stone, you won't be able to build and repair these towers indefinitely, but you will inherit excellent stone deposits as you take more territory from the Izumo.

Your secondary defense should come from your towers and your axemen. As you develop your village, build a siege workshop and a government center. Having these buildings will qualify you to enter the Iron Age once you have 800 units of gold, but more importantly, they will enable you to build powerful catapults.

Your catapult's first mission should be to open the way to the southeast. The Izumo have a tower just south of your village. Send five axemen and three villagers with your catapult and destroy that tower. Next, move down the map toward the gold deposits at 7:00.

Move your ships close to shore to kill soldiers who come to defend their territory, then move your invasion force within catapult range of the Izumo towers. Destroy the Izumo towers and storage pit and build a storage pit of your own, then send your catapult back to town.

The yellow Izumo will send several villagers to try to reclaim the area by erecting towers and other buildings. Kill them and destroy their buildings. They will send soldiers, too. Your ships should have no trouble defending your claim as the Izumo will exhaust their population trying to reclaim it. Once the Izumo stop challenging your territory, you'll encounter little resistance when you march into their city, claim their stone deposits, and destroy their buildings.

The battle may not go quite so smoothly along the northern half of the map. The brown Izumo have a dock, a siege workshop, and enough gold to manufacture several catapults. They will continue to harass your ships with archers and catapults and to challenge your fleets with ships of their own.

Once you've emptied the small gold deposit just north of your mission, send your ships, catapult, and foot soldiers to clear the way for the next deposit, which is located at 11:00 on the map. This deposit is guarded by two towers. Have your catapult destroy the towers while your ships and men guard against Izumo soldiers arriving to protect their territory. Then have your villagers build a storage pit and begin harvesting the gold.

Wait until you have enough gold to advance to the Iron Age, then upgrade your galleys to triremes. You may even want to upgrade your dock to build catapult triremes so that you can include that additional firepower when you attack.

Once you've upgraded your navy, have your ships move slowly down the northeastern shore destroying all enemies that challenge them and all buildings that come within range. The Izumo will throw all of their resources into attacking your fleet, but they will be unequipped to stop you. Just be careful to destroy catapults as soon as they appear. An unchecked catapult can destroy an entire fleet of ships.

Like the yellow Izumo, the brown Izumo will exhaust their resources trying to fight off your invasion. Once your ships have destroyed their dock and most of their city, your ground forces will encounter only minimal resistance when you send them in to finish the job.

The final phase of this mission involves attacking the red Izumo stronghold in the center of the map. This stronghold is built on an island with sheer cliffs on all sides. The only entrance to the island is a tiny pass that's blocked by a wall and guarded by four heavy towers.

Begin your assault on this island by destroying the two towers guarding its rear. You can make this assault with a catapult trireme or a juggernaut. Either way, you'll find that these towers can absorb lots of damage before collapsing.

You will also discover that the island is guarded by three ballistas. There is no need to look for these ballistas—attack the towers and the ballistas will find you. Because these ballistas are very capable of sinking your ships, concentrate your fire on them as they arrive, then send your ships back for repairs as needed until you've destroyed the ballistas and all four of the towers guarding the island.

Once the ballistas and towers are gone, the only enemies remaining on the island will be four Izumo phalanxes. If you've upgraded to juggernauts, you'll be able to kill these foot soldiers wherever they go. If you have catapults, they may be able to hide from you in the center of the island.

Either way, the next step of your invasion is to raze the first wall blocking the entrance of the island. March a priest and a catapult past the destroyed wall. You can convert the phalanxes with your priest, then let them kill each other or try to shoot them with your catapult. The only way they'll be able to move out of your priest's and catapult's range will be to move in range of your ships.

Once the phalanxes are dead, have your ships destroy the second protective wall at the front of the island. Once it is gone, march in and claim the artifact and the mission is over.

Ways to Lose

Play this mission gingerly, and the Izumo will triumph. You have to be prepared to expand and take enemy land so that you can offset the imbalance of natural resources. You will need 800 units of gold to move into the Iron Age and more gold to build catapult triremes. Again, the only way to get that gold is to take it, and take it quickly, before the Izumo mine it for themselves.

The second danger in this mission is not preparing for invasions. When you break into the Izumo harbor, assuming you break in early enough, you'll discover they have several transport ships as well as galleys. These transports were not built to take tourists sightseeing along the picturesque coastline.

Make sure that your ships are deployed where they can stop any transports from landing and kill any troops that march into your village. Have sufficient ground strength to finish the Izumo that slip past your ships. They will destroy your village if you give them the chance, so be sure to defend your property carefully.

Additional Hints

Use your granary to upgrade your towers as quickly as possible—you will need towers to secure outposts throughout this mission.

Do not bother building farms in this mission. The waters in this map are filled with great fishing sites. Just be careful to protect your fishing boats.

There are large groves of berry bushes near the gold deposits at 7:00 and 1:00 on the map. If you need more food quickly after conquering the yellow and brown Izumo, build granaries in these areas and have your villagers forage for food.

Watch out for catapults. The Izumo will send several to sink your fleets. When you hear a warning trumpet, check your small map and see where the action is. If it involves your fleets, chances are the Izumo have sent a catapult.

Have either your ships or your catapult kill the elephant at the top of the screen. Left on its own, it will crush your villagers if you do not kill it.

In the first part of the mission, the only civilizations that matter are the yellow and brown Izumo, located at 3:00 and 6:00 on the map, respectively. They have better resources than your village and will expand quickly to find more resources. Let them get too big and you'll be unable to regain control of this mission. (The red Izumo are trapped on their island and will not try to invade you.)

Do not let your fishing boats or galleys go near the center of the lake or the Izumos' heavy towers will sink them.

Mission 4: Mountain Temple

You begin this mission with a Stone Age village consisting of a town center, two towers, and three villagers. Your village is located on a ridge on one side of a small island. The Kibi, a clan allied with the Izumo, have a village on the other side of the island.

Assign one of your villagers to forage while your other villagers build barracks. Once they have finished the barracks, assign your builders to erect three houses, then forage. You need to build an army of clubmen and march east to destroy the Kibi before they harvest the gold and wood in their village. You need it more than they do.

From the outset of this mission, there will be two axemen and three clubmen defending the Kibi village. It will not take them long to develop this army—they will add 15 more clubmen if you let them. Begin leading the Kibis' soldiers into your towers as early as possible, then invade them when you have enough clubmen.

You will need at least ten clubmen to wage a successful invasion The Kibi will have stationed several clubmen along the beach on the northern edge of the island. Try to slip your army past the southern ridges so that you can overwhelm the clubmen in the village and begin destroying their barracks as the clubmen from the beach straggle in.

Once you have destroyed their army and their barracks, destroy any villagers left in the village and send your villagers over. It will not be long before enemy galleys will begin patrolling the shores and attempting to kill your men and destroy your buildings, so try to keep away from the edges of the island as you move east. Your objectives will be to forage for 500 units of food so that you can enter the Tool Age, then to build a dock and two scout ships to clear your shores.

Don't expect the Kibi to sit by idly while you do this. They will send invaders, mostly archers, to your shores, so have your men ready to meet their transports and destroy them as they land. They will also continue sending galleys to patrol your shores.

The only way to keep the Kibi off your island is to build a dock and chase them away. To do this, you must find a secure area that the Kibi are unlikely to discover until after your dock is completed. There is a small stretch of beach on the western end of your island. Send soldiers along your ridges to lure the Kibi ships east, then send a villager to build a dock. Build three scout ships, and prepare for a sea battle.

You do not want to build ships and engage the Kibi navy until you have three ships and enough wood to repair your ships during the battle. Their galleys will be more powerful than your scout ships, so make sure you have a villager and at least 100 units

of wood ready as you send your ships out to fight. Once you take these precautions, you'll be able to clear the Kibi from your waters. Taking control of the seas and destroying the Kibi dock will require more preparation.

The first thing you need to do is advance to the Iron Age, an act that requires 1000 units of food and 800 units of gold. You can find the gold you need on an island just west of your home base. Build a transport and send three villagers to the island. Have them run toward the island quickly—there are three alligators along the beach. They may come in handy for food later, but at this point they simply pose a low-grade threat to your villagers' safety.

Have your villagers build a storage pit on the island—there is a gold deposit on the back side. Have two villagers mine it while your third villager cuts wood. As soon as you have enough gold, advance to the Iron Age and upgrade your ships from galleys to triremes.

The Kibi dock is in a corner of land between the Izumos' mountainous territory and the Kibis' island. An Izumo tower overlooks the dock, and another tower looms near enough to strike your ships when you move in for the attack. In order to destroy the dock and raze the town, you will need to attack from the south and fight your way across the Kibis' island.

You will not need a lot of men for this attack, just a stone thrower, a priest, and a lot of patience. Rather than staging a full invasion, you should simply destroy everything with your stone thrower. What you have to do is unload your stone thrower along the island and destroy towers, buildings, and people as you work your way across the island.

Start by destroying the towers along the eastern edge of the island. You can demolish the first one from the beach of your island, then transport your stone thrower across the channel and start destroying the other towers. If your stone thrower takes damage, send it back to your island and have a priest repair it. Never let your stone thrower stray far from your transport. That way you will be able to load your stone thrower quickly and send it to safety if Kibi archers close in on you.

Destroying the Kibi after this fashion is downright dull, but it gets the job done with a minimum of casualties, protecting your limited resources. After you annihilate the Kibi, your next task is to mount an attack on the Izumos sacred (and well-guarded) hill. Begin by using your triremes to destroy the towers guarding the Izumo shoreline. Fire at everything you see—cavalrymen, towers, and stone throwers. The cavalry and soldiers may simply step out of range, but you'll be glad you hurt them later on.

Now comes the hard decision. With very little gold and no chance of finding any more, you must decide whether you want to build several stone throwers and attack the Izumo mountain with stone throwers and scouts or strengthen your priest and try to convert your way in. Either way, you're in for a fight.

The final assault will send you up a winding path past five stone throwers, three ballistas, four priests, 12 composite bowmen, and four heavy towers. Don't expect to charge in and win. No matter how many scouts and archers you train, your priests and stone throwers will ultimately decide whether you win or lose.

Upgrading your priest's range is probably the better choice since it will enable you to convert a stone thrower or two during your assault. It will also enable you to convert some very expensive cavalrymen who are guarding the cliffs. With these men on your side, you stand a better chance of accomplishing your ultimate mission.

Once you've knocked down the towers guarding the coast of the Izumo island, you can send your priest to convert their men. Have your transport unload him along the beach toward the west side of the island. You'll see two cavalrymen. With their path to the beach blocked by boulders, they will not be able to attack your priest as he chants to them.

Convert the first cavalryman, then have your transport pick him up. The second one will attempt to reach your priest. Load the priest into your transport—the boulders at the front of the beach usually block the cavalrymen, but they sometimes find their way around it. When you think your priest's faith is recharged, unload him at the far edge of the beach and have him convert the second cavalryman, then have your priest heal both soldiers before you transport them to safety.

With his added range, your priest will be able to convert some of the archers lining the first part of the mountain pass leading to the Izumo temple. Convert as many as you can. Their fellow archers will kill them, but that still thins the Izumo ranks.

A stone thrower will attempt to kill your priest. Dodge its barrage of stones and convert it. Though the Izumo cavalry will eventually destroy it, your stone thrower should be able to clear all of the archers along the first stretch of the path.

Use your priest wisely and you should be able to acquire seven or eight cavalrymen before you even begin your final invasion. That will strengthen your landing force considerably. (Remember, cavalrymen are catapult-killers.)

Now you need to get serious about this invasion. There is a spot not too far from the western edge of the Izumo coastline where the path between the cliffs and the coastline is very narrow. Your triremes should be able to shoot anything moving through that area. Move the entire fleet to that spot. Now transport your entire population to the island.

Have your villagers build stables on the island. From this moment on, the only type of units you should build are scouts, and you should build as many of them as possible. Next, move one of your catapults along the edge of the cliffs to kill the archers and towers along the first terrace on the sacred mountain. Retreat to the safety of your triremes at the first sign of retaliation. Your ships will be able to destroy anything chasing you.

Next, put your extremely expensive priest to work converting the row of stone throwers along the next ledge of the trail. The Izumo will destroy each stone thrower as you convert it, but you would probably rather have them shoot each other than your army.

The first two stone throwers are along the wall on the third tier of the trail. Have your priest inch up until one is in sight, then have him convert it. As soon as it is converted, have it turn and fire at the stone thrower beside it. Chances are they will destroy each other, but you may get lucky and kill a couple of Izumo composite bowmen before your stone thrower is destroyed.

Next, have your priest move down along the bottom of the first cliff and convert the remaining cavalryman. (If you run into an archer before you reach the cavalryman, convert the archer and send him to your stocking area while your priest recharges his faith.) Send him to join your forces at the western edge of the island, then have a stone thrower come and annihilate the remaining archers, completely clearing out the first ridge of the sacred mountain.

The Izumos' two final stone throwers are just above the area where you slaughtered the archers. Send your stone thrower up to that area and destroy the first one that attacks you. (Remember to move your stone thrower back and forth after every shot so that it doesn't get hit.) The second stone thrower will also join the battle, but do not destroy it. With the other three stone throwers destroyed, this last one will be able to do a lot of damage if you convert it. Send your priest in and make it yours. (Again, remember to move as you chant or that stone thrower can make juice out of your priest with its first shot.)

Move your stone thrower east the moment it's converted, then take it north and use it to destroy the first tower that comes in sight. The Izumo will send a ballista, three composite bowmen, and a priest to kill it, but the converted throwers should be able to take the tower and a few bowmen before going down.

Once the stone thrower is dead, allow your priest to recharge, then send him to convert the ballista. Once you've gotten the ballista, turn it on the Izumo priest before he reconverts it. With a little luck, the ballista will get the priest and two bowmen before dying. Use your priest to convert the final bowman—you never know what may turn the tide of the rather treacherous battle that looms ahead.

Having destroyed the archers lining the first terrace and the stone throwers overlooking it, you're ready to march your forces toward the Izumo temple. Bear in mind that the Izumo still have three towers, three priests, and a lot of composite bowmen waiting for you, so this will not be easy.

The first target that will come in range will be a tower. Have your scouts form a ring around your stone thrower to protect it, then move in and destroy the tower. If bowmen come down to attack, send your scouts after them and move your stone thrower to safety. Remember, you cannot afford to build more stone throwers.

The next target will be two composite bowmen stationed two thirds of the way up the final hill. Have your stone thrower kill them, then move it to safety and bring the rest of your forces up.

There's an old proverb among martial artists that says that you should never take a weapon to a fight unless you know how to take it away from your opponent. The idea behind the proverb is that if your opponent gets hold of your weapon, you'll need to know how to defend yourself against it.

This adage is quite appropriate for this part of this scenario. The Izumo have three priests waiting for you to attack. Whatever you send at them, you can bet they will try to convert it—so make your next attack a weak one so that the Izumo use their faith on disposable targets—scouts and axemen. (Cavalrymen take too many hits to kill and you don't want to risk a stone thrower.)

Send five or six scouts up the hill to destroy the Izumos' remaining ballistas. Chances are that between the ballistas, the bowmen, the priests, and the towers, your five scouts will not achieve their goal, but they will cause the priests to use up their faith temporarily.

There's no room for elegance in a moment like this—send all of your cavalry, axemen, and remaining scouts up the hill to kill the priests, the ballistas, and as many bowmen as possible. The towers will kill several of your men during this strike, but not before they get the priests and ballistas. And with those threats out of the way, your stone throwers can march up the hill, kill the remaining bowmen, and destroy the Izumo towers and temple.

Once you've finished this demolition job, send some villagers up the hill to build a temple over the spot in which the Izumo temple once stood. You have accomplished your mission when the new temple is built.

Ways to Lose

Give them the chance and the Kibi will end this mission for you in a hurry. If you wait too long to attack the first Kibi town, they will develop a large enough army to overwhelm your forces. They will also use up the resources you need to continue the mission.

The brown Kibi, on the eastern island, pose an equally dangerous threat. They will send galleys to patrol your waters and transports with composite bowmen to invade your island. These are dangerous threats. Even if the galleys do not get your men, they can shoot buildings and cause you to expend resources you'll need later.

You will face the standard perils as you ascend the Izumo mountain, but there may be one additional threat you've overlooked. Do not run out of wood at the end of this mission. Ridiculous as it sounds, you'll need enough wood to erect a temple over the ruins of the Izumo temple or you'll have to start again.

Additional Hints

The Izumo have no villagers or barracks. Their army is in place the moment this scenario begins, so there is no value in rushing to attack before you have sufficient forces.

Build your first houses and barracks as far inland as possible so that enemy ships cannot destroy them from offshore.

Use your storage pit to upgrade your soldiers and armor as soon as you enter the Tool Age.

Use your market to upgrade your woodcutting and farming throughout the scenario.

The Kibi navy will attack your repairmen and try to kill them before attacking your ships, so have your repairmen walk to a safe spot between naval battles.

Do not try to convert the Kibi composite bowmen on the eastern island. There are too many of them and they will kill your priests before they are in range. Kill the bowmen with a catapult.

The cavalrymen and scouts in this game are downright stupid. Do not trust them to go places—once you assign them a destination watch, make sure they make it or they will get lost.

You will mine less than 2000 units of gold in this mission. That means that priests and catapults are irreplaceable—keep them safe and healthy.

Build a government workshop and upgrade your catapults and missile weapons. Having powerful projectile weapons will serve you well during the final assault.

After you have converted all of the cavalry near the cliffs, send cavalrymen up to lure additional suckers into your priest's range.

Mission 5: Canyon of Death

Your next battle will be with the Shikoku, a southern clan who has stolen an artifact from the Yamato. Your job is to lead a small army through treacherous grounds. Make it through this trap and you'll be given a large enough army to defeat the Shikoku and recover your treasure.

You begin this mission with six cavalrymen, four composite bowmen, four horse archers, and four short swordsmen. Your immediate opposition includes axemen, archers, composite bowmen, stone throwers, horse archers, towers, short swordsmen, and lions. Survive all of that and you'll face a small but potent force with composite bowmen, cavalrymen, stone throwers, and phalanxes.

As the mission opens, you'll hear a lion attacking off in the distance. Believe it or not, this is good news. The lion has just killed two Shikoku archers.

Your first task will be to clear a path for your men. The lion that killed the Shikoku archers is just west of your men. Just beyond the lion is a ridge overlooking three enemy archers. Two more archers and two axemen await your army beyond some trees to the north. None of these threats will destroy your force, but they will chip away at it. What you need most is to keep your army intact for as long as possible.

Send two composite bowmen to clear all of these threats. Keep tight control on both men and have them concentrate their fire on the same targets. This will ensure that the lion and axemen do not reach them, and that the archers will be killed before they get in range to fire back.

Now move your men north to the base of the hill. From here you can either move north or west. If you head north, you'll have to fight your way past several bowmen, two towers, and a stone thrower. This approach is a bargain compared to what you'll meet if you head west. Have your archers clear the three lions just beyond the trees, then start moving toward the top of the map.

You'll see a rock ledge as you get past the trees. Two lions are resting just to the west—do not let your archers kill them. You can use these lions to save some of your Yamato lives.

There are four Shikoku composite bowmen and a tower at the top of the cliff and a stone thrower and tower on the next ledge up. The first tower and bowmen will see your men coming, so you have no range advantage. This is the time to make a strategic sacrifice.

Send a cavalryman to attract the lions, then send him up the hill toward the Shikoku bowmen and have him attack their tower. The tower and bowmen will attack your cavalryman, but the lion will attack the bowmen. If you get really lucky, the stone thrower will descend from the next ledge and the lion will destroy it. (Your men will have to kill any archers who survived the lion. That goes for the stone thrower as well.)

The next task involves threading your men up the hill and trying to slip them past the first tower. There is a safe spot at the top of the hill against the edge of the map. Send a horse archer to that spot and have it kill the lion hiding beyond the trees at the top of the hill. Now send three swordsmen to that spot, then have the swordsmen raze the upper tower to clear the way for the rest of your army. As soon as they engage the tower, send your cavalry to assist them. (You will unavoidably take casualties at this point.)

Once you make it past the towers, you'll encounter a horse archer and three composite bowmen. Have your cavalry swarm and overwhelm them.

The next part of the mission is the toughest. You must lead your men down a long slope to the west until they reach the seashore. There they will be greeted by swordsmen, bowmen, two stone throwers, four towers, and a wall. You need only one man to make it past these obstacles to complete your mission—that will not make this task any easier.

Three things that can make this part of the trek a bit less perilous. There are three lions hiding behind the trees. Have a horse archer lead these lions along the shore and they will kill the swordsmen and one of the stone throwers. There are no clever tricks after that—your cavalry and swordsmen will have to hack through the remaining Shikoku and break through the wall to get to the transports. (They may also have to put some wounded-but-useful lions out of their misery.)

Once you hack through the wall, quickly lead your men to the end of the peninsula. There you will find two heavy transports waiting for you. Your fortunes in this mission are about to take a serious turn for the better.

Have the transports move along the southwest edge of the map and you'll find a tiny island crawling with blue soldiers. Unload your remaining men and have the priests heal them, then load everybody on the transports.

Take your transports north to the Shikoku stronghold. Unload one of your stone throwers on the southern shore and have them destroy the Shikoku towers, then bring your entire army to the island.

The landing force you picked up on the last island is strong, but not strong enough to go toe-to-toe with the Shikoku. Use your transports to shuttle one of your stone throwers along the side of the island to harass the Shikoku and shoot at their stone throwers. When they send bowmen down to investigate, have your stone throwers kill them. This will enable you to thin their numbers.

Your harassment will also cause the Shikoku to move their stone throwers to the ledge of the cliff. By keeping your transport nearby as an escape hatch, you should be able to engage and destroy one or both of the Shikoku stone throwers. This will give you a decided edge during the final fight.

After you have destroyed the stone throwers, go after the Shikoku archers and horse archers. If you're able to kill them, the Shikoku will no longer be able to shoot arrows at your stone throwers. The only way they'll be able to attack them will be to send slow-moving phalanxes down the slope. (The bowmen and horse archers may wound your stone thrower—be sure to send it back to the priests before it takes too much damage.)

Once your stone throwers have eliminated the archers and bowmen, send your priests in the transport to convert the Shikoku cavalrymen. Cavalry are adept at destroying catapults, so converting their cavalry will improve your chances of protecting your stone throwers. (Remember to keep your transport nearby should your priest need a quick escape.)

At this point, you'll be able to overwhelm the Shikoku with your forces or you can continue to whittle their numbers with your priests and stone throwers. Once you're ready to finish the scenario, send a stone thrower to destroy the tower at the top of the hill and cavalrymen to capture the artifact. Once the artifact is safely deposited on your island, the mission ends in your favor.

Ways to Lose

You spend the first half of this mission hoping to survive so that you can spend the second half of this mission fighting an uphill battle.

Simple mistakes can cost you this entire mission. Head west instead of north, and you'll find yourself fighting much stronger forces. You may well beat them, but the fight will be harder and your men will be in much rougher shape as they sprint along the beach and attack the wall.

Do not kill the lions. The Shikoku are trained to kill your men as soon as they see them—they will not necessarily attack the lions, and the big cats may clear a lot of enemies out of your way. They are particularly good at clawing catapults.

Finally, do not waste your priests by sending them after large forces when you invade the Shikoku stronghold. Remember that your priests need to recharge after every conversion. Send them to convert two or three bowmen, and the unconverted bowmen will likely kill them as soon as they stop chanting.

Additional Hints

Move very slowly and methodically through this mission. If your men bunch up and move along a wide path, they will attract additional lions and archers.

Have your men hug the water as they move along the shore. If you do not get too close to the trees at the end of the peninsula, you will not be attacked by the stone thrower and five bowmen who move along the edge of the cliff at the end of the beach.

Remember to save your progress often throughout this game. You should save your progress as you make your way to the transports, then save your progress again after you destroy the Shikoku stone throwers that are guarding the artifact.

Mission 6: Oppression

You begin this mission with four villagers and a Stone Age village. You have 400 units each of wood, food, gold, and stone. As a menacing reminder of just how primitive your forces are, your enemies have six phalanxes and a catapult stationed around your village.

Assign your first villagers to forage the berries by your granary and cut wood. Make more villagers, build a dock and fish for food. Build trading boats and trade food for gold with the yellow town at the top of the screen. You will not finish any of this, however, before you receive a message stating that the Kyushu demand a tribute of 200 units of gold. Pay it.

Advance to the Tool Age as quickly as possible, then to the Bronze Age. The latter will enable you to upgrade the size of your ships. Your upgraded trading boats will

bring in more gold, and your upgraded fishing boats will bring in more food. When you have 1000 units of gold, you can stop trading and build your food supply.

As you build up your food, you might want to send two or three villagers to the small island along the northwest edge of the map to mine for gold. Also send your fishing boats to the western corner of the map. As the scenario winds down, you may decide that you need more villagers. Good news! The yellow civilization on the north island has no army, so you don't have to worry about the military ramifications of that group changing its diplomatic stance. Just send over a priest and make as many converts as you like. Consider it a good source of cheap labor.

With your tributes paid, the Kyushu will leave you alone. This is your chance to go after all of the resources on the map as aggressively as possible. Mine the rock deposits and wood to the west. Fish and farm until you have thousands of units of food. Develop a large army of bowmen, and upgrade your ships to juggernauts.

The Kyushu (the fools!) trust you. Use this trust to your advantage. Build towers beside their walls—seal the north, south, and east entrances to their city. Station your juggernaughts beside their port. Place priests near the catapults they have sent to various outposts. By the time you finish preparing for this fight, it should be like shooting fish in a barrel.

As soon as all of your forces are in place, begin the battle by changing your diplomatic stance to that of an enemy and converting their catapults. The entire scenario map will instantly light up with conflicts as your towers attack their towers and men.

Lead your bowmen to their city wall and spray the Kyushu phalanxes and catapults with arrows. Have your juggernaughts demolish their dock and government center. This battle ends the moment you destroy the Kyushu government center.

Ways to Lose

The biggest danger in this scenario is aggravating the Kyushu before you're ready to fight them. You need to pay them off because you won't have any forces that can stand up to their phalanxes and catapults until you enter the Iron Age.

Build your trading fleet quickly and make sure you always have enough gold to meet their demands.

As long as you pay your tributes and do not attempt to attack or convert any red Kyushu units, you will be able to co-habitate with your oppressors.

Additional Hints

Do not build your dock next to the Kyushu guard tower or it will attack your dock as soon as you miss a tribute payment.

Several lions inhabit the northwest island with the gold deposits. Send a scout ship to kill the lions and clear the island.

You may need to destroy your own dock if the Kyushu send too many trading boats and start depleting your gold supply.

When you run out of wood and gold on the northwestern island, build a granary and farms.

There is a lake with several schools of fish in it near the west corner of the map. You can build a dock in the lake if you need food.

Play your cards right throughout this mission and you should have thousands of units of wood, gold, and food by the end of the mission. If you are aggressive about mining stone, you should have nearly 2000 units as you prepare for the final showdown.

Upgrade your villagers so that they can destroy walls and towers. You should have a surplus of villagers as you enter the fight.

Build a siege workshop and upgrade your projectile weapons. This will give your towers a fighting chance against the Kyushu's sturdier but less powerful heavy towers.

Mission 7: A Friend in Need

Having gained control over most of Japan, the Yamato have turned their attention to Korea. They founded a colony in Korea and formed an alliance with the Paekche Kingdom, a non-aggressive civilization struggling to maintain its foothold in Korea's shifting balance of power. Another Korean nation, the Scilla, are threatening the Paekche, so the Yamato have decided to intervene.

Your first task is to save the Paekche government center from destruction. The mission opens with the Scilla attacking their city, which is located along the northwest edge of the screen. Scilla cavalry have entered the city, and more importantly, two Scilla catapults are firing into the city from behind its western wall.

Most of your soldiers and workers are safely tucked away inside your village as the mission opens—you have six axemen in the Paechke village. Send them through the entrance to the city to attack the catapults. Have them charge one catapult and strike at it until the second catapult fires at them. As soon as it does, have your men turn and attack the second catapult—the shot from the second catapult will destroy the first one.

Scilla cavalrymen will descend on your axemen and kill them as they destroy the second catapult, but you will have given the Paekche government center a reprieve. With the catapults destroyed, the Paechke will be able to mount a decent defense while you send your cavalry and short swordsmen to chase them away.

Once the Paechke government center is safe, it's time to focus your attention on building your city and army. You have an Iron Age village with eight short swordsmen, eight composite bowmen, four cavalrymen, and nine villagers. You have 200 units each of wood, food, gold, and stone, and there are forests around your village and berry

bushes to the east, near your granary. There's also a small gold deposit near the south corner of the map and a stone deposit along the western edge of the map, just north of your village.

As you develop your army, create enough villagers to cut wood, forage food, and mine the various mineral deposits around your village.

You will find that your village is protected by natural barriers—a small row of trees extending from the northwest edge of the map and a long row of trees along your northeastern flank. These trees form a strong wall with two breaks—one north of your village and one along the southeastern edge of the map. Since Scilla Central is located in the eastern corner of the map, expect most of their attacks to come through that second break.

Build a wall to seal that entrance. Build towers along the wall and send composite bowmen to fend off attackers. Once you've built a siege workshop, you may want to send a couple of stone throwers to protect the wall. This area will be a weak link if you do not seal it off properly. The Scilla will attack it repeatedly, sending catapults and horse archers to destroy the wall if possible.

Once you have sealed that area, it will be time to take control of more territory. There is a large gold deposit (3600 units) in the center of the map. Send a large squad of composite bowmen, a priest, a stone thrower, and four villagers to take control of that area.

Two towers guard the gold—have your stone thrower attack them. (The towers will have better range than your stone thrower, so you'll have to send your stone thrower to be healed halfway through each attack.) Once the towers are down, have your villagers erect three guard towers around the site and place your bowmen beside your towers. Next, have your villagers build a storage pit and begin mining.

The Scilla will continually challenge your hold of the central gold deposit. They will start by sending horse archers. Wait until the horse archers begin shooting at your towers, then have your priest convert them. You'll be able to amass a fairly sizable army this way.

Once you've assembled a strong enough army around the gold in the center of the map, send villagers and cavalry to build an outpost beside the Paechke city. There is a large stone deposit just south of their city and a grove of bushes to the north.

Paechke towers and soldiers will offer your forces some protection, but you should expect the Scilla army to invade your outpost. Build additional towers and either an archery range or stables so that you can expand your forces.

If you have enough stone, you will discover that the easiest way to move east toward the Scilla city is by building towers, then converting the soldiers the Scilla sent to destroy them. You'll want at least three priests for this operation. Starting with the towers you built around the central gold deposits, build two towers at the very edge of your existing towers' range. The Scilla will send horse archers and long swordsmen to

destroy them. Have your priests convert as many of the Scilla as possible, then have your archers kill the rest.

Your eastward trek will be blocked by sheer cliffs about three-fourths of the way across the map. The Scilla have built their city at the top of these bluffs—go too close and they'll shoot arrows at you. For a better look, send a horse archer to ride by the base of the cliff. This will help you locate the towers and buildings.

The Scilla have built a walled city on the top of a large plateau which they've also carpeted with towers. Have your stone throwers attack the towers along the edge of the plateau. The Scilla will send cavalry to attack your throwers, so send composite bowmen and converted long swordsmen to protect them. Sending a large battery of composite bowmen is a particularly effective way to protect catapults and stone throwers because the bowmen can kill enemies before they reach their target.

The rest of this mission is a simple clean-up operation. Send your force up the southern slope of the plateau and have your bowmen form a line behind your stone throwers. (Don't worry, these lines never stay straight. As long as your bowmen do not get between your stone throwers and any attackers, you'll be fine.) Have a priest beside your stone throwers throughout this operation so that you can heal your throwers as they take damage.

Have your stone throwers attack all towers and military buildings first. (Remember, the towers can shoot their arrows farther than your stone throwers can toss their loads, so you will need to have a priest heal your throwers as they attack each tower.) Leave the houses for your cavalry and swordsmen. Work your way across the plateau, killing every man, beast, and building that you pass. The mission ends when you have razed every building on the plateau.

Ways to Lose

You will lose this mission in a hurry if you do not stop the Scilla catapults from destroying the Paechke government center. This is not a difficult task on the easier levels—the Paechke will pretty much fend for themselves. On the more difficult levels, however, the Scilla are not so easily turned away.

The Scillas' catapults are their main weapon of destruction. Left alone, they will destroy dozens of Scilla soldiers as they shoot at the Paechke. More often than not, one of the Scilla catapults will destroy the other while shooting at Paechke soldiers—but the remaining catapult will be within range of the Paechkes' government center.

On the hardest level, the Scilla will try to bolster their invasion by sending additional forces. You will need to send most of your army to meet them while assigning your villagers to forage and cut wood. The Scilla may even visit your village while you rebuild, so have villagers concentrate on gathering food while you rebuild your cavalry. (You'll lose if you don't have an army when the Scilla roll into your

village, too. They will annihilate your villagers, then destroy your buildings. Very methodical.)

If you succeed at controlling the center of the map and the gold deposits therein, you will avoid some very nasty pitfalls. With tons of towers around their city, the Scilla are well prepared to fight off an archer and cavalry invasion. You will need stone throwers to destroy their towers and gold to make those stone throwers.

Additional Hints

Don't assume that your farms and villagers have been upgraded simply because you are starting with an Iron Age village. Build a market and upgrade your farms. Also, upgrade your villagers' siege ability and wood cutting.

Even though the priests in this mission have a limited range of abilities, they're extremely potent at converting enemies. Build a temple early in the mission and have fully upgraded priests available.

Once you have enough gold, use your storage pits to upgrade your soldiers' armor and fighting ability. The Scilla have powerful soldiers—you will need those upgrades to match them.

If you have the gold and resources, don't be afraid to upgrade your horsemen to cataphracts or your horse archers to heavy horse archers. These fast and powerful units can pay for themselves when the fighting gets heavy.

Controlling the gold supply in the center of the map is similar to controlling the center of a chessboard. This will allow you to cut the Scilla off from everything but the gold and stone within their city walls. (They have 2400 units of gold within their walls—more than enough to build an army of catapults.)

If you move east by building towers to attract the Scilla, have villagers handy to repair the towers after every attack. Scilla long swordsmen can damage or destroy a tower very quickly.

Mission 8: Tang Invasion

To beat this scenario, you will have to build a huge army to defeat a very large army that has a decided home-court advantage.

The map for this mission is divided into three horizontal strips. Your village is located on the southern strip. While there is a lot of timber and wildlife on your land, your territory has very little gold and stone. Both deposits are located on a butte near the southern corner of the map.

The middle portion of the map is uninhabited and has multiple deposits of gold and stone. Most of these mineral deposits are located on buttes and are guarded by Shang towers.

The Shang inhabit the northern third of the map. They have a large village with large foraging areas. There are two gold deposits near their village that hold a combined 42,000 units of gold. The Shang also have large stone deposits. In short, don't try to starve them out.

The Shang will gather their considerable forces into one spot along the river as the mission opens. It's an immense army with chariot archers, chariots, stone throwers, scouts, cavalry and more. On the easier levels, they will gather along the north shore of their river and stop, sending only a lone stone thrower to harass your village. On the more difficult levels, they will send villagers to inspect your lands, followed by cavalrymen, scouts, and swordsmen.

You can launch an early offensive to claim the center region on the easier levels, but on the more difficult settings, you will need to build walls along the land bridges along the river and build your army before you attempt to take more land.

Unfortunately, the 100 units of stone you're allotted as you begin this mission is not nearly enough to wall off the three land bridges leading to your area. If you send a villager to look for the stone deposits near the southern corner of the map, he will discover a storage pit with three villagers standing beside it. Send the villagers to mine stone. When they finish with the stone, have them mine gold.

Build your first wall at the mouth of the land bridge in the middle of the map. When that one is closed, send most of your soldiers to block the bridge on the western side of the map while your archers and villagers seal the bridge in the east. Once that is sealed, send your villagers to seal the western bridge. This will not keep the Shang out forever, but it will buy you enough time to develop an army.

There are two weapons that can give you an edge to help control your shores at this point. The safest choice is to build a dock and have galleys patrol the waters. Galleys are smart weapons. They will stalk villagers and foot soldiers, and you can use them to destroy Shang stone throwers as they attempt to breach your walls.

Unfortunately, galleys are susceptible to attacks from stone throwers and archers, and they sometimes get so close to shore that cavalrymen can ride up and attack them. On the other hand, you'll want juggernaughts before this mission ends, and upgrading to galleys is the first step to building juggernauts.

If you don't want to waste wood building a dock and ships in a river, you can train priests. You'll need to increase their range by purchasing the Afterlife upgrade from their temple. Once upgraded, your priests will be able to convert enemy units all the way across the river.

Converting enemies is good because it weakens the Shang while it strengthens the Yamato. Convert a Shang stone thrower and you'll be able to start clearing the towers from the buttes in the center of the map, clearing the way for you to mine the gold. If you convert a Shang villager, you can have him build a storage pit and mine enough

gold to move on to the Iron Age. (Once you're in the Iron Age, you can have him build a town center and start an entire village.)

As powerful as priests are, they have an inherent weakness: they are costly and fragile. They're great at converting foot soldiers and cavalry, and they can be used effectively against stone throwers, but they're too slow to convert archers and bowmen.

The galleys are probably the better choice, largely because you need to save 800 units of gold to move to the Iron Age, and you only need wood to make a galley. Either way, your job is to beat the Shang away from your shores, then the villagers and stone throwers across the river. (If you build a dock, you can send them in transports—otherwise, you'll need to blast holes in the walls you built to block the land bridges.)

There are four large buttes in the center strip of the map. The westernmost butte has 1500 units of gold and stone guarded by one Shang tower. The entrance to this butte faces the Shang side of the river, and there is a land bridge to the Shang homeland that ends near that entrance. Sneaking onto the butte may be difficult, and holding it will be nearly impossible.

The entrance to the next butte faces the Yamato side of the map and there are no towers on it—unfortunately, the only thing on this butte is a herd of gazelles. Though it will have strategic value later, the butte is not worth taking at this point in the mission.

Just like the first butte, the third butte has 1500 units of gold, a tower, and a land bridge. There is an excellent chance that you could slip men on to it, but it won't be easy to defend.

The easternmost butte has 1500 units of gold and stone and faces the Yamato side of the map. There are no land bridges that spill directly on to it, and you could defend it with one or two towers and a stone thrower.

Slip two villagers and a stone thrower across the river. Have the stone thrower destroy the tower on the eastern butte, then have your men build a storage pit and towers on the butte. You'll only need two towers along the northern ledge initially, but you may want to build more as the Shang begin their invasions.

Once you've taken the eastern butte, slip three villagers and a stone thrower on to the western butte. This one will be a bit trickier to take. The Shang use the western land bridge frequently and they've built a tower on their side of that bridge.

Send your stone thrower around the east side of the butte. You won't be able to shoot at the tower guarding the gold until your stone thrower begins moving up the sloped entrance to the butte. Send your villagers on to the butte as soon as your stone thrower destroys the tower.

Because the Shang are so close and the resources on this butte are so valuable, you should take special precautions to insure that the gold and stone do not fall into Shang hands. Have your villagers seal the entrance to the butte with a stone wall, then have one of them build five towers along the northeastern ledge while the other erects a storage pit and begins mining the gold and stone.

Once you have control of the first and fourth buttes, you should begin sending reinforcements. Have your men take control of the second butte, even though there is no stone or gold on it. By building a row of towers along its western ledge, you'll create a gauntlet that will prevent the Shang from slipping past you.

After your men have begun mining the other buttes, send villagers and a stone thrower to take the final butte. Seal this one with a wall, and build several towers on it. The Shang will be especially keen about trying to recapture this piece of real estate.

Build lots of towers and move your other units into position—the Shang will send waves of invaders to try to recapture the center of the map. With all of the gold you are mining, you'll be able to build two special weapons that will break the Shang offense. The first weapon is the heavy horse archer. Go to your archery range and purchase that upgrade.

Next, have one of your villagers construct a dock at the widest point in the river that separates the Shang homeland from the second strip of land. (The widest part of the river is just a little north of the middle land bridge.) Once the dock is built, upgrade your ships to juggernauts.

Build two or three juggernaughts and a trireme. These units will allow you to destroy most of the Shang buildings, including more than half of their towers. The Shang will send stone throwers to attack your juggernauts, but they won't have enough range to defend themselves against your ships.

Once you've forced the Shang into the top of the map, send a party of ten heavy horse archers to finish them off. You accomplish your mission and finish the campaigns when you've killed the Shang and razed their buildings.

Ways to Lose

Do not let the Shang get a foothold in your land. They enter this battle with a larger and more powerful army than you, and if they slip into your land, you won't get them out again.

Your goal in this mission should be to move into the second strip of land and take control of the buttes as quickly as possible. The more gold and stone you control, the easier you'll find your task.

Additional Hints

There is a storage pit with three villagers hidden near the southern corner of the map. Send a villager to find them. Assign your newly discovered villagers to mine stone while your original villager cuts down trees.

Use the trees around the center land bridge as part of your wall. The Shang will not fire at them, so the trees will become the strongest and least costly part of your defense.

Upgrade your walls and towers—you're going to need them. Even with towers and walls, the Shang will continue to try to attack you. Use priests to convert their stone throwers and foot soldiers.

There are no fish in the streams—don't bother building fishing boats. Build a government center during your Bronze Age so that you can access its upgrades the moment you move into the Iron Age. Purchase engineering so that you can build juggernaughts and upgrade your projectile weapons.

Build an archery range and a siege workshop as soon as you make it to the middle of the map. From this point on in this mission, your new units will come out of those buildings.

Remember to move all of your combat units to the middle strip of the map to protect your dock and mining efforts.

Index

to help everyone— from new users to seasoned developers—

Step by Step Series
Self-paced tutorials for classroom instruction or individualized study

Starts Here™ Series
Interactive instruction on CD-ROM that helps students learn by doing

Field Guide Series
Concise, task-oriented A–Z references for quick, easy answers—anywhere

Official Series
Timely books on a wide variety of Internet topics geared for advanced users

All User Training   All User Reference

Quick Course® Series
Fast, to-the-point instruction for new users

At a Glance Series
Quick visual guides for task-oriented instruction

Running Series
A comprehensive curriculum alternative to standard documentation books